Matters of Opinion

When a government announces that it will 'listen to the public', we are reminded that public opinion, and not just voting, underpins democracy. *Matters of Opinion* offers an interesting new insight into 'public opinion' as reported in the media, asking where these opinions actually come from, and how they have their effects. Drawing on the analysis of conversations from focus groups, phone-ins, and broadcast interviews with members of the public, Greg Myers argues that we must go back to these encounters, asking questions such as what members of the public thought they were being asked, whom they were talking as, and whom they were talking to. He suggests that people don't carry a store of opinions, ready to tell strangers; they use opinions in order to get along with other people, and how they say things is as important as what they say. Engaging and informative, this book illuminates current debates on research methods, the public sphere, and deliberative democracy, on broadcast talk, and on what it means to participate in public life.

GREG MYERS is Senior Lecturer in the Department of Linguistics and Modern English Language, University of Lancaster, where he has taught a variety of courses on text analysis and the language of the media since 1989. His previous books include *Writing Biology: Texts in the Social Construction of Scientific Knowledge* (1990), *Words in Ads* (1994), and *Ad Worlds: Brands, Media, Audiences* (1999), and he has published in a wide variety of journals. From 1998–2002 he was Honorary Secretary of the British Association of Applied Linguistics.

Studies in Interactional Sociolinguistics

EDITORS

Paul Drew, Marjorie Harness Goodwin, John J. Gumperz, Deborah Schiffrin

Matters of Opinion

Talking about Public Issues

GREG MYERS

CAMBRIDGE
UNIVERSITY PRESS

PUBLISHED BY THE PRESS SYNDICATE OF THE UNIVERSITY OF CAMBRIDGE
The Pitt Building, Trumpington Street, Cambridge, United Kingdom

CAMBRIDGE UNIVERSITY PRESS
The Edinburgh Building, Cambridge, CB2 2RU, UK
32 Avenue of the Americas, New York, NY 10013–2473, USA
477 Williamstown Road, Port Melbourne, VIC 3207, Australia
Ruiz de Alarcón 13, 28014 Madrid, Spain
Dock House, The Waterfront, Cape Town 8001, South Africa

http://www.cambridge.org
Information on this title: www.cambridge.org/9780521793124

© Greg Myers 2004

First published 2004
Reprinted 2006

Printed in the United Kingdom at the University Press, Cambridge

Typeface Sabon 10/13 pt.   *System* LATEX 2_ε [TB]

A catalogue record for this book is available from the British Library

Library of Congress Cataloguing in Publication data
Myers, Greg, 1954–
Matters of Opinion: Talking About Public Issues / Greg Myers.
p.   cm. – (Studies in interactional sociolinguistics; 19)
Includes bibliographical references and index.
ISBN 0-521-79312-2 (hb)
1. Mass media and public opinion. I. Title. II. Series.
P96.P83M94 2004
302.23 – dc22 2004047296

ISBN-13 978-0-521-79312-4 hardback
ISBN-10 0-521-79312-2 hardback

For Nan Myers, Scott Myers, and Mark Myers

Contents

Acknowledgments

This book is about the ways people express opinions in groups and in broadcast media. With such a topic, I am lucky to be working at a university with a lively interdisciplinary social science research community, especially in the Centre for the Study of Environmental Change and the Institute for Cultural Research. I owe thanks to the colleagues with whom I worked on research projects that provided much of the data for this book: Phil Macnaghten, Peter Simmons, Bronislaw Szerszynski, Mark Toogood, John Urry, and Brian Wynne. They tried patiently, if not always successfully, to get me to look at broader issues and applications.

I am also grateful to colleagues on the courses I teach, who have shaped my thinking more than they probably know: Anne Cronin, Rob Shields, John Soyland, and the late Dede Boden in Culture Media and Communication, and Jonathan Culpeper, Roz Ivanic, Norman Fairclough and Jane Sunderland in Linguistics. I have also benefitted from comments of PhD students on the Faculty of Social Sciences courses on qualitative methods, and from examining some relevant PhD dissertations, especially Philip Mitchell on reported speech (Cardiff) and Claudia Puchta on focus groups (Loughborough).

I have learned a great deal from comments on papers by audiences at the British Association for Applied Linguistics (Manchester, Edinburgh, Cambridge, Reading, Leeds), the American Association for Applied Linguistics (Seattle, Arlington), the Sociolinguistics Symposium (London, Bristol, Ghent), the BAAL/CUP seminar on Analysing Conversation (Open University), and seminars held by Linguistics and by CSEC at Lancaster University, the English Department at the University of Illinois, Champaign-Urbana, the

Centre for Language and Communication at Cardiff University, the English Department at Gothenberg University, Science Studies at the University of Basel, Applied Linguistics at Reading University, English Language at the University of Tampere, and the Discourse and Social Interaction group at King's College London. My thanks to the organizers and participants at these events.

I am especially grateful to the Broadcast Talk Seminar, held each September at Ross Priory, which provided the occasion for early versions of Chapters 9 and 10, and also showed me a model of committed scholarship and fierce, wide-ranging debate that carries over, I hope, to some of the other chapters. My thanks to Andrew Tolson for first inviting me, to Stephanie Marriott and Joanna Thornborrow for keeping it going year after year, and to Shoshana Blum-Kulka, Ian Hutchby, Tamar Liebes, Ulrike Meinhof, Kay Richardson, Paddy Scannell, Theo van Leeuwen, and all the others who kept up such entertaining arguments while we watched clouds scudding across Loch Lomond.

I am aware of some special debts to people who commented on some version of these chapters, or provided key references or insights: Chapters 1 and 2: Susan Condor, Jonathan Potter, and Mark Toogood; Chapter 4: Phil Macnaghten and Bronislaw Szerszynski; Chapters 5 and 6: Michael Agar, Dede Boden, Jenny Kitzinger, Jonathan Potter, and two anonymous referees at *Language in Society* who made detailed suggestions; Chapter 7: Mike Baynham, Carol Berkenkotter (who made a key suggestion), Elizabeth Holt, Geoffrey Leech, Gregory Matoesian, Srikant Sarangi, Elena Semino, Mick Short, Stef Slembrouck, and an anonymous referee at *Applied Linguistics* who made detailed re-analyses of some examples; Chapter 8: Lorenza Mendoza, Tom Horlick-Jones; Chapter 9: Andrew Tolson and Joanna Thornborrow; Chapter 10: Brent Macgregor, and Nan Myers, Pat Myers, and Dan Calef for videotapes; Chapter 11: Ben Rampton. Christine Räisänen made a number of suggestions to improve the readability of Chapters 1–4. The editor of this series made crucial suggestions for Chapters 9, 10, and 11, especially 10.

Besides these specific debts, I would like to acknowledge the general inspiration from the published works of Jenny Kitzinger, Jacqueline Burgess, Michael Billig, John Heritage, and Paddy Scannell, which suggested in different ways that a project such as this might be possible. I proposed the study at the suggestion of Andrew Winnard of Cambridge University Press. And though I am now working in a rather different area from him, I always owe a debt, personal and intellectual, to my mentor Charles Bazerman.

Tess Cosslett and Alice Myers put up with this book as it changed from seed to flood to cloud to beast to box to ball. H. A. P. and Pat Myers offered support from afar. I have dedicated the book to three people who taught me, among other things, to have opinions.

The data in Chapters 5 to 8 are drawn from three studies: 'Public perceptions and sustainability', done for the Lancashire Environmental Forum and Lancashire County Council by the Centre for the Study of Environmental Change (Phil Macnaghten, Robin Grove-White, Michael Jacobs, Brian Wynne); 'Public rhetorics of environmental sustainability', UK Economic and Social Research Council grant R000221347 (Phil Macnaghten, Greg Myers, Brian Wynne); and 'Global citizenship and the environment', UK Economic and Social Research Council grant R000236768 (Greg Myers, Bronislaw Szerszynski, John Urry). Chapters 5 and 6 began as 'Displaying opinions: topics and disagreement in focus groups', *Language in Society* 27: 85–111 (Cambridge University Press). Chapter 7 draws on material from 'Functions of reported speech in focus groups', *Applied Linguistics* 20: 376–401 (Oxford University Press). All these chapters have been completely rewritten, with new material.

Transcription conventions

.	pause less than a second long
(2)	pauses more than a second long, in seconds
/	beginning of overlap
=	latching turns, with no interval between them
=	
((laughter))	transcriber's description of sound or manner
( )	uncertain transcription (sometimes with the best guess in parentheses)
(xxx)	unintelligible words
<u>underline</u>	emphasised syllable
>talk<	quieter talk
word-	apparently truncated word
→	turn referred to in the discussion
. . .	part of the turn omitted
3.2.1.31	reference numbers to the transcripts (see section on data)
M/F	unidentified male or female participant
M1/F2	identified participants
IR	interviewer
IE	interviewee
[Alan]	all names of participants are pseudonyms; these names are substituted in brackets for any real names referred to in transcripts
CU	close-up
MS	medium shot
LS	long shot
VO	voice over

– – –	interviewee response edited before any terminal contour
*	index marks in the transcript showing
* *	approximately where the gesture or movement described in the visual column occurred
.	full stop at the end of a phrase shows falling intonation
?	question mark at the end of a phrase shows rising intonation, not a question

Focus-group data

More details on these groups are found in the reports of the projects. Transcripts are cited in this form:

study number . group number . session number [if there were two sessions] . transcript page

Sustainability indicators

Lancashire County Council / Centre for the Study of Environmental Change
Groups conducted September–October 1994

1.1. Young Men, 17–19, on YTS schemes, Morecambe
1.2. Asian Women, 30–40, Preston
1.3. Mothers, 25–40, with children under five, Thornton
1.4. Unemployed men, Preston
1.5. Retired men and women, 50–70, Thornton
1.6. Professional men and women living in rural areas, 40–60, Lytham St Anne
1.7. Working-class women, 45–60, children grown, Blackburn
1.8. Young professionals, 25–35, Thornton

Public rhetorics of environmental sustainability

Economic and Social Research Council Award number R0000221347
Groups conducted March 1995

2.1. Mothers, 25–40, Thornton
2.2. Men, C1/C2, 35–45, Preston

2.3. Men and women, A/B, 45–60, Silverdale
2.4. Professionals, 25–35, Manchester
2.5. Professionals, 25–35, Brighton (not recorded)
2.6. Men and women, A/B, 45–60, Brighton
2.7. Mothers, 25–40, Brighton
2.8. Men, C1/C2, 35–45, Brighton

Global citizenship and the environment

Economic and Social Research Council Award number
R0000236768
Groups conducted December 1997 – February 1998

3.1. Women, 20–40, involved in local charities and clubs, Great
      Eccleston
3.2. Men and women, 55+, regular foreign holidays, Thornton
3.3. Young women, 16–18, sixth-form college, Blackpool
3.4. Men, 35–55, small business owners, Preston
3.5. Men, 35+, active in trade unions, Preston
3.6. Men and women, 20–40, from an EU country besides the UK,
      Preston
3.7. Men and women, 25–40, work in media-related fields, Man-
      chester
3.8. Men and women, 40–55, public-sector professionals, Man-
      chester
3.9. Men and women, 45–60, corporate professionals, Manchester

Radio phone-ins

BBC Radio Lancashire *Lunchtime Phone-in* with Brett Davison
(26/2/03; 2/9/03; 9/9/03)
BBC Radio Wales *Lunchtime Phone-in* with Nicola Heywood
Thomas (12/2/03)
BBC Radio 4 *Any Questions / Any Answers* (26/10/02; 20/9/03)
BBC Radio 4 *Straw Poll / Talkback* (30/8/03)
Magic 999 (Blackpool) *Late-Night Phone-in* with Pete Price (9/9/03;
11/9/03)
WRIF (Detroit) *Night Call* with Peter Werbe (24/8/03)
WABC (New York) *Sean Hannity* (9/9/03)

Television vox pops

BBC – Inauguration of President Clinton (20/1/93)
GMTV – 'Working mums' (27/2/97)
BBC – Death of Princess Diana (31/8/97)
Channel 4 – *The mourning* (9/97)
CBS – Presidential Address (Clinton on Lewinsky) (18/8/98)
KOIN (Portland) – local evening news (18/8/98)
BBC – Solar eclipse (11/8/99)
BBC – US election (7/11/00)
BBC – Attacks on World Trade Centre and Pentagon (11/9/01)
Channel 4 – *When She Died* (25/8/02)
BBC Breakfast News – 'Pensions' (27/11/02)

1

Paradoxes of opinion

'No opinion'.

That's the last box the survey offers, after all the choices the researcher can imagine, and the humiliating 'Don't know'. The British news magazine *The Economist* used to have an advertisement saying simply:

No Economist. No opinion.

Apparently readers are terrified at the thought of being unable to give an opinion on some topic when challenged, even if that opinion has to be provided by a magazine. Somehow it is important in a society that considers itself democratic that everyone have an opinion on certain issues, and that they be willing and able to tell other people what it is. Yet everyone must control their expressions of opinion as well; it is never a compliment to call someone 'opinionated'.

If we ask why we should have these opinions, why we need them ready for conversation, or why we should read a magazine to find them, we come to a series of paradoxes in our opinions about opinions:

- We cherish our own opinions, but we can also dismiss opinions as a poor substitute for facts.
- Opinions are meant for public discussion, but are also private, individual, protected.
- Opinions are personal, but shared with a group.
- Opinions display one point of view, but the same speaker can express two contradictory opinions.
- Expressions of opinions are assumed to be ephemeral, but are also part of the on-going structure of society.

- Each individual expression of an opinion is limited to a particular space and time, but 'public opinion' has broad effects on national or global events.

In this book, I argue that all these paradoxes arise because we often overlook two aspects of opinions: opinions are always expressed in some interaction between two or more people, and opinions have to be collected and transmitted in some way to become public opinion. We need to look at how people say things, and how this saying is transformed, as well as what they say.

Imagine filling out a survey: there's a man with a clipboard on your front doorstep (he's standing one step below you, as you hold open the door), or a woman on a street in a shopping area (wary shoppers pass by quickly), or a voice on the phone interrupting your dinner, or a questionnaire arrives in the post and you sit with it at the kitchen table. When you respond you may want to impress the interviewer, or get rid of them, or present yourself as a certain type, or avoid revealing anything about yourself, or turn the conversation to something more interesting. The interviewee can treat the survey as a way of accomplishing any of these interactive goals.

The complexities of interaction are not restricted to surveys. A person may be expressing an opinion at a public meeting, or at a dinner party, or across an empty room at the television set. If we are interested in the distribution of opinions, how they are maintained and how they change, we need to know about these interactions too. When researchers, or readers of research, or policy-makers, or theorists of public opinion ignore this immediate context, and treat opinions as if they were things inside us, or as if they were things out there in the social structure, the opinions become puzzling. What seems straightforward enough, at the time and in the place we hear it and respond to it, gets caught up in problematic slides between opinion and fact, or gaps between the public and private, or irrational contradictions.

When I say opinion is a matter of interaction, it is not just my opinion. It has been emerging as sociologists discuss the construction of *facts*, as social psychologists question the concept of *attitudes*, as political philosophers try to define the *public sphere*, as conversation analysts look at *talk*, as media studies scholars look at *broadcast talk*, and as social scientists reflect on their use of *methods* such as interviews, oral history, focus groups, surveys, or experiments. I am not saying that the work of all these researchers converges, but they have all come to take seriously the particular ways opinions are expressed in context and transformed by media, whether television, tape, or paper and pencil. In the next chapter I will discuss analytical methods. In the rest of the book, I will present detailed analyses of specific cases in which opinions are expressed or packaged. But first, in this chapter, I will identify some of the strands of this wider research project by discussing each of the paradoxes I have raised and considering some of the wider implications of this approach, such as why opinions matter in the study of language, in the study of society, or in our own roles as citizens.

Facts and opinions

In an early episode of the television situation comedy *Friends*, Phoebe, a stereotypical enthusiast for New Age beliefs, mentions in passing that the reality of evolution is a matter of opinion. Her friend Ross, who works as a palaeontologist in a natural history museum, is shocked by such an unwillingness to face facts. The situation becomes more and more comic, as he fills his briefcase with bones from the museum to demonstrate that evolution is something out there, not something conditional on anyone's belief or lack of belief. For Ross, Phoebe's resistance to facts is a barrier to any kind of talk about anything else. How can one talk to someone for whom *everything* is just a matter of personal opinion? ('Don't get me started on gravity,' Phoebe says). Surely there must be some distinction between matters of opinion and matters of fact?

The word *opinion* has multiple and complex meanings (see Myers 2002); in one sense it is 'just opinion', not knowledge or demonstration:

Opinion . . . 1. What one opines; judgement resting on grounds insufficient for complete demonstration; belief of something as probable or as seeming to one's own mind to be true (Dist. from *knowledge, conviction,* or *certainty*; occas. = *belief.*) (OED)

Opinions aren't facts. As Harvey Sacks remarks in his *Lectures on Conversation,* 'one of the characteristics of opinion is that it's something lay people are entitled to have when they're not entitled to have knowledge' (1992: I.33). Everyone is entitled to their own opinion, on all those matters that are matters of opinion. One can, of course, disagree with the opinion they hold, but to deny their entitlement to have an opinion is to challenge their individual identity (that is why Phoebe gets so angry). Facts, on the other hand, are what people already agree on, what they can demonstrate; one doesn't need to argue about them, but just to inform people (that is why Ross gets angry). Facts are kept tidily on display for company in the living room; opinions are stacked up in a kind of back room, where company need not visit, and where they have no right to criticize.

Because of this long-standing opposition between facts and opinions (it can be found in Aristotle as well as on *Friends*), the meaning of *opinion* changes if the meaning of *fact* changes. And the meaning of *fact* has been changing, both in the academic study of science and in the way members of the public understand scientific facts. Some sociologists, historians, and philosophers of science have argued that scientific facts are established through social processes of persuasion (Latour and Woolgar 1979; Mulkay 1979; Brannigan 1981; Collins 1985; Latour 1987; Potter 1996). In this view, facts are something like opinions; instead of saying we believe a statement because it is a fact, these researchers say we hold a statement to be a fact because of the way we believe it (Woolgar 1988).

There have been ferocious arguments, in science studies and between science studies and scientists, about this view of science as socially constructed (for one of the most interesting and readable responses from scientists, see Dunbar 1995). These disputes would not matter to most non-scientists (or to scientists) if they were confined to the academic fields of science studies. But issues of expert and lay fact and opinion appear in all areas of our lives, from financial predictions to radiation risks to nutrition. A statement given the authority of an expert is another of the senses of *opinion* given in the OED:

3. The formal statement by an expert or professional man of what he thinks, judges or advises on a matter submitted to him; considered advice.

Experts have their own rhetorical strengths and their own institutional channels. As Walter Lippmann observed, in his classic essay on the formation of public opinion, 'Except on a few subjects where our own knowledge is great, we cannot choose between true and false accounts. So we choose between trustworthy and untrustworthy reporters' (1922). But experts do not settle the matter; their assertions just lead to further rhetoric about their trustworthiness, their own motives, limitations, and biases (see Chapter 8). If we want to pursue the ways the boundary between fact and opinion is drawn, we need to look at how claims are made and supported as people talk, what they take and don't take as a matter of opinion.

Private and public

There is something personal and distinctive about your own opinion, in the dictionary sense of 'what one opines'. It is yours, it is different from that of other people, and it is part of what marks you as an individual, like your style of dress or hair. But the *OED* has another sense of *opinion*, besides the sense opposed to fact and the sense associated with experts: as something collective and social.

Opinion . . . b. what is generally thought about something. Often qualified by *common, general, public, vulgar.*   (OED)

When *opinion* is used in this sense, it is apparently both generalized and potentially criticized. The *common opinion* is just what one doesn't want to have, and *vulgar opinion*, in the sense *vulgar* now has, would be even worse. And yet for all this denigration, public opinion has an essential role in any democratic society. Democratic states depend on representation, and what the representatives represent is some form of the will of the people (Barber 1996). The will of the people is not just the sum of the opinions of individuals; it is assumed to be something collective, more considered, less ephemeral (see Chapter 4). Hannah Arendt traces the very idea of opinion to the American and French Revolutions and says that these events taught a cautionary lesson:

Even though opinions are formed by individuals and must remain, as it were, their property, no single individual – neither the wise man of the philosophers nor the divinely informed reason, common to all men, of the Enlightenment – can ever be equal to the task of sifting opinions, of passing them through the sieve of intelligence which will separate the arbitrary and idiosyncratic, and thus purify them into public views.   (Arendt 1963)

What sort of forum best provides for this sifting of opinion? It's clearly not Congress or Parliament (though Arendt argues the Senate was intended for just this purpose), not newspaper editorials or leading articles, not 30-second election spot advertising, not public enquiries, not private talk over coffee or a beer. Much of the academic debate on possible forums has followed from Jurgen Habermas's argument that there is and should be a *public sphere* apart from the state and the market; Habermas first developed this argument in an early book, and it has been much debated since it was translated into English as *The Structural Transformation of the Public Sphere* (1962/1989). He gives a historical sketch to show how the word *public* shifted from being associated with the court (public vs. private authority) to it being associated with the kind of discussion and opinion found in coffee houses and newspapers emerging in the eighteenth century. He then argues that this emerging forum for discussion was colonized by mass media such as large newspapers or broadcasters, so that discussion, when freed from the state and the church, becomes dominated by commercial interests.

There are many controversial aspects of this overview (Dahlgren and Sparks 1991; Calhoun 1992; McGuigan 1998; Sparks 1998), including the idealization of one stage and class of bourgeois society, and the view of mass media as one-way, centralized, and manipulative. John Thompson (1995) distinguishes between the public imagined by Habermas, one defined by its separateness from the state and openness to discussion, and a new sphere opened up by electronic media: 'These new media create a new kind of publicness which consists of what we might describe as *the space of the visible*' (1995: 245). An example of an intervention in 'the space of the visible' might be a television report on road protesters (Szerszynski 1999) – an apparently local and procedural issue of building a road becomes a public issue of values because we *see* it.

There are also questions about what issues are matters of public as opposed to personal concern. Feminists extending these discussions (Fraser 1992) have argued that the idea of a single unitary public sphere is itself gendered. It is not just that men have opportunities and models that enable them to dominate much of public discussion, and that they therefore have a disproportionate amount of influence. More fundamentally, the realm of 'public affairs' has been defined as excluding domestic and affective realms as the affairs of women, and the preferred style of discussion privileges a gendered idea of rationality (Young 1996). Lauren Berlant has argued that what has developed in the US is an 'intimate public sphere': 'No longer valuing personhood as something directed toward public life, contemporary nationalist ideology recognizes a public good only in a particularly constricted nation of simultaneously lived private worlds' (Berlant 1997: 5). In this view, the blurring of the boundary of public and private is not a liberating expansion of the political, but a contraction of what is public. Institutions of opinion play their part in making isolated people spectators to citizenship.

These realms of public and private, civic and domestic, masculine and feminine are not just matters of political theory; people refer to available categories and draw on them when talking in groups and when presenting themselves. In a group recruited from women picking up toddlers at day care, a woman says 'as a mother you just tend to step back from it'; in a group of male small-business owners, a couple weeks later in a nearby city, a man justifies his own list of concerns in terms of specialist knowledge from his job: 'working as I do in the petrol industry, I have to think of . . .' These approaches suggest that we must be careful not to take the 'public' in 'public opinion' as given (see Chapter 10). The ways people define the public can vary with different experiences, different purposes, and different forums. The boundaries of public and private are also open to moment-to-moment negotiation, as participants decide what is appropriate to say next.

Individual opinions and group identities

The reason a survey researcher asks for your view is that you are assumed to have one as an individual, potentially a different one from that of the next person down the street. But the organization doing the survey is only interested because this response can stand for many others. As an old textbook on public opinion research put it, 'Opinions cluster by groups: regional, national origin, race, religion, urban-rural status, and social class or status. Consciously or unconsciously people tend to identify with such groups as these (and many more specific ones: unions, trade associations, sporting clubs, and so forth) and to draw their opinions from these identifications' (Lane and Sears 1964: 2). There are two claims here, that the opinions correlate with group membership, and that the identification with the group shapes the individual opinion. These claims relate to an underlying political purpose of public opinion research in its formative period; the relation of the individual to the group opinion is a major problem for the American liberalism of the 1950s, and for the research on opinion that developed in this climate (e.g., Katz and Lazarsfeld 1955). If individuals generally conform to groups, how can they be said to hold an opinion? If they don't conform to groups, how can single statements of opinion be aggregated or generalized at all?

Researchers have often turned for an answer to these questions to social psychological work on the ways groups shape individuals. But this work deals with attitudes, not opinions. The terms *opinion* and *attitude* are often used interchangeably in other fields, but for these social psychological researchers they are distinct. 'Attitude is a psychological tendency that is expressed by evaluating a particular entity with some degree of favor or disfavor' (Eagly and Chaiken 1993: 1). Opinions are the cognitive, affective, or behavioural responses that reveal these underlying psychological attitudes. In this view, opinions are indeed tied to a particular situation, and may be transitory, as I have been arguing, but attitudes are carried by individuals, and remain stable over time. The social psychological distinction is a useful corrective to methods that would mistake the instrument (polls, focus groups, experiments) for the entity itself. But from the point of view of discourse analysis, there are no grounds to propose or know about such entities as attitudes (or traits, emotions, or habits), apart from the way they are manifested in discourse and action (Potter and Wetherell 1987).

I need, then, a view that defines the self in terms of how it emerges in social interactions and I find such a view in the work of Erving Goffman (1959; 1963; 1971). Goffman conceived of the self as a role each of us plays, a way we present ourselves in encounters with others. This presentation varies from situation to situation, so that, for instance, a waiter may have a very different manner in the kitchen and out in the dining room taking orders from guests; Goffman was fascinated with the possible gap between 'frontstage' and 'backstage' performances. These performances take work, a constant attention to the way we stand or pass someone, say hello or good-bye, tell stories, or look away. Even our sense of what is real and what is just practice, a joke, or a game is a matter of signals we give off and interpret moment to moment (Goffman 1974). Goffman also suggested that participants in interaction could take on different roles, so that I might shift, for instance, between speaking for myself and voicing the concerns of others, between being the person who is being talked to and being an eavesdropper. I will discuss these distinctions in Chapter 2 and Chapter 7.

Goffman's work has had its critics, who have seen it as individualistic, or unsystematic, or limited in its central metaphors (as we will see in the next section). But it has remained enormously influential, as it has been extended to other fields (Meyrowitz 1985; Drew and Wootton 1988; Malone 1997). After reading Goffman, it is hard to imagine a naive self who simply reveals pre-existing opinions to a neutral stranger who asks for them. Normal people are quite capable of managing the impressions they give; indeed people who cannot manage these impressions are considered abnormal (mental health institutions are another area of Goffman's interest). We will see this self-presentation in the talk about experts in Chapter 8, the phone-ins in Chapter 9, and the analysis of vox pop interviews in Chapter 10.

Much of the painstaking work of quantitative public opinion research is an attempt to get around these little dramas of self-presentation, to bracket them off as a kind of bias so that one can get to the real opinions underlying them (See Chapter 4). But if we take Goffman's project seriously, we see that self-presentation is not methodological noise to be corrected, it is an inevitable part of any elicitation of opinion. The very fact that people produce opinions is a matter of self-presentation. Walter Bagehot noted more than a hundred years ago that people would obligingly produce opinions even where they could not have had any opinion before: 'It has been said that if you can only get a middle-class Englishman to think whether there are "snails on Sirius", he will soon have an opinion on it. It will be difficult to make him think, but if he does think, he cannot rest in a negative, he will come soon to some decision' (quoted in Lippmann 1922: 224). Bagehot takes this as an indication that the middle-class Englishman (like the reader of *The Economist* apparently) likes to have opinions. We on the other hand might take it as an indication of the way a question projects the possibility of an opinion for the answerer to take up. Constraint on opinions is also a matter of self-presentation; no one wants to be considered *opinionated* in ordinary social settings. (According to the *OED*, Milton coined a term for holding excessive opinions that is now, alas, archaic: *opinionastrous*). In either case, the opinion emerges or is buried because of the interaction.

Goffman's concepts of roles and performances were grounded in his ethnographies of institutions such as a Shetland Island hotel and a mental hospital and illustrated with a vast collection of clips from his reading of newspapers and non-fiction. But they are more useful as methodological and theoretical suggestions than as templates for practical analysis. For more systematic linguistic categories we can turn to another influential line in the study of interaction, the ethnography of communication, which focuses on speech in its cultural context (Hymes 1972; Gumperz 1982; Moerman 1988; Saville-Troike 1989; Duranti and Goodwin 1992; Lucy 1993). Dell Hymes specified a range of dimensions in which one might describe a speech event (a wedding, a party, a theatrical performance, a class), partly as an aid to systematic comparison of such events across cultures. I consider this approach, and tensions between it and other approaches to the context for talk, when I consider speech acts involving opinions in Chapter 3.

Consistent and contradictory

The social psychological work on attitudes seeks to explain consistency: why someone says one thing today, and something rather similar on a different issue and to someone else tomorrow. Discourse analytical work tries to explain contradiction: why someone can say one thing today, and something different tomorrow, or even a few minutes later. The nineteenth-century American poet Walt Whitman announced at the end of 'Song of Myself':

> Do I contradict myself?
> Very well then, I contradict myself.
>   (I am large, I can contain multitudes)

There are a number of reasons why Mr Whitman would provide problems for a survey researcher. One of them is that surveys assume that underlying attitudes remain consistent from moment to moment, even if stated opinions may change gradually over

time, under identifiable influences. If someone holds two opposite
opinions at the same time, as Whitman claims to do, then on the
survey it is assumed he or she has no strong opinion, or is undecided.
But ordinary people (and not just nineteenth-century poets) do con-
tradict themselves, even if they are not always this proud to admit
it. And there are often contradictions in just those opinions that a
person might say they felt most strongly about, those that were most
central to their identity: the environmentalist with the big car, the
socialist who distrusts workers, the conservative opponent of big
government who wants central control over the school curriculum.

   The importance of contradiction in our thinking and talk has
been explored by the British social psychologist Michael Billig. His
interest began with his study of the ideologies of anti-Semitism and
racism in right-wing movements (Billig 1978) and has continued
in studies of how royalty enters into the everyday lives of British
people (1991b) and of the ordinary, daily aspects of nationalism.
Researchers on racist discourse point out the way people say 'I'm
no racist but . . .' before going on to make disparaging remarks
about members of other groups (Wetherell and Potter 1992; van
Dijk et al. 1997). More surprisingly, Billig finds examples of people
who do claim to be prejudiced, but who can justify being humane or
admiring in dealings with a particular representative of the groups
they despise. This kind of contradiction leads beyond social psychological research on attitudes and stereotyping, and back to the
history of rhetoric. Rhetoric is the craft of persuasion; for Billig,
what is crucial is that the rhetorician acknowledges and responds to
the opposing argument.

   This spirit of contradiction, Billig argues, occurs not only in the
law courts, the legislature, and formal debates, but also in our own
thinking, where we typically argue back and forth, always aware
of alternatives (1991a: Ch. 1). The result is not confusion, or the
survey questionnaire's 'Undecided'. Opinions tend to fall into pairs,
structured by our search for oppositions. Or as Whitman puts it:

> I find one side a balance and the antipodal side a balance,
> Soft doctrine as steady help as stable doctrine
> > ('Song of Myself')

As a psychologist, Billig is concerned with the way this restless play
with language and persuasion undermines the study of attitudes as

stable entities. But he is also interested in how such contradictions structure our everyday experience of political issues – for instance, how the daily news and weather report reinforces a sense of taken-for-granted national identity, even for someone who (like me) is not a citizen of the nation in which they live (Billig 1995).

Billig distinguishes his approach from that of Goffman, with whom he might be expected to agree (1987: Ch. 1). Goffman's metaphor of roles on the stage, he says, treats performances as regular, scripted, and coordinated; it does not encourage us to see conflicts within the theatre or ways people work out their roles. And it focuses on the individual; Billig's emphasis on rhetoric brings the public forum in contact with private life. Despite these differences, Goffman and Billig are similar in stressing the way opinion emerges in interaction (even interaction with oneself), rather than existing as an attribute. As Goffman shows how opinions are designed as self-presentation, Billig shows how they are shaped in an on-going and not always harmonious dialogue, and how certain familiar arguments recur, echo, and are inverted, often in witty play.

Billig's perspective will help us make sense of many contradictions we will encounter later in the book, in talk about the environment, immigration, poverty, and community. For instance, a participant in a group says that instead of giving money to help people abroad, money should go to people in this country on hospital waiting lists: 'I'm sorry but they must come first.' The moderator points out a contradiction:

```
Mod:  But that, you can see obviously that runs
      against sort of what we were saying earlier
      when we were discussing the landmines.
```

The participant is not bothered by this contradiction:

```
Mike:  I'm caring for people here in Manchester and
       in the UK, you know, frequently, I am really
       caring for those people, you can't care for
       them all unfortunately.
```

Mike reformulates what he has said, from a matter of exclusion to a matter of priorities. Both he and the moderator are invoking familiar arguments, one that treats all humans as having the same claim on us, the other saying that the claim is weaker the further away the needy person is (Ginzberg 1994; Myers and Macnaghten 1998).

Billig draws our attention to such interplay, points out the historical and literary lineage of everyday encounters, and links the internal tensions of thought to the external tensions of argument. But he does not give us a way of analysing the sequence of such arguments. Why is it taken as a criticism in this context when the moderator says this runs against what they were saying earlier? Why is Mike's response taken as a response? How can we tell when what is going on is an argument, and when it is banter, or storytelling, or interrogation? For these sorts of questions we will need a more detailed analysis of the way people agree and disagree.

Structural and ephemeral

It may seem from the review so far that a detailed analysis of talk will break down any sense of the structure of public opinion, revealing how each expression of opinion is unsupported, private, designed for a particular encounter, and potentially self-contradictory. This detailed analysis leads us to criticize the abstraction, reification, generalization, and aggregation that go on in the processing of public opinion. Are we left, then, with just a lot of disparate occasions, this encounter on the doorstep and that rant in the pub, each dinner party or each interview different from every other? Fortunately, we find that the talk is both fleeting, and also tightly and regularly structured. What people say remains unpredictable, complex, contradictory; the way they say it is surprisingly predictable, down to fractions of a second. This predictability can provide an empirical basis for Goffman's approach to self-presentation and Billig's approach to argumentation (but see Billig 1999).

The study of these predictable patterns in talk has been the project of ethnomethodological conversation analysis over the last thirty years. I will discuss some of the analytical detail of conversation analysis in Chapter 2; here I want to go back to the beginnings to suggest how the approach fills a gap left by the other approaches I have been discussing. For all the hundreds of people who have written on conversation analysis, the liveliest and broadest discussions are still the first ones, the lectures given by the young Harvey Sacks at the University of California between 1964 and 1972, and recorded and transcribed by other researchers (Sacks 1992; Silverman 1998). In these lectures, Sacks raised big issues: what does it mean to be ordinary, to go about one's life normally, to be needed, to make sense, to be in one category of person or another? And in pursuit of these big questions, he took apart bits of conversation in the most excruciating detail, week by week on the same extracts: How do participants interpret a silence, or a glance, or a question? Who is entitled to talk about what? How do they open a conversation and close it? Unlike linguistic analysts who sought an elaborate underlying grammar for dialogue, as for sentence structure (see Chapter 2), Sacks and his colleagues looked only at how one speaker's turn of talk followed that of another. The question is always, 'Why just that just then?' The aim in asking this question is not to construct a system of rules known to analysts but to see how the participants themselves interpret the talk as orderly.

Sacks's answer to the question I mentioned earlier, of how we know when an argument is going on, is to look at how the participants are treating the talk. When someone says, 'I still say though ...' they are not just asserting something, they are treating the interaction as an argument (perhaps to the surprise of the other participants) (Sacks 1992: I.344; see also Antaki (1994; 1998)). All this might seem obvious enough, but Sacks's task is to get these social observations out of the transcript, not to bring to it what he knows about, say, the power relations between interviewer and interviewee, or the pressure that groups can put on individuals. For Sacks the talk is central and has its own structuring, brought about by participants in the course of talking; it is not just an epiphenomenon of something else, such as social power or stratification. This does not mean that conversation analysis ignores social structure; as we will see in Chapter 2, there have been a number of studies devoted to conversation in different kinds of institutions: classrooms, courtrooms, doctors' surgeries. All the talk I will analyse in this book is, to one degree or another, within an institution: focus groups (Chapters 5–8), radio phone-ins (Chapter 9), or broadcast interviews (Chapter 10). I will return to Sacks and other conversation analysts to try to untangle what is institutional about these interactions – and what is not.

Local and global

When the survey researcher leaves your doorstep, he or she takes away a piece of paper (or now a computer file) with your responses on it. Opinions become concrete in other forms: bumper stickers, ballots, letters to the editor, T-shirts. They are collected in various forms in which they can be summed up at a glance: percentages in headlines, tables in yearbooks, bar charts on the front page of *USA Today*. They can then be used to explain or justify some action in the public arena, or lack of action. Thus there is another paradox of opinion, between its local powerlessness, and its potentially national and global effects. Sitting in a pub with other wise people, I can complain eloquently about the treatment of refugees, the funding of schools, or Third World debt, but I know nothing I say will have any influence on what happens. The paradox is that when the government makes – or avoids – a decision on refugees, schools, or debt, it is often attributed to 'public opinion', which we are told (for instance in Gallup and Rae (1940)) is the aggregated form of all the conversations in pubs, on buses, and over backyard fences. This form of public opinion is played back to us in interviews with people on the street, in poll results, in interpretations of focus groups or local meetings. How does talk that is so weak become so strong?

There are two related processes here: the way the world is represented to us as material for opinions, and the way opinions are packaged for presentation to the world. These are complex processes, but clearly in the societies I am discussing, mass media play a central role. Traditional studies of the media tried to account for the ways their representations channelled opinion (Lippmann 1922). Early media research was modelled on propaganda studies during the Second World War and focused on misrepresentation and stereotyping on the one hand, or the promotion of citizenship and internationalism on the other (Blumler and Gurevitch 1996). There are many insights in this literature, but it tends to characterize audiences as passive recipients of messages (for critical reflections, see Katz et al. 2003).

More recently, media theorists have taken a more interactive view of how people receive and construct news and public issues, and in particular on the effects of new electronic media. So, for instance, Meyrowitz (1985) has argued that the intense scrutiny that television gives us of the moment-to-moment impression management by public figures, and the intrusion into what had been backstage regions, does more than any scandal to undermine confidence in leaders; once one sees the President scratching his nose, it is never possible to go back to the heroic image on the election poster. Dayan and Katz (1992) analyse the live, continuous broadcasting of major events to show how these events enter into our conceptions of history, nationhood, and our own lives. Boltanski argues that we can reconcile the demand for a moral and emotional relation to distant others with universalistic ideas of justice (the problem some call 'compassion fatigue') only by understanding the way we relate to suffering through media (1999).

What about the other side of this process, the way opinions are packaged for playing back to the public? I will be turning to a range of studies concerned with broadcast talk, for models of how people express opinions when they have a microphone or camera in front of them, and of how these expressions are used in programmes (see references in Chapter 2, and also Bell 1991; Bell and van Leeuwen 1994; Fairclough 1995; Bell and Garrett 1998; Scollon 1998). How do questions and answers constrain the discussion in interviews? What makes an interviewee seem evasive? How do people perform sincerity? How does one remark get replayed as representative of the public, and another as a personal view? Often these analyses concern major events: an influential speech, a meeting at a crucial turning point, the outbreak or end of war, or a mass protest. But they can also be about the daily, quickly forgotten dialogues on talk radio, or chat shows, or press conferences, dialogues that shape our sense of what the issues are and how they are to be discussed.

I have referred to the problems in democratic theory of dividing public from private affairs; these problems are intensified by our involvement with media. What was considered private (family squabbles, illnesses, royal divorces, drug habits) are now conducted in the full attention of broadcast media; what was considered public (wars, bombings, Parliamentary and Congressional hearings, trials, state ceremonies, sporting events) can now be brought into daily lives (Dayan and Katz 1992; Liebes and Curran 1998). The way people talk about news – Diana's death, Clinton's impeachment, or the UK Government's Iraq dossier – is an important part of any political process, and this way of talking cannot be separated from broadcast talk. Expressions of opinion are part of a cycle in which people on television model their talk on everyday conversation, people in everyday conversation model their talk on broadcast chat, and both are seen as performances in which one constructs a preferred self (Thompson 1995; Abercrombie and Longhurst 1998; Luhmann 2000). Like the playground basketballer imagining himself sailing up to the hoop in slow motion, we find our everyday activities are tied up with their mediated images. It is these mediated images that make 'public opinion' a powerful force for (or against) change. So we need to attend both to the forms of expression of opinion (Chapters 5–8) and to the packaging of these expressions in the media (Chapters 9–10).

Social science data as talk

I have argued that most research on opinions starts with some sort of encounter between the researcher and a member of the public, and that traditional methods tend to strip away all the details of this encounter to leave a simple statement, or to put these statements together to get numbers. The introductions that produce surveys, interviews, and focus groups are reduced to clear findings, and in the process we lose any sense of who said what to whom, after what, and to what end. More subtly, we lose the pace and feel of people talking, and this pace and feel are crucial to how we interpret how they might have meant their statements. When I began this book, there were already whispers in various corners pointing out that most social science methods, for researching opinion and other topics too, were based on talk. As I have been writing, these whispers have grown into an impressive chorus, even if not everyone is singing from the same song sheet. Actually, though I was not aware of it when I began, this attention to talk began much earlier than I thought, back with the origins of such methods as polling and focus groups.

If this attention to talk in social science data is not yet recognized as a field, school, or polemical turn, it may be because these various methodologists, analysts, and critics are pursuing different agendas, trying to understand objectivity, power, institutions, or writing. Some researchers are trying to improve traditional methods of interviewing by eliminating possible areas of bias, or to improve analysis by closer attention to what is transcribed from tapes. Others are concerned with power relations between the researcher and the researched, the way an approach to questioning can determine some kinds of answers and silence others. Some are applying the study of the language of institutions and professions, which had taken on the courts, doctor's offices, and schools, to institutions closer to home, those of academic research, and finding that these questions and answers also work within unstated constraints.

Questions have been raised from the very beginnings of social science surveys about how they are conducted, often in the context of the ancient battles between quantitative and qualitative methods in the social sciences. It is interesting that Paul Lazersfeld, one of the pioneers of survey methods, also made a perceptive list of possible problems with surveys interviews (1944). But he proposed 'depth interviews' as a complementary method only to remove ambiguities from the surveys and improve the statistical analyses of the results. A classic critique by Lucy Suchman and Brigitte Jordan, based more on conversation analysis, challenges the way opinions are defined and gathered (1990). I will discuss this line of critique in Chapter 4.

The critiques of survey methods do not mean that more qualitative interviews have been left unscathed. In a classic of linguistic ethnography, *Learning How to Ask*, Charles Briggs argues that 'because the interview is an accepted speech event in our own native speech communities, we take for granted that we know what it is and what it produces' (1986: 2). When researchers interview in another culture, they may miss the signals they are getting about the kind of communication that is going on; they may structure the interview by their own norms and miss the hybrid and conflicting norms of speech events – for instance testimony or teaching or performance rather than interview. My problem is different, but the issue Briggs raises still applies; I am dealing with members of a culture in which several forms of interview are well established, so we see participants slipping into what they assume to be the role demanded of them. What Briggs says of the anthropological interview applies more widely: 'What is said is seen as a reflection of what is "out there" rather than as an interpretation which is jointly produced by interviewer and respondent' (3). Linguistic anthropologists have pursued Briggs's questions about how the research interaction shapes findings about culture (Duranti and Goodwin 1992). The most extensive study of anthropological data from the perspective of conversation analysis is by Moerman (1988).

Researchers in other social sciences have considered interaction between members of the same culture. Gilbert and Mulkay (1984) influenced a whole range of work in science studies with their decision to look, not just at what was said by the scientists they interviewed, but at how they said it, for instance how they shifted from one kind of explanation of a scientist's actions to another. Marjorie Goodwin (1990) gives detailed attention to her part as researcher in the talk among black children that she studies. Schiffrin (1984; 1990; 1993; 1996) and Johnstone (1993) both consider the interactional as well as the linguistic features of their sociolinguistic interviews. Oral historians once tried to keep the interviewer in the background, to let the interviewee speak for him/herself; now some historians see issues of self-presentation as speakers remember. Summerfield (1998) for instance, discusses the way speakers achieve *composure*, both in the sense of feeling at ease and in the sense of composing their memories. Hutchby and Wooffitt (1998: Ch. 7) devote a whole chapter of their introduction to conversation analysis to applying it to research data, in this case to interviews on paranormal experiences (Wooffitt 1992).

Most of the data in this book are from focus groups, and as with surveys, they received close attention from one of the founders, Robert Merton (Merton and Kendall 1946; Merton et al. 1956; Merton 1987), who pointed out, for instance, the crucial effects of sequencing of questions. Morrison (1998) has provided both a detailed history of the method and an account of how it has been used; I will return to his comments on how the moderator can affect the interaction. Burgess (Burgess et al. 1988a; Burgess et al. 1988b) has applied her experience as a trained therapist to the development of a group's identity. Kitzinger (1994; 1995), in her work on health studies and media studies, has urged analysts not to ignore the interactions between participants. Michael Agar and James MacDonald (1995) have applied to focus-group research the insights of the ethnographer. Wodak and her colleagues (1999) consider the way participants in groups work together to co-construct aspects of national identity. Greg Matoesian and Chip Coldren, Jr have analysed non-verbal cues in focus-group interaction (2002). Claudia Puchta, a professional focus-group researcher as well as a discourse analyst, has with Jonathan Potter done the most careful study of the genre from a conversation analytic perspective (Puchta and Potter 1999; Puchta and Potter 2003), and I have taken up various aspects of interaction in the studies leading up to this book (Myers 1998; 1999b; 2000a; 2000d; Myers and Macnaghten 1998; Myers and Macnaghten 1999; Macnaghten and Myers 2004). The most recent handbook of focus-group research contains a number of insights on interaction (Bloor et al. 2001).

All these references may make it seem that the talk in social science research data is of highly specialized methodological interest to other academics. But the issues raised in these discussions are of much broader interest. They tell us about the construction of 'public opinion' in polls and focus groups that play an important – and controversial – role in the day-to-day running of modern democracies. They remind us that social science research more generally crucially involves questions about just what the researcher and the researched think is going on. When we hear of an academic study showing changes in attitudes towards sexuality, television violence, the environment, or foreigners, we need to be able to reconstruct some of the interactions that might have produced this new knowledge. And on a deeper level, we need to consider how institutions of opinion and the mediated representations of this talk both draw on and shape our everyday interactions.

Plan of the Book

The book is structured in three parts: an overview of analytical issues and methods (Chapters 2–4), analyses of expression of opinions in group discussions (Chapters 5–8), and analyses of the ways these expressions are performed and packaged in media texts (Chapters 9–10). The first section begins with a review of some of the resources for analysing group discussions (Chapter 2). I use this framework to compare discussions in different kinds of groups, such as focus groups, consensus panels, and seminars (Chapter 3). I then put these discussions within the wider framework of the institutions that commission and use public opinion polls and focus groups (Chapter 4).

The core of the book is the chapters dealing with detailed analyses of focus-group interactions, considering the ways participants define and close topics (Chapter 5), the patterns of agreement and disagreement (Chapter 6), and the various uses of reported speech (Chapter 7). Finally, I consider the ways these people talk about the broadcast and reported opinions of experts (Chapter 8).

To deal with the ways opinions are packaged and reproduced, I focus especially on phone-ins as 'sociable argument' (Chapter 9) and vox pop 'man on the street' interviews, showing how public opinion is constructed as a category through the categorization work on and with interviewees. Finally, in Chapter 11, I return to some of the issues raised in this chapter, and consider some of the wider implications of treating opinions as talk.

2

A tool kit for analysing group discussions

The transcriber of our focus-group tapes broke down at one point and recorded several minutes of talk with the words, 'STILL MORE ABOUT RUBBISH BINS'. Any of us who read this particular set of transcripts, with its repetitive complaints about local government services, can sympathize with her exasperation. But we might wish for a rather more detailed account than this curt summary.

This transcription is an extreme case of what I noted in Chapter 1, the way researchers reduce transcripts to content categories, losing the details of talk. I argued there for analysis that would tell us about how people said things as well as about what they said. This chapter introduces some of the tools used for analysing group discussions, in conversation analysis, discourse analysis, pragmatics, and rhetoric. Instead of introducing each of these fields of research separately, I will look at the same passage in various ways. I will start with one participant's statement of an opinion, as it appears in a transcript, and the ways it might be coded. Then I will give a much more detailed transcription, including what was said by the preceding and following speakers, and consider some aspects of turn-taking, to see how this utterance was elaborated, echoed, and transformed. But I would also like to go beyond conversation analysis to look at how words and sentences relate to what we know about the structure of language, and to identify uses of persuasive language such as commonplaces. These levels of analysis – turns, words, and rhetorical devices – by no means exhaust the possibilities for interpreting this passage, but they illustrate the range of approaches I will take in later chapters.

Analysis and reporting of spoken data usually have to deal with written transcripts, not with audiotapes, videotapes, or live talk.

The whole analysis depends on the way the talk is written down; as Ochs put it in a much-quoted chapter title, it depends on treating 'Transcription as theory' (1979). I will argue at the end of this chapter that we need more detail than is standard in most transcripts that are made for non-linguistic research.

An opinion

Let's start with just one participant's response to a question and see what it can tell us. This is from a focus group, a discussion held for research purposes, with eight participants in this case, led by a moderator who follows a standard list of questions called a topic guide. This group includes upper-middle-class men and women over fifty-five years old, living in a village in an attractive rural part of Lancashire near the Lake District. The village has a station on the railway line that goes around the Cumbrian coast to Sellafield, a large nuclear reprocessing plant that has been the subject of environmental controversy for more than twenty years. At this point in the session, the moderator has already gone around the group once, asking participants about where they live; now he has asked them if there are 'any environmental issues that concern you individually'. Here is the first response, as it appears in the transcript used by researchers for their analysis and report:

```
Lynne:  Something that came to me the other day. I
        was reading about houses being built at the
        station, and I suddenly thought about trains
        carrying the nuclear waste up to Sellafield -
        and I've never thought about it before -
        but then I thought, you know, because I was
        thinking - ooh, (laughter) that was just
        something that I did think about. You know.
        I think people worry about the pollution on
        the shore.
```

One way to interpret this bit of data is to code it according to a systematic scheme: this might be marked as environmental concerns / nuclear / waste / transport / Sellafield (on the methods of such coding, and ways of extending it, see Hoijer 1990; Bertrand et al. 1992; Catterall and MacLaren 1997; Titscher et al. 2000: Ch. 5; Bloor et al. 2001). The coding can stop at that, and often does, and it can be useful; the researcher could then count up all the mentions of Sellafield or nuclear waste transport and compare them to mentions in this group and others of environmental problems such as car fumes, sewage on the beach, or erosion of footpaths. The coding would take into account some aspects of the research situation (the age, gender, location, and class of participants) but not others (what was asked, how other people responded, how they were sitting). The problem with such coding is that it fits what Lynne said into the categories determined by the analyst. An attention to the way she said it, for instance the way she starts talking about one issue and ends with another one, might be more of a clue to the categories that are relevant to her and to the group.

An opinion in interaction

To look at the interaction involved in Lynne's opinion, we will need a more detailed transcript that can show us, for instance, where participants overlap or pause. I have also continued the transcript through another three minutes of talk, so that we can see how the topic shifts and how the moderator makes her come back to what she has said. The transcriber punctuated the talk in grammatical prose sentences; I have left it unpunctuated, but have put in full stops (.) to indicate pauses (see 'Transcription conventions' at the beginning of the book). This is the longest example in the book; it might help if I indicate with arrows some of the turns on which I will focus in the analysis.

2.3.8
```
  1. Mod:   ok . that's very helpful . gives me .
            a different sense of the place now .
            I mean given that we are going to be
            talking a bit about the environment
            this evening . what would be quite .
            helpful I think . just a just again
            to go round . just to see if there
            are any particular environmental
            issues that concern you individually
            . that can mean anything . that can
            be something very local or something
            much broader that affects other
            people as well . um so maybe can we
            start on this side this time around
```

```
  2. Lynne: um . ((laughs)) oh all right .
             something that came to me the other
             day I was reading about houses being
             built at the station
  3. F:     yeah
  4. Lynne: and . uh I suddenly thought about
             trains carrying the . nuclear waste
             up to Sellaf- and I've never thought
             about it before
  5. Mod:   right
→ 6. Lynne: but then I thought . you know .
             because I was thinking oh:
  7.        ((laughter))
  8. Geo:   anything can happen=
  9. Lynne:                        =yes
 10. Alice: they go through at four /in the
             morning
 11. Lynne:                         /that was
             just something that I did think about
             . sort of you know . um
 12. Mod:   right
 13. Lynne: I think . people worry about the
→            pollution on the shore=
 14. Alice:                          =yes . that I
             think of what
 15. Lynne: mm
 16. Alice: comes down from Sellafield
 17. Lynne: yeah
 18. Alice: that concerns me . And I was down on
             the beach today and there's just
             the=
 19. Lynne:     =sleaze
 20. Alice: apart from the stuff you can see
 21. F:     mm
 22. Alice: the stuff you can't see
 23. F:     mm
 24. Alice: there's a lot of plastic litter down
             there
 25. Mod:   yeah
 26. Lynne: but I don't think it actually stops
             people using it . to I don't know .
             /I do know a few people who won't
 27. Paul:  /don't think they swim there as much
             as they used to
 28. Lynne: oh no
```

```
29.             ((overlapping talk - 2 seconds))
30. Paul:    we used to we used to
31. Alice:   but the estuary would be different
             then /(the sewage situation)
32.                  /((overlapping talk))
33. Amy:     and the oil now the oil . you can't
             paddle /the kids can't paddle in the
             sand
34. Mark:    /it was always horrible . even when
             we were boys
35. Paul:    muddy
36. Mark:    it was always muddy . muddy and
             shallow . / you never saw your feet
37. Paul:    /(xxx) that never bothered us
38. Amy:     the other thing was . for the most
             part I mean apart from where the um
             that goes u- the thing goes out .
             jetty . stone wall . most of the
             grass et cetera was way out . so you
             had to go a long way out . to even
             find the sea . but that was a seventy
             year cycle so of course at the minute
             it's as far in as it can get
39. Mod:     ah: right
40. Amy:     so the sea comes right up to the .
             what you say is the shore . the
             houses at the . shore line
41. Susan:   might we have our . boats back to
             Morecambe then . and go by boat to
             Morecambe again . couldn't it
42. Lynne:   yes . yes
43. Mod:     yes [Lynne] when you said about the
             trains . you suddenly started
             thinking about it=
44. Lynne:                       =yes
             which I hadn't really thought
             about /
45. Mod:            /yeah . does that
46. Lynne:   before . then I suddenly thought .
             well . I wouldn't want to live .
             actually right next to the railway
             line . you know
47. Alice:   /makes no difference if the railway
             in the end
48.          /((overlapping talk))
```

```
     49. Lynne: /no . it wouldn't . rationally it
                doesn't make any difference if you're
                here or there . but it did make a
                difference
     50.        ((overlapping talk))
     51. Lynne: (xxx) so there's nothing you can do
                about it
→    52. Paul:  the only thing there is . there is
                one . school of thought . that if it
                weren't for Sellafield and the need
                to keep the line open/
     53. Amy:   /oh yeah
     54. Paul:  they wouldn't have the line/
     55. Amy:                            /yeah
     56. Paul:  at all the first time /
     57. F:                           /oh no
     58. Paul:  they wanted to close  /we'd lose it
     59. Mod:                         /right
     60. F:     yeah
     61. Amy:   because they have to keep a ring
                don't they as well
     62. F:     mm mm
     63. Amy:   an obvious escape route /
     64. F:                             /yeah
     65. Amy:   they can't have one ro . route/
     66. Mod:                               /right
     67. Amy:   they have to have a . a ring  /(as
                well)
     68. Lynne:                               /there's
                always a sort of clash between the
                environment and people's lives isn't
                there this is the thing/
     69. Mod:   /right
     70. Lynne: you can't /come down on one side or
                the other
→    71. Paul:            /you ask people in
                Sellafield you ask people in Sellafield
                whether they want it to go /
     72. Amy:                               /exactly
     73. Paul:  and stop they say they don't
     74. Alice: well we used to live up at Whitehaven
                and it was just the factory . and
                everyone was for it . they were for
                Nirex up there .
     75. Paul:  well they'd have to be
```

```
     76. Alice: because it was jobs
     77. F:     yes
     78. Alice: and the unemployment's appalling the
                pits the last pits closed . when . uh
                Workington steel closed
     79. Mod:   so when you said about a clash
                between . people and the environment
     80. Lynne: mm mm
→    81. Mod:   what exactly were you thinking=
     82. Lynne:                              =well
                people's lives . people's jobs .
                people's homes you know/
     83. Mod:   /right right
     84. Lynne: /they all clash with . with
                environmentalists in in . you know in
                some degree
     85. Mod:   right
→    86. Lynne: so. you know it's it's trying to get
                the balance I think between . between
                /all of them really
     87. Geo:   /so you're arguing in favour of the
                environment provided it's somewhere
                else that doesn't affect you /you
                know
     88. Lynne:                               /yes
                well that's . that's what people feel
                isn't it
```

Turn-taking

Conversation analysis, the origins of which I traced in Chapter 1, has produced a huge body of work on the regularities of everyday talk-in-interaction (for introductions and overviews, see Atkinson and Heritage 1984; Button and Lee 1987; Psathas 1995; Hutchby and Wooffitt 1998; Silverman 1998; ten Have 1999a; Wooffitt 2001). Conversation analysts start with the simple observation that in conversation, one person speaks and then another. Thus the unit for them is not the sentence, with a capital letter and full stop, or the clause, with a subject and verb, but the *turn*, what one person says after someone and before someone, whether 'mm mm' or a long speech at a party conference. They can then look at how the speaker is chosen or chooses themselves to speak in each turn, how participants deal with overlapping talk, and how one turn relates to the previous turn. In this example, we see three minutes of talk that

seems rather repetitive; on closer examination we see the participants near the beginning of a group sounding each other out.

Turns and continuers

It may seem trivial to note that one person talks and then another.
But in this passage it is crucial. One reason that lines 2–11 look so
much longer than the first version of the example (p. 23) is that I
have added in the brief words and sounds the listener utters while
someone is speaking. Conversation analysts call these 'continuers'
(Schegloff 1982; Hutchby and Wooffitt 1998: 106), because they
typically come at a possible transition point, where one speaker
could stop and another could start, and they signal that other speakers will not take the floor then and the current speaker can continue.
When Lynne comes to the first possible transition point (at the end
of turn 2), a place where she might stop and someone else might
speak, there is a falling pitch contour on 'station', and the moderator says 'yeah'. The moderator's 'yeah' signals that she is saying
something relevant, as far as he is concerned, to the question he has
just asked, and she continues. He does this again when she pauses
after turn 4. Moderators are trained to use such continuers (*right,
yeah, okay, uh huh*), and they use them even more frequently at this
stage of the talk, when a participant has just begun hesitantly.

Continuers occur throughout each speaker's talk, with this regular rhythm. Often it is the moderator responding to the speaker (see,
for instance, 83, 84); sometimes other participants take on the role
of listener and give the continuers (for instance 21, 23, 53, 55, 57).
But no one makes such noises while the moderator is talking. This
is a strong indication that the moderator's talk, however carefully
casual, is different from that of the participants. It is not that the
participants are not listening, but that he is assumed to have the right
to talk as long as he wishes, until he asks them a question, so they
do not need to make any signal at each possible transition point (cf.
broadcast interviews, Greatbatch 1988). Note that we arrive at this
conclusion, not by assuming the moderator must have power over
the discourse, because of the nature of focus groups, but by looking
at the transcript, seeing how participants treat him, and establishing
the nature of the group interaction from that.

Transcribers usually cut continuers out, because as you can see,
they considerably interrupt the flow of talk on the page. And indeed,

we tend to edit them out in our own recollection of talk, or even
listening to a tape, because they are so much a normal part of
conversation; it takes concentration to hear them as one transcribes.
The moderator in this session (Peter Simmons) noted that when he
included them in a transcript for another study, they were misin-
terpreted. The client thought that when he said 'right' or 'yeah',
he was agreeing with everything the participants said. On the page
they come across more emphatically, more as utterances meaningful for themselves, while in the course of conversation they seem
to be heard as part of the on-going rhythm and structure. (That's
why Yngve (1970) and Gumperz (1982) called them 'back-channel'
utterances, a constant flow complementary to the front channel of
speakers to whom we are attending). But however easy it is to let
them pass unnoticed, they are crucial for our purposes: they indicate
how other participants do or do not present themselves as listeners.

Overlaps and keeping the floor

The moderator selects the speaker three times in this example, starting with Lynne (2), going back to her opening comment after talk
about the shore (43) and going back to her comment on the need for
balance (79). But for the rest of the example, it is the participants
who self-select. While some passages may sound anarchic, the turn-
taking follows predictable patterns (Schegloff 2000). There are several points in this example when the overlapping talk was too much
to transcribe (29, 32, 48, 50), but fairly quickly in each case (two
seconds or less) one participant gets the floor and the turn-taking
continues. Conversation analysts don't say that two people won't
ever talk at once, but that when they do, the speakers acknowledge
in some way that something odd is going on – typically by talking
louder, or trailing off, or apologizing, or demanding the right to
speak. Usually the transitions are managed more subtly.

Here, though the first transcriber didn't record it, there are three
interruptions while Lynne is first speaking, and she treats them in
different ways. She seems to take the laughter (7) as indicating that
the others understood what she means by 'oh:' (6), since she doesn't
go on to elaborate. When the man says 'anything can happen' (8),
she responds quickly before going on, confirming that that is another
way of saying what she was saying. But when Alice comments on

another aspect of the trains (10), Lynne continues speaking without waiting for a falling intonation, a transition point (11). She asserts in this way that she still has the floor, and the moderator confirms it by providing a continuer to her rather than to Alice (12). When Alice does enter (14), it is in direct response to Lynne, and from here it is Lynne, not the moderator, who is giving the continuers. Since these 'mm's are said without a falling intonation, they leave open the possibility that Lynne is merely acknowledging the relevance of Alice's contribution, and that she is not yet done with what she had to say.

Turn-taking is not all a matter of fighting for the floor. In 56–61, Amy begins her turn while Paul is still talking, but after a possible completion point.

```
Paul:   the first time they wanted to close we'd lose
        it
Amy:    because they have to keep a ring don't they as
        well
```

In one interpretation, Amy is suggesting something quite different from Paul. He is saying that Sellafield benefits the community by keeping its rail line open; she is suggesting that they keep it open for escape from any accidents. But with the tag question ('don't they') she seems to offer it as an extension of what he was saying, and Amy goes on with supportive continuers from other participants.

This passage illustrates an important stage in any group, when the participants start talking to each other rather than to the moderator (Myers 2000a). It is not just a matter of the moderator deciding who gets to speak and who doesn't. The group has complex ways of negotiating the floor, and the moderator usually steps in to start it up (1), to close it off, or to bring back a topic for more discussion (as he does in 43 and 79). Work on talk in groups of women (Tannen 1993; Coates 1996; Wilkinson 1998; 1999) has been useful here, not just because some of our groups are all women, but also because these researchers have been particularly interested in revaluing the kinds of rapid overlapping group discussion characteristic of 'gossip' or 'small-talk' (Coupland 2000). Analyses of interactions between men and women (such as Edelsky 1981; Blum-Kulka 1997a; Eggins and Slade 1997; Malone 1997) have also focused on issues of turn-taking and control of the floor to explore how gender enters into interaction.

Adjacency pairs and preference

Lynne begins with 'oh all right' and a pause. How do we interpret this? Conversation analysts note that certain turns are regularly followed by others in *adjacency pairs*: greetings by greetings, invitations by responses, and, here, a question by an answer. Where there are two possible responses, it is typically the case that one type of response is made quickly and without modification (for instance accepting an invitation), the other made with pauses, particles like *well*, and reasons before the response (for instance rejecting an invitation). The first type of response is called *preferred*, and the second *dispreferred*, not because the speaker or hearer must want this answer, but because the preferred response comes in this unmarked form (Bilmes 1988; Kotthoff 1993; Boyle 2000).

Here the moderator's question (though it is not syntactically in the form of a question) would typically be followed by a quick and direct answer, as it is when the participants are asked at the beginning of the group where they're from and what they do. The kind of hesitant response we see here ('um . oh all right') arises, not when the participant doesn't know the answer, but where the participant isn't sure this is what the moderator wants. Thus there is typically a pause early on in the response, as there is here, in which the participant waits for some response from the moderator.

There is a more subtle adjacency pairing at work in turns 11–13. An evaluative statement (an assessment) is typically followed rapidly with agreement, often in strengthened form, while any disagreement is marked as dispreferred (Pomerantz 1984). Lynne has a point at which she has stated that this story is her response:

```
that was just something I did think about
```

But no one comes in at this possible transition point, despite several possible openings:

```
. sort of you know . um
```

Instead the moderator's continuer (12) leaves her to go on. It is then that she tries another kind of response, not what worries her ('the trains'), but what worries people in general ('the shore') (13). To this, Alice agrees, breaking in without a pause or preface (14):

```
Lynne:  I think . people worry about the pollution on
        the shore=
Alice:              =yes . that I think of what
```

We will often see participants structuring their turns so as to end with something that others can take up this way. This analysis of preference will be important later when we look at agreement and disagreement (Chapter 6).

Let us look again at the moderator's question to Lynne in 81, taking her back to 70:

```
Mod:  what exactly were you thinking
```

This is odd. There are very few situations in which one can ask someone to say exactly what they mean; the sociologist Harold Garfinkel made such a question the subject of one of his famous breaching experiments (1967). It is hard to imagine such a question outside an institutional situation such as a focus group (or an interview, interrogation, or an oral examination) in which the questioner has the power to control the terms of the questioning. In casual conversation, it is assumed that people have said as much as they need to say (Grice 1989; Thomas 1995: Ch. 4). The stress on *you* makes it even more problematic. Lynne's response (82) is quick but marked (with *well*) as dispreferred. Such signs lead us to look back to the previous turn to see what the problem could be.

Conversation analysis is central to the study of opinions in interaction because it provides a middle level between the kinds of details that we observe in the text – pauses, overlaps, continuers, laughter – and the kinds of issues we want to study – the statement of opinions, the evaluation of these opinions, the role of the moderator, the opening or closing or shifts in topic. What the first transcriber left out of Lynne's response was crucial in helping us to see what sort of response she takes it to be, and what she and other participants take to be an adequate response. In terms of the paradoxes discussed in Chapter 1, conversation analysis helps us see the way individuals offer some opinion as shared, and how other people take it up or don't, the way contradictory statements arise in the course of turn-taking, and the underlying structure in what seems ephemeral talk.

Conversation analysis has its own programme of social research, demonstrating how people make a social order moment to moment.

It has also developed in the direction of what Paul ten Have has called 'applied conversation analysis' (1999a: 162), using the findings of conversation analysis across a range of data to understand the special constraints within institutions, as in doctor–patient interactions, talk to therapists and advisors, courtrooms, or classrooms (for examples and reviews, see McHoul 1978; Atkinson and Drew 1979; Maynard 1984; Heath 1986; Boden and Zimmerman 1991; Drew and Heritage 1992; Boden 1994; Jacquemet 1996; Drew and Sorjonen 1997; Heritage 1997; Maynard 1997; Hutchby and Wooffitt 1998: Ch. 6; ten Have 1999a: Ch. 8). Conversation analysis was concerned with such talk from its origins (Sacks's analysis of calls to a suicide prevention line; Schegloff's analysis of calls to an emergency line), and it can be argued there is no line of demarcation between 'everyday' and 'institutional' talk. The difference in applied conversation analysis is the intention to tell us, not only about talk, but about the nature of the institutions involved.

One line of applied conversation analysis that has been particularly relevant to opinions is that concerned with broadcast talk (e.g., Heritage 1985; Clayman 1988; Greatbatch 1988; Scannell 1991; Hutchby 1996; Clayman and Heritage 2002; Thornborrow 2002). For instance, Greatbatch notes that turn-taking between interviewers (IRs) and interviewees (IEs) in UK news interviews differs in significant ways from that in ordinary conversation:

1. IRs and IEs systematically confine themselves to producing turns that are at least minimally recognisable as questions and answers, respectively.
2. IRs systematically withhold a range of responses that are routinely produced by questioners in mundane conversation.
3a. Although IRs regularly produce statement turn components, these are normally issued prior to the production of questioning turn components.
3b. IEs routinely treat IRs' statement turn components as preliminaries to questioning turn components.
4. The allocation of turns in multiparty interviews is ordinarily managed by IRs.
5. Interviews are overwhelmingly opened by IRs.
6. Interviews are customarily closed by IRs.
7. Departures from the standard question-and-answer format are frequently attended to as accountable and are characteristically repaired.
(Greatbatch 1988).

These are not, of course, external rules to which participants always conform (if you think they do, turn on BBC Radio 4 any weekday at 8:10 GMT (available on the web) for an example of the kind of adversarial interview associated with the *Today* programme). For our purposes, the key to Greatbatch's argument is in his point 7: when participants do not do as in points 1–6 (for instance, if the interviewer does not seem to be asking a question, or the interviewee to be answering), someone usually initiates repair, or offers an explanation, or notes in some way that something is odd. So the technique of analysis (for Greatbatch, Heritage, Clayman, and others) is not just a matter of showing, statistically, that these regularities are usually followed, but also a matter of looking at what participants do when they aren't. Another observation by analysts of broadcast interviews is that many of the turns make sense only in terms of the participants taking into account an additional unseen participant, the broadcast audience (Clayman 1991). The same sort of approach has been taken with talk shows (Thornborrow 1997; Haarman 1999; Thornborrow 2000; Tolson 2001), and I return to some of this work in Chapters 9 and 10.

Categories

One way of looking at my data of talk in groups is to categorize the people and see what kinds of utterances are made by people in each category: male or female, old or young, urban or rural. The distinctions could continue endlessly as a given theory demanded. Another way is to look for the categories participants use, and how they use them, in the talk; for instance in the example, participants talk about 'people' (13, 26), 'boys' (34), 'people in Sellafield' (71), 'everyone' (74), and 'environmentalists' (84). While Harvey Sacks was developing what is now conversation analysis, he was also working on an approach to what he called Membership Categorization Devices (Sacks 1972; Sacks 1992; Hester and Eglin 1997; Silverman 1998). Membership Categorization Devices are systematic ways of classifying, for instance by gender, age, family relationship, occupation. Sacks's first examples come from suicide phone helplines; he asks how the caller and the advisor jointly construct categories of other people available to the caller. Sacks argues that callers systematically go through members of these categories to show that in the end there is 'No one I can turn to,' that is, that there is no one in the category of people from whom one is

entitled by relationship to ask for help (family, friends), and that
those in another category, of people who know about the problem
(co-workers, counsellors), are not required to help.

Sacks's point is that we do not need to impose theoretical categories on conversational data and hope that they are relevant.
Participants use these and other categories in interaction in a way
that shows their shared understanding of how this category relates
to others, and what actions or other predicates go with it. Three
further developments of this insight are relevant here. One is a rule
of 'adequate reference' (Sacks 1992) or 'economy' (Sacks 1972):
in practice one category ('black' or 'female' or 'democrat') is often
enough to identify a person conversationally. Another is a rule of
'consistency', so that if a categorization device is used for one member of a population, it may be used for another (if the first interviewee
is categorized as 'black', then another person who is not black may
be taken for present purposes as 'white', while in a different context
they might be taken as 'young' or 'Californian') (Sacks 1972: 34;
Sacks 1992: I.248). Sacks also suggests that participants can refer to
'category-bound activities'. In the case of the suicide prevention line,
the caller assumes we share assumptions about what activities are
or are not appropriate for, say, a mother, a partner, an acquaintance
from work, or the person who answers the phone at the helpline:
only certain categories of people need to help him.

Consider the way the participants talk about 'people in Sellafield'
in lines 71–8 of my example. They could be categorizing these people
by place, job, risk, or economic status, and which of these ways
of categorizing they mean can only emerge in the discussion. We
could start with the observation that Amy seems to know what Paul
is going to say before he says it, because she interrupts to agree
before he completes his utterance (72). But what is it about 'people
in Sellafield' that makes their view (that they don't want the plant
to close) relevant to the argument here? There are several ways of
taking this: they know better because they live there, they have
the right to say, they might be expected to say otherwise. Alice's
turn (74) starts with 'well', as a possible dispreferred response to
Paul (not an agreement). She presents herself as one of this category (Whitehaven is the nearest large town to Sellafield) and says
'it was just the factory'. This too is interpretable in many ways (a
factory like any other, the only factory in town, the town was just

the factory). Paul comes back in (73) with another 'well', another potential disagreement: 'they'd have to be' [for the Nirex nuclear waste storage facility]. Now Alice's turn (76) parallels his. Together, three people have sorted out what 'people in Sellafield' means; for them the operative categories are the economic depression of the area and its reliance on an industry which people in other areas might oppose. We will see such work on categorization again and again in the transcripts, and it plays a particularly important role in vox pop interviews (Chapter 10).

Participant roles

Conversation analysis and Membership Categorization Analysis are not the only approaches to talk, though they are the core of the approach taken here (for debates and comparisons, see Schegloff 1997; Titscher et al. 2000; van Dijk 1997a; van Dijk 1997b; Wetherell et al. 2002). Another approach, mentioned in Chapter 1, starts with frames, what it is that participants take to be going on in an encounter. Goffman's work on frames (1974) led him to unpack the way linguists traditionally refer to the participants in communication as the 'speaker' and the 'hearer'. Goffman argued that there were in fact several possible roles under each of these labels, what he later called different 'footings' on which one could participate (Goffman 1981; Levinson 1988; Antaki, C. et al. 1996; Leudar and Antaki 1996; Matoesian 2000).

Consider, for instance, the moderator's words at the beginning of my example. We could think of him as saying these words for himself, as the *principal*, or as just reading out more or less the words someone wrote for him and other moderators to read. In that case, he would be the *animator*, and someone else the *author*. Less obviously, there are different roles for hearers. The people in the group are the moderator's addressed audience. But there is a co-moderator there, a *bystander* who is not addressed but someone whom everyone can see is there, listening. And there are listeners like me, transcribing the tape of a group I never saw; we are *eavesdroppers*. Many other distinctions are possible; the key insight is that participants may shift roles in an interaction, and other participants can generally follow these shifts (as we will see in Chapter 7). The idea of the overhearing audience has been taken up in research on broadcast talk to account for ways interviewers and interviewees talk *to* each other but *for* an unseen audience (Chapters 9 and 10). It could be argued that the broadcast audience cannot really be said to be eavesdropping, since the participants are aware of them even if the audience is not physically present; the same point could be made about the way focus-group participants are aware of the microphone. But this is to say that participants can make more subtle distinctions than we find in Goffman's original essay, not that such distinctions don't matter.

Words

Conversation analysis and Membership Categorization Analysis are committed to a project that takes into account only those features which participants themselves show they are noticing, in that particular interaction. On the one hand, this means that they reject analyses that assume that some social categories, such as class, gender, or professional power, are necessarily relevant (e.g., Fairclough 1988; 1992; Wodak 1996; Fairclough and Wodak 1997; Wodak et al. 1999; Wodak and Meyer 2001; Fairclough 2003). On the other hand, it means that they reject analyses that interpret talk in terms of the meaning a word or sentence might have in other contexts, in any real or imaginary dictionaries or grammars. In the strongest form of this approach, meaning is always indexical; that is, it arises from its particular use then and there (that is how I interpret Schegloff (1984)). This amounts to throwing out linguistics, the study of language as a system. I would not want to do that, not just because I am a linguist, but because I think we can show that people bring to an interaction a rich sense of the structures of language, including ways that one word might be different from others closely related to it, or ways one sentence structure conveys something different from another. Detailed linguistic description is one way of showing how other uses of expressions, and past uses, may enter into play, a way of linking different uses, in talk, print, or electronic media, past and present. I will draw on four areas of description relevant to the example: discourse markers, politeness, pronouns, and reported speech. (For more comprehensive outlines of linguistic text analysis, see Schiffrin 1994; Stubbs 1996; Georgakopoulou and Goutsos 1997; Delin 2000; Titscher et al. 2000; Stubbs 2001.)

Discourse markers

The difference in approach between conversation analysis and linguistics can be illustrated with the work of Deborah Schiffrin (1987) on discourse markers like *oh* and *well* (see Antaki 1994 for contrasting approaches to similar material; Jucker 1993). She defines *discourse markers* as 'sequentially dependent elements that bracket units of talk' (Schiffrin 1987: 31); that is, they are elements that have their meaning because of where they are placed in the interaction, not because of their place in the sentence. The emphasis on sequential dependence shows she is drawing on conversation analysis. But she starts each of her analyses with a consideration of various uses of the element and its systematic place in relation to alternatives.

If we go back to a turn discussed earlier, we might ask, what does *oh* mean in these phrases?

```
oh all right . something that came to me the other
(turn 2)
because I was thinking oh: (turn 6)
```

Schiffrin develops an interpretation of *oh* as serving various 'information management tasks', and links these tasks to its traditional grammatical categorization as an exclamation. In turn 2, Lynne is responding to a question, and as we have seen in the previous section, she gives signs of hesitation. Schiffrin comments, 'answers to questions are prefaced with *oh* when a question forces an answerer to reorient him/herself to information' (86). The moderator has assumed that they each have a personal environmental problem and can talk about it; the *oh* notes the gap between this question and what was expected. The *oh* in turn 6 works differently, as what Schiffrin calls 'recognition display' (91). Lynne is reporting what she thought to herself then. The elongated *oh:* conveys nothing but the fact that she had a sudden recognition; she leaves it to listeners to figure out what it was she recognized.

We will see that particles and exclamations are common in reported speech used for reporting opinions (Chapter 7); the point here is that such devices are so strongly associated with interaction that they can convey a process of interaction even when just one person is involved. Schiffrin's pragmatic analysis is not very different from Heritage's conversation analysis treatment of *oh* as a 'change

of state token' (Heritage 1984a), purely in terms of its function.
But Schiffrin's analysis (1987: 99) leads in a different direction from
Heritage's, towards Goffman's concept of different roles the same
person can take in an interaction, as the person talking and the
person talked about.

Similarly, *you know* (or *y'know* as Schiffrin transcribes it) might
seem to be an empty filler (and is often criticized as such by teachers
marking students' writing). Schiffrin starts with its literal sense as
'do you know?' and traces it as a marker of background information
(1987: Ch. 9). So while *oh* can signal to a questioner that information assumed isn't already shared, *y'know* can propose to a listener
that some information is or might be shared. Lynne uses *you know*
twice, before and after giving her response to the realization of what
the railway meant.

```
but then I thought . you know . because I was
thinking (6)
that was just something that I did think about . sort
of you know . um (11)
```

The first 'you know' (6) proposes what she is about to think as
something that will be recognizable to her audience. The second
(11), with falling intonation, as for a statement, is part of closing
off her response and turning it over to others: she need not say more
because this is part of an apparent consensus. So 'you know', here
and later in the example, seems not to have a fixed meaning, but
to have several functions in signalling the proposed relation of this
statement to listeners.

Similarly, Schiffrin points out that *so* (and the related *because*)
have logical functions indicating cause and effect, but can also
have structural functions in the discourse, turning the interactional
responsibility over to the other participants. Lynne's 'so' in turn 51
seems to be an attempt at summing up and closing the topic – since
the railway is going to be used for this purpose, 'there's nothing you
can do about it'. The moderator's 'so' in turn 79 functions in what
Schiffrin calls the *participation structure*, shifting the responsibility
for answering the question back to Lynne, because he presents the
question as following from what she has already said. That's why
he can break off in the middle of his turn and expect her to pick up
his question. There is clearly no logical structure to the argument

here, and we can't look to logical connectors like *so* and *because* to provide such logical connections. Discourse markers both indicate the argument and mark the flow of the interaction.

Schiffrin's approach, by starting with the linguistic element *oh* or *y'know* instead of the temporal sequence of turns, can lead to a range of related functions, linking what people are saying and how they are participating. Her approach is an example of how linguists try to support Goffman's insights into encounters with systematic detail. We will find in discussing shifts in topic (Chapter 5 and Chapter 9) that linguistic study of markers complements the conversation analysis approach to turn by turn sequence.

Politeness

Another area of intense linguistic study that is relevant to the analysis of group discussions is the use of *hedges*, words or phrases that weaken or strengthen a statement, such as *probably, maybe,* or *certainly* (Lakoff, G. 1973; Hyland 1998). Hedges clearly play a role in indicating certainty and uncertainty, but they can also be used to signal politeness, a desire not to impose a view on others (Lakoff, R. 1973; Brown and Levinson 1987; Kasper 1990; Blum-Kulka 1997b). Consider the way Lynne sums up what she has said:

```
that was just something that I did think about . sort
of you know . um
```

This is typical of the way someone might offer a potentially controversial opinion in these groups. The use of *just* minimizes the importance of her thought, while *sort of* renders it vague. The use of *did* on the other hand (rather than *might* or *could*) usually emphasizes the factual nature – she certainly and sincerely did have this response. Lynne's use of such hedges suggests that offering an opinion at all is potentially an imposition on others (even though two other participants have chimed in with their agreement). Conversation analysis does deal with such weakening of assessments (Pomerantz 1984), but as a function of sequential position, not as a function of this category of linguistic items.

One could look also at Lynne's handling of disagreement in 49. She has restated her worry about the railway line (46), and Alice (and perhaps others) have disagreed (47), perhaps because if there is a

nuclear accident, its effects will reach far beyond the railway. Lynne
makes a concession by contrasting two views of what she has said:

```
rationally it doesn't make any difference if you're
here or there
but it did make a difference
```

The verb tense is the key here: it *doesn't* make a difference (as a
general rational rule), but it *did* make a difference, in her account of
her moment of realization. Concession is another politeness device
(we will see it in Chapters 6 and 9).

Pronouns and reference

Even in this short example, we see a range of ways of referring
to people, using pronouns ('*I* think', 'the stuff *you* can see', '*we*
used to', '*they* have to keep a ring', '*everyone* was for it') or general references to 'people' (1, 13, 26, 68, 71, 82, 88). Sacks (1992)
was fascinated with the ways groups categorize people in conversation, including and excluding. But of course the use of pronouns is
also open to systematic linguistic study (Brown and Gilman 1960;
Muhlhausler and Harre 1990). Lynne contrasts 'something I did
think about' with 'people worry about', to shift from her own concerns to general concerns. *You* is potentially ambiguous, referring to
the people here present (not including the speaker) or to a general
group (including the speaker). Alice uses 'the stuff you can see' (20)
to include others in this observation of the pollution; we will find
this general indefinite use of *you* often in statements of opinions
and of repeated typical experiences. There is a slippage from 'you
can't paddle' to 'the kids can't paddle' in 33, perhaps because Amy
realizes as she says it that 'paddling' is something typically done by
a more specific category of people, kids. Indeed it is the potential of
all these references for ambiguity that makes them useful in offering
points of view in a group.

Reported speech and thought

Reported speech has been extensively analysed in literary and linguistic studies, but I am particularly interested in those studies that

focus on how it is used in interaction. As we will see in Chapter 7, representations of speech and thought play a crucial role in allowing participants to try out and shift possible opinions. The speech or thoughts reported may be those of the current speaker, someone else, or some typical figure; they may be reports of actual, possible, or even imaginary thought or words. Lynne's opening response involves enacting the response she had at the time, thinking 'oh:'. The transcriber takes this as an indication that this is a report of her thought, setting it off as a dash (elsewhere she might transcribe this with quotation marks). Analysis of reported speech and thought is a way into opinion as performance. In the second part of this passage, the participants use reported speech, not to dramatize their own responses, but to imagine the views of others: 'one school of thought' (52), and then the hypothetical 'you ask people in Sellafield' (71), and then 'we used to live up at Whitehaven' (74). We will consider in Chapter 7 how these reports function in the interaction. The main point here is that the ability of people to take on these various voices is another aspect of opinion lost in a survey interview, where they are asked to speak only for themselves.

Rhetoric

So what is Lynne's opinion? After this retranscription, and analysis of some of the features of interaction, we can see that something more is going on than is easily content coded. Part of what is going on is her attempt to present her proposed problem in a way that is effective for this setting and group, an attempt that can be studied under the heading of 'rhetoric'. Of course this ancient craft of persuasion and its modern versions have something to say about many of the issues I have discussed in this chapter under other headings: self-presentation, audiences, relevant contexts. Here I will focus on just one legacy of this tradition that has recently been taken up by social researchers: the study of commonplaces. In everyday usage, this may be a synonym for 'cliché', but rhetoricians use the term *commonplace* ('a statement generally accepted, a stock theme, a platitude' (*OED*)) for arguments that can be applied to a wide range of situations. For instance in the example we see Lynne uses various versions of a general argument:

```
there's always a sort of a clash between the
environment and people's lives isn't there (68)
```

The tag question, 'isn't there', is a cue that we are to take this as an assertion that anyone, environmentalist or developer, will accept, especially when she rephrases it as 'trying to get the balance' (86) – balance is always a good thing, isn't it? Lynne can even accept it when George gives it an ironic reformulation (87). We will see later appeals to such commonplaces as the argument that one should take care of problems close to home before dealing with problems far away, or that one should think of future generations before one's own comfort (Myers and Macnaghten 1998). In this case, Lynne's commonplace draws on the feeling these people have that there are two conflicting demands, 'environment' and 'people's lives'. The same argument is made at other points in this group about the noisy and dusty quarry that is a major employer, and the beautiful coast that attracts tourist coaches with their engines spewing fumes. John Shotter has argued that a commonplace is not just a reference to a conventional list of arguments, as one might get in Aristotle's *Rhetoric*; it can evoke a shared experience. I will return to Shotter's use of the concept in Chapter 4.

This brief example shows that a tool kit drawing on several disciplines can take us from detailed analysis of linguistic features such as discourse markers and reported speech, to turn-taking and the kinds of possible participation, and to larger rhetorical issues of how participants frame arguments. We find, even in this short exchange, that participants express their opinions in relation to the other people, in time with the on-going interaction, and in terms of what they think is the purpose of the event.

Transcription

We have seen in comparing the first and second versions of my first example that a more detailed transcription of a statement, in its interactional context, can allow for a richer interpretation. Even such lexical items as *yeah*, *oh*, or *you know*, which are left out of some transcriptions as empty fillers but included here as discourse markers, can vary in meaning with different intonations, rising or falling.

So how much detail do we need? Conversation analysts provide guides that allow for a remarkable amount of detail on timing, pitch, pace, loudness, and voice quality, in a system developed largely by Gail Jefferson (Hutchby and Wooffitt 1998: Ch. 3; ten Have 1999a). The generous principle is that other analysts should be able to use one's transcriptions for their own studies of completely different topics, such as laughter or dispreferred turns or side sequences. But I have not given that much detail here (see 'Transcription conventions'). First, it is impractical – for a hundred hours of tape, it would take a full working year just to transcribe it fully (assuming it didn't drive me or the transcriber mad). And even if I did include all this detail, it would be insufficient and inconsistent in many ways; conversation analysts give rough spellings of pronunciations that seem subjective and ethnocentric to linguists, giving as they do a highly inconsistent lay recording of some relevant phonemic features and not others (O'Connell and Kowal 2000). Should I show the difference between the British 'Received Pronunciation' of the moderator and some participants here, and the various Lancashire or Scots or Yorkshire or Geordie accents of many participants in other groups? Indications of accent are potentially useful (they enabled the transcriber to distinguish participants' voices), and though they were seldom remarked on in the groups, they could be relevant to interpretation (I know they were curious about my US English when I moderated). Rather than record a few features of accents and not others, I have chosen instead to use ordinary spelling.

We should remember that this and other choices depend on theoretical and political assumptions (Ochs 1979; Cook 1995; Coates and Thornborrow 1999; Bucholtz 2000), as well as on the exigencies of transcription, printing, and readership. As a practical matter, I give in this book just the level of detail necessary to make my own arguments. I think there is a principle in this as well: that researchers shouldn't claim in the transcripts more refined analysis than they provide in the text.

Since the transcripts in Chapters 5–9 are based on audiotapes, I am not transcribing actions, gaze, or other features alongside the words. Much of the most exciting current work in discourse analysis is based on video and considers non-verbal as well as verbal features (Buttny 1999; Goodwin 2000; Kress et al. 2001; Kress and van Leeuwen 2001; Matoesian and Coldren 2002). We will get an idea of some of the potential richness in Chapter 10, which does include some aspects of the visual, such as framing, gaze, movements, and gestures, in the analysis.

Analysing opinions in interaction

My aim in looking at this example has been to show that a range of approaches from discourse analysis, conversation analysis, and pragmatics can inform the issues I identified in Chapter 1 as characteristic of opinions.

- Opinions vs. facts. Even these short analyses do show how participants try to warrant the factuality of some statements, by grounding them in their own experience and that of others, while marking others as matters of opinion.
- Public vs. private. They treat some opinions as appropriate for public discussion with strangers and try moment to moment to define the bounds of this forum (for instance, Lynne's doubts about whether her own private worry is of general concern).
- Individual vs. group. They are careful about distinguishing their own views ('what I did think about') from those of their group ('people think'), and they present their views in relation to what they take to be the present group.
- Consistency vs. contradiction. They try to show that one of their utterances is consistent with another but are tolerant of contradiction as a feature of on-going talk and of opinions (Lynne accepting George's ironic remark about her willingness to preserve the environment only when it doesn't affect her).
- Local vs. global. Participants refer to local experiences (the mud on the seashore) but also draw on commonplaces they take to be generally persuasive (the appeal to balance).

Of course the example I have given is not just any conversation; it is a focus group, with all the resources and constraints that might involve. We need to ask how different groups, from focus groups to dinner tables, provide different kinds of occasions for talk and opinions.

3

Forums for opinion: 'What is it that's going on here?'

It is evening, after dinner, and you knock timidly at the door of a bungalow in Thornton, a town near the Lancashire coast. A friendly woman in her 40s shows you into a living room with a floral carpet, a gas fire, and a big television set in the corner. It is the first time you have let yourself be talked into going to a focus group.

How do you know what is going to happen? You might think of tupperware parties, club meetings, reading groups, perhaps therapy groups. Whatever is going on, it is unlikely to be completely new; you try to treat it as a version of a familiar practice. But how do we describe such practices, which could include such a range of familiar and unfamiliar events? Erving Goffman warns us that 'the question "What is it that's going on here?" is considerably suspect. Any event can be described in terms of a focus that includes a wide swath or a narrow one and – as a related but not identical matter – in terms of a focus that is close-up or distant' (1974: 8). I will try to take a more distant focus first, and then a close-up.

First I will compare various kinds of events in which opinions are displayed, drawing on frameworks from the ethnography of communication that have been used to compare speech events in different cultures. This framework can serve as a heuristic to point out what is different and, less obviously, what might be similar between different forums. In this section we are in effect starting from a distance, taking categories of speech events as contexts, and outlining what sorts of discourse practices go with these events. In the second part of the chapter, I will look at one focus group session in detail, to see how participants define it as a focus group, and how they recontextualize language from other kinds of interaction

and shape it to fit this forum. We find then that even in the most
rigidly conventionalized event, participants must constantly signal
whom they are talking to and listening to at this moment, how a
contribution is meant and how they take it, what they take to be
the current rules governing who speaks next and what responses
are appropriate. We can define and name a forum, but it won't hold
still.

Contexts for opinions

If we are looking for opinion statements, we might look first in
public meetings, paper and pencil surveys, or newspaper letters to
the editor, institutions designed to gather a range of opinions. But
we could also find them in talk at dinner tables, on broadcast talk
shows, on bumper stickers and T-shirts, in pop-song lyrics, in boxes
to tick on web pages, in banners hung from the tops of buildings,
or the gathering volume of the slow handclap during a politician's
speech to members of the Women's Institute. Most of this book is
about focus groups, so it will be useful to compare them with other
forums for opinions where the settings, participants, exchanges, and
norms of interpretation might be similar but different. Of the many
possible forums for comparison, I will focus on some kinds of interactions that have already been analysed in detail: classroom discussions (e.g., Sinclair and Coulthard 1975; McHoul 1978; Mehan
1979; Mercer 2000; Kress et al. 2001); business meetings (e.g.,
Boden 1994; Holmes et al. 1999; Tracy and Naughton 2000); and
dinner-table discussions (Tannen 1984; Blum-Kulka 1997a; Eggins
and Slade 1997: Ch. 5; Aukrust and Snow 1998).

In a classic essay, Dell Hymes (1972) packaged eight components
with the mnemonic SPEAKING, which has helped generations of
students recall it in examinations, though it makes for a rather cum-
bersome list. (Saville-Troike (1989) among others has rearranged
and elaborated the components for pedagogical purposes.) Hymes's
schema remains useful in allowing us to think in broad compara-
tive terms, not just distinguishing events in terms of, say, the setting,
or the participant roles, or the goals. To keep the overview brief, I
will consider just five of his components: Situation, Participants,
Acts, Norms, and Key (giving the rather unfortunate mnemonic
SPANK).

Situation – marked and unmarked spaces

Hymes groups under Situation both Setting, the place and time of the event, and Scene, the 'psychological setting'. For instance, the same Setting, a large oblong room in Lancaster, could be several different Scenes through the week as it is used as Methodist chapel, church hall, old age centre, polling station, and a meeting room for Girl Guides. Despite this potential for ambiguity, Setting would seem to be the most evident and definite way of distinguishing some of the events on our list (Scollon and Scollon 2003). For instance, family *dinners* are typically held at a table and in a room set aside for this purpose; newspaper commentators and other moralists complain when it is replaced by a meal eaten in front of the television which is not, in their view, a family dinner. Times are also set; there is a conventional 'dinner time' whether is is 7 pm, 6 pm, or noon. *Classes* are usually held in rooms set aside for this purpose, at fixed times in the schedule. In our university, seminars used to be held in staff offices, which suddenly stopped being offices and became classrooms for the fifty minutes. As with dinners, one can vary this setting, but the teacher who takes the class to a new setting (perhaps to sit outside on a rare sunny day) is redefining the event. The place and time of a business *meeting* is usually written on top of the agenda and the minutes, as significant in defining which meeting this is; managers know it is a different sort of meeting when it is held in a room set aside for this purpose, the manager's office, or a public space. So far, it seems that the events that interest us can be defined in terms of place and time.

Focus groups may be held with existing groups in their usual meeting places, such as community centres or workplaces (e.g., Holbrook and Jackson 1996). But they often try to establish some neutral space in a pub or dedicated research room with comfortable furniture and one-way mirrors; we know it is neutral because researchers almost never say *where* the words that they quote were said. Rothenberg (1994) describes the setting for market-research groups conducted by Wieden and Kennedy for Subaru:

There was nothing in the room to distract them. It was purposefully bland, its mottled walls, gray carpeting, blond oval table and blue fabric chairs designed to facilitate conversation by giving no resting place for wandering eyes ... The point of a focus group, after all, was to focus. And Wieden &

Kennedy had trekked north from Portland, to an unadorned low-rise office building adjacent to an undistinguished intersection in a nondescript suburb of Seattle, to get people to focus on cars.   (Rothenburg 1994: 390)

Our own groups were held in the recruiter's living room (as I have mentioned), in hotel meeting rooms, or in upstairs rooms of pubs. We learned that there is no neutral space when the recruiter booked us into one of two pubs in a village to talk to readers of *The Times* or *Telegraph* (two centre-right national newspapers). The moderator realized as soon as he walked in and saw the signs of social class in this pub – lager, darts, loud TV, fruit (gambling) machines – that the upper-middle-class participants in this group would be the sort who would go to the other pub in the village, the one with the wood fire, horse brasses, and traditional ales. It was marked, not neutral space.

I have never seen a survey or a focus group report that said what time of day a statement was made. But just as there are no neutral spaces, there are no neutral times; the evening marks this event as something apart from work, school and chores, after the kids are in bed, an alternative to watching TV or going to the pub. And however the moderator tries to create a relaxed and autonomous world, participants are often highly conscious of the time passing outside the room, the programmes or football missed, the babysitter waiting, or the chance for a social evening. So focus groups, which try to present a neutral Situation, cannot keep participants from interpreting the place and time in their different ways, and drawing on these interpretations as conversational resources.

Participants – roles and groups

The roles assigned to participants, teachers and pupils, interviewer and interviewee, might also seem to define forums. Formal *meetings* are constituted by the presence of specified participants: a chair, maybe a secretary, and a quorum of members. (At my university, the minutes of management meetings describe administrative officers who are not academics as 'in attendance', not as present, even though they are often the most active and powerful participants.) Without a quorum, talk may happen but it isn't a meeting. Similarly, a *class* includes both teacher(s) and student(s); the teacher may leave the classroom as students do some exercise or lab activity but remains the official sponsor of the activity. Pupils learn early, in their first days at school, that others (parents, friends, pets) are excluded from classes. A family *dinner* is by definition one that includes two or more family members from different generations; non-members of the family are usually treated as guests (as the researchers were in Blum-Kulka's (1997a) study), and the dinners of couples, parties, boarding houses, and meetings are different kinds of events, even if they all happen to be eating lasagna.

Categorization of participants in a focus group is problematic, because participants, unlike respondents in surveys, have the opportunity to find out, or guess, why they have been brought together. Sometimes they are an existing group, such as retired people at a day centre, or mothers picking up kids at a preschool centre. But even when they are not, they are aware of themselves as a group in the way another crowd of strangers, queuing for a bus or watching a movie, is not. Many focus-group researchers worry about this group influence, as the contamination of individual opinions; on the other hand Bloor and his colleagues argue that what a focus group does best is the exploration of norms and meanings held by the group, not individual responses (Bloor et al. 2001: 4–8). The participants are interested as well in the researchers and the invisible over-hearers; there is no pretence that they are saying this just for each other or for the benefit of the moderator. Some of their comments don't make sense unless one assumes a wider audience (see Chapter 5), and some of their comments show self-categorization work in the course of a group (see Chapter 8).

Acts – questions and interpretations

If Situation and Participants do not always serve to categorize forums, clearly we may need to look more closely at just what the participants are doing. Hymes takes Act sequence as a general term for both message content and message form – that is, the whole of what linguistics usually studies. Of course the content of messages may vary widely across such diverse settings as classrooms, meetings, and dinner-tables. What they typically have in common is a form, often a sequence of questions and answers, even when they differ in the way these sequences are interpreted (see 'Norms' below).

In *classrooms*, there is a well-documented three-part pattern of
Initiation – Response – Feedback, built around the inevitability
of the teacher's evaluation (Sinclair and Coulthard 1975; McHoul
1978; Mehan 1979). Neil Mercer has questioned some of the tabu-
lation of acts that followed these classic studies: 'If one is interested
in what teachers actually do and say with language, the value of categorizing and quantifying "questions" is limited. Unfortunately for
language researchers, people do not reliably use the same grammatical forms of speech to pursue the same purposes' (2000: 29–30). So,
for instance, the same utterance by a student could be intended as
a question, an answer, or an ironic remark, and neither the analyst
nor the teacher may be sure which. The same problems arise in all
attempts to reduce on-going interactions to discrete acts.

Acts in more formal *meetings* are specified by conventional or
written rules: who may open or close a meeting, who may participate
and when, what sorts of contributions are allowed and what sorts
are minuted. Of course many meetings are less formal than this,
but participants can move them back towards the formal end of
the continuum by, for instance, addressing the chair (as in formal
meetings) rather than participants. A *dinner-table* conversation has
many things going on: scolding, praising, storytelling, planning, and
complaints. Blum-Kulka (1997a: Ch. 3) lists a series of 'topical acts':
initiations, elaborations, backshifts, digressions, readaptations, and
closings. In her data from family dinners, most of these acts are
initiated by parents' questions, so that they are similar in some ways
to school. One of the functions of the moderator's introduction to
a *focus group* is to forestall any expectation of similar patterns to
classrooms; we will see this in the second part of the chapter.

So far I have treated speech events in terms of the language used in
them, but all the forums I have discussed involve acts besides speaking, and analysts have repeatedly urged attention to these non-verbal
actions (Heath 1986; Goodwin 1990; Goodwin 2000; Kress and van
Leeuwen 2001; Scollon and Scollon 2003). Dinners involve serving
and eating food, and that is understandably the focus of much of the
talk. Classrooms may involve writing, drawing, or experimenting
(see Kress et al. 2001 on science classrooms). Even meetings, where
the scope for movement would seem to be constrained, involve
highly significant non-verbal actions. Gregory Matoesian and James
Coldren Jr (2002) have carried out a particularly perceptive analysis

of the non-verbal communication in a focus group. But talk remains central, it is talk that is recorded and evaluated, and in most cases the purpose of other activities is to give the participants something to talk about.

Norms – sequences and interpretations

We have seen that the study of individual acts, even acts as apparently straightforward as questions and answers, does not take us far in characterizing speech events, because the acts, taken by themselves, are hard to define. What may be more characteristic of a particular forum are the norms used to interpret these acts. So, for instance, what counts as 'answering the question' could vary between a news interview, a courtroom, a classroom, and a dinner table; the acceptability of the response is not determined by any general rules for questions and answers, but by awareness of the goals of the activity type (Levinson 1992) in which one is engaged. We will see in Chapter 9 that even the exchange of greetings, which would seem to be the simplest of sequences, can be multifunctional in phone-ins.

In a similar way, the conventions governing overlapping talk and silences, as explored by conversational analysis, operate in different ways under institutional constraints (see Chapter 2). Turns are typically assigned by the teacher in a classroom, by the chair in a meeting, and the teacher or chair but not others may interrupt. Silences may be interpreted as directives to speak, as when a seminar tutor waits for ages for a response from students, or when an administrative task has come at a departmental meeting and my colleagues and I wait to see who will crack first, speak up, and take it on. Dinner-table conversations vary widely in their norms, from families that eat almost silently, to those in which one parent directs a range of questions to the children (see Blum-Kulka 1997a).

Focus groups are hybrids of the conventions of institutional and everyday norms of interpretation. Moderators are given instructions on choosing speakers, encouraging reluctant participants, restraining domineering participants, opening and closing topics (Krueger 1998: Ch. 9; Bloor et al. 2001; Macnaghten and Myers 2004). They may sort out overlapping talk by responding to only one participant, echoing one of the phrases, turning to one part of the group, or breaking in at a specific point (see Chapter 4). That the norms of the interaction allow these interventions is shown by participants' responses; they treat these echoes as invitations to develop a topic further, and they never, in my experience, object to being interrupted by the moderator. This kind of tight control is anathema to some researchers; they may use different styles, have the group moderate itself, or allow the group to develop its own agenda. Burgess, Limb, and Harrison (1988a; 1988b), and Wilkinson (1999), among others, have shown that shifts in the norms of interaction of focus groups can be valuable or essential for some topics, some groups, or some theoretical goals. But by definition, focus groups are focused. Morrison observes that even where the moderator avoids signalling directly what kind of answer he or she wants, there is a second-level 'moderator demand' in which participants accommodate what they believe to be the values and interests of the researcher (1998: 186). As Agar and MacDonald say: 'We thought that a moderator should keep his nose out whenever possible. We might as well have started to drive by deciding it wasn't a good idea to steer' (1995: 81).

Key – enacting vs. rehearsing

Key is the hardest of Hymes's components to pin down: 'the tone, manner, or spirit in which an act is done' (1972: 64). And yet there is clearly a difference between a dialogue in a language classroom and a real dialogue with a shopkeeper, between a wedding rehearsal and the real wedding the next day, between a straw poll and a real election, between Swift's 'A modest proposal' and a cookbook. The problem for analysts is the range of different qualities Hymes suggests as possible alternatives of key, such as *mock* and *serious* or *perfunctory* and *painstaking*. Goffman (1974) brings some order to these oppositions by suggesting (following Bateson 1972) that we see key in terms of a recontextualization, as 'a set of conventions by which a given activity, one already meaningful in terms of some primary framework, is transformed into something patterned on this activity but seen by participants to be something quite else' (1974: 44). In this definition, some sort of re-keying is going on in theatre, parodies, political demonstrations, and rehearsals. Goffman is particularly interested in what he calls *laminations*, the layering of one frame of interpretation on another, as when a real speech becomes part of a fiction, or a mock demonstration has real effects. But re-keying need not be so dramatic; almost any department meeting can shift from serious business to jokes and back again, and the joking suggestions are a part of getting the serious work done.

At the core of all explorations of public opinion is some implicit *primary framework* in which one person speaks to another without any irony or marked modality, imagined perhaps as a soapbox speaker on Hyde Park Corner, or as talk over a back fence or over a coffee. All public opinion research has to make do with one of the laminations of this imagined primary situation, recording a practice for what they would say, a rehearsal of how they will act, an imitation of how they think they argue, or a verbalization of the arguments going on in their heads. But an awareness of these laminations does not mean that we as analysts should try to get back to the *real* opinions. Goffman's (1974) point is that our daily experience is full of such frame shifts, that it is incomprehensible without them, and that understanding of our roles and relations is gained, not by stripping away interactions to their real core, but by following the ways frame shifts are signalled and interpreted.

That focus groups are framed as rehearsals of opinions is apparent in three sorts of shifts. (1) In every group, participants offer opinions, not as their own but as views of others that need to be taken into account. They are, in effect, monitoring their own performances and supplying any missing views. (2) In some groups (as in our groups of younger participants, sixth formers and Youth Training Scheme participants) there is a kind of joking send-up of the discussion, as it is re-keyed from serious research to playful banter. (Kitzinger (1994) and Waterton and Wynne (1999) point out some of the serious implications of such joking in a focus group.) (3) There are rare but unforgettable moments when the key shifts in the other direction and one remembers what it is like for a participant to speak seriously, as in our groups when a woman tells how she had to leave her home, or a man insists on his need to protect his children from any threat of BSE (cf. Kitzinger and Farquhar 1999). In these moments, the temperature of the room changes, as participants strip away laminations over the event and speak as if what they say suddenly matters.

Why analyse components of speech events?

Hymes's programmatic essay, which I have been taking as a basis, may seem dated today in its optimism about finding one overall structure in which to analyse speech events (cf. Auer and di Luzio 1992; Duranti and Goodwin 1992). It is now commonplace in discourse analysis to describe situations as hybrid, participants as having multiple identities, acts and norms as open to contest and negotiation, and analysts are skeptical about structures built of formal components modelled on phonology. But if we do not have any map of the overall terrain of speech events, we cannot know when a practice is moved from one kind of event to another. This overview does show us the need for a more detailed look at just how participants orient to what they are doing and negotiate the complex shifts. If we as analysts have trouble answering the question 'What is it that's going on here?', then how do participants answer it and signal to others what they think it is? For that we need to start at the other end of analysis, not with the broad ethnographic overview but with the details of turn-taking.

Contextualizing focus groups

The moderator of a focus group enters the room with a clear idea of what Acts and Norms to expect. But for participants, the session is two hours of 'What is it that's going on here?' This would be extremely uncomfortable for all concerned if they were not able to fall back on some conventional understandings of why people do this sort of thing, and what norms apply, as we saw in the first half of the chapter. They may have models for such events from talk shows, dinners, or classrooms. But these understandings change, so they need to signal to each other and to the moderator what they think is going on at the moment, in this turn or exchange. Instead of a given context, then, we have a process of contextualization, a process that may not be over until participants finally leave the room (and may, indeed, continue afterwards).

Goffman says that we should look at 'the way individuals then proceed to get on with the affairs at hand' (Goffman 1974: 8). Gumperz, working at the same time as Hymes and in a similar project, provides one of the vocabularies for pinning down this process of 'getting on' in the text as *contextualization* (Gumperz 1982; see also Auer and di Luzio 1992; Roberts 2000). Gumperz argues that

> constellations of surface features of message form are the means by which speakers signal and listeners interpret what an activity is, how semantic content is to be understood and *how* each sentence relates to what precedes or follows. These features are referred to as *contextualisation cues*. For the most part they are habitually used and received but rarely consciously noted and almost never talked about directly. (1982: 131)

Gumperz was particularly interested in code-switching, shifts between different languages or dialects (Auer 1998), and the way such shifts could cue different functions or roles. But we can apply such cues more broadly, for instance to the use of markedly increased pace to indicate a borrowed or quoted phrase, relatively flat intonation to indicate reading aloud from a card, 'anyway' to mark a shift of topic, 'well' to suggest discomfort with the kind of question being asked. Gumperz is specifically interested in the unnoticed cues, rather than the explicit indicators or direct challenges, for it is with these cues that misunderstandings are most likely.

Focus groups, like classrooms, exams, and broadcasting studios, are sites of constant contextualization. A participant raising his or her hand cues a classroom frame. A participant saying, in a group of union members, 'so we're all agreed then', cues a shift to the frame of a meeting rather than a focus group. Side questions about common acquaintances suggest a coffee morning. The moderator may also recontextualize practices; when a moderator gives participants 'homework' (such as collecting news articles or writing in a diary) to do before the next session of a focus group, it carries with it something of the school, even if it is introduced and responded to in a joking key. I will consider cues and interpretations of these cues in key moments of a focus group:

- how they are to speak [the moderator's introduction]
- where they are speaking from [participants' introductions]
- what they are speaking about [prompts]
- who they are speaking to [closing]

At each of these stages, I will consider specific linguistic features used as cues:

- negatives in the moderator's introduction
- receipts in participants' introductions
- lists in response to prompts
- questions to the moderator in closings

I will look at the transcript of one group, one I moderated in 1998, with eight men aged 35–55, all owners of small businesses, at a pub in the centre of Preston, from 7 to 9 pm. This is not an account of the dynamics of a whole focus group, but it is perhaps enough to suggest how the definition of the event is up for grabs.

Opening – how do we talk?

My introduction in this group is very similar to those done by the other moderators on the project. The most striking textual feature of this monologue is the string of negatives, each assuming some preconception on the part of participants that needs to be forestalled (I will highlight the negatives in this passage). The moderator begins with an assurance of anonymity:

3.4.1.1
as you can see rather obviously we are recording this but it's still um . entirely confidential and **anonymous** . we need the tapes to transcribe it . so that we can talk about it in our research group . they **don't go outside** of our university and when we refer to you in the transcripts we refer to you by first names . so that it's **not a . trackable sort of thing**

No one has asked about the tape recorder. It is our assumption that the participants will want to be treated as anonymous representatives of a type of person, not as identifiable individuals; yet in many opinion forums, such as petitions or phone-ins, being identified by name is the whole point. The introduction continues to define the speech event in terms of what it's *not*.

the basic idea and the reason we have gotten together is that we want to hear people um talk about these issues . so there are **no right or wrong answers** we're **not looking for something** . in particular and **don't**

```
worry that it isn't sort of what we . have in mind
so . as far as the topics, they will probably go all
over the place but I'll I'll try to guide it somewhat
. so don't you worry that oh this must not be what
they're um what they're interested in
```

The statement on topic is rather complex; on the one hand the moderator will take responsibility for guiding it (and thus topic is constrained), but on the other hand they are not to worry about whether they are on or off topic. The moderator dramatizes this worry in reported speech which is attributed hypothetically to the participants ('this must not be what they're . . .' – the 'they' refers to the moderator and researchers). He then explicitly sets aside one possible frame for the event.

```
now the reason we are in a circle like this feel free
if somebody else says something to respond to them .
it's not like a classroom where you've got to . talk
to teacher all the time . um . so if somebody else
says something and you want to say something back .
that's fine
```

So it is not like a classroom, and there are no right or wrong answers, but the moderator sets the topics. After some rules on not talking at once, the moderator ends by saying he won't be telling them, yet, who the researchers are.

```
OK I hope that gives you some idea of the background
. we'll tell you more about who we are and what we
are doing at the end of next week's session . we
don't want to give too much away on that because it
might influence what you say
```

This raises what is for me one of the puzzles of focus-group research: why are they willing to talk when they don't know who they are talking to? We will see that, despite this attempt to set the issue aside, it remains in participants' minds to the end of the session. But that seems to be part of the definition of *opinion* that is implicitly offered here: it is offered by representative members of the public, anonymously, to anyone, with no right or wrong, in a form for possible transcription.

Each of these negatives implies some assumption on the part of the participants, who haven't spoken yet: that the tapes might go outside or their identities be tracked, that there are right answers, that the researchers have some specific answers in mind, and so on. So implicit in this monologue is a possible dialogue. In a few groups, the participants break in with questions, and this can give us some idea of what they are thinking, as opposed to the preconceptions the researchers are attributing to them. For instance, in one group, a participant asks a question based on the questions she was asked when she was recruited for the group:

```
[why is it] limited to Times and Telegraph
readers?
```

This suggests, in one group at least, a rather different set of worries from those attributed by my introduction: they want to know who they are supposed to represent, whether the research is fair, and whether it is local issues, that is, issues of particular concern to them. So it may be that participants remain vague about the researchers' identities and aims, not because they don't want to know, but because no conversational slot is created in which they can ask.

Participants' introductions – where are we talking from?

Fortunately for researchers, the interaction with participants does not usually begin with this kind of challenging of the moderator; usually it begins with each participant being asked in turn to introduce themselves, and perhaps with an unproblematic question. In the group I am using as an example, the moderator put the question this way:

```
um . well what I want to start with is just some
introductions . where you live and your names . so
probably the simplest thing is just to go round
starting at the left here
```

But even this apparently straightforward opening leaves participants several choices. They can give first name or second name, or both, as on a form. They can define 'where you live' in terms of street address, neighbourhood, or town, or they could describe the kind

of house (a tower block, a pebbledashed semi). They have to check
what amount of knowledge the moderator has of the area, and how
best to orient him or her. And of course the question asked by some
other moderators, 'where are you from' is even more ambiguous.
It requires cues on both sides to determine which response is to be
given and what it means here. Here are the first three participants
(names changed):

```
3.4.1.1
1. Charles: yeah . my name is Charles Martin and I
            come from Leyland and I have a travel
            business
2. Mod:     OK and
3. Adam:    Adam . Adam Hampson . I live in Ashton at
            Preston .  I am a retailer hardware
            retailer
4. Joe:     my name is Joe Thomas and I come from
            Fulwood . I have an upholstery business
            in upholstery
5. Mod:     OK?  in Fulwood
```

Given the possible ambiguities, participants seem to rely on the moderator's receipts after their responses. Charles keeps adding information until the moderator says 'OK' and signals that this is the sort
of introduction expected. Adam introduces himself both ways, by
first and full name, and also introduces his business in more general (retailer) and more specific (hardware retailer) terms. This time
there is no receipt signalling that this is the sort of answer wanted.
Joe just follows the pattern set by the first two. The moderator
repeats Joe's naming of a neighbourhood as he writes 'Fulwood',
signalling that such designations are an acceptable form of 'where
you live' to him, someone from outside Preston. By listening to the
moderator's receipts ('OK') and patterning their responses on previous, acceptable responses, they can treat the issue of 'where you
live' as unproblematic. (In another group, a participant answers
the questions 'Where are you from?' with another question: 'do you
mean which company or which country?' (Myers 2000c).) For some
groups, it could be said that 'where are you from?' is not just an easy
introduction, it is what the whole group is about.

The complexity of locating place (Mondada 1995; Schegloff
1972) is one instance of a general problem for social research. All

the interactions on which such research is based begin with the attribution of some identities to participants, if only a label on the cas-
sette 'Preston unemployed'. But where participants see themselves
as from may vary among the group, and where they see themselves
as from for the purposes of this particular group may change in the
course of the interaction. They may draw on identities established
earlier to make arguments later, so one can present oneself as being
from a rough inner-city neighbourhood, or from near a disputed
airport, or as having lived near a disputed nuclear plant, or as having grown up 'here'. Other aspects of demographic identity – age,
gender, ethnicity, religion, even family relations – are potentially just
as problematic as a participant's address; the category in which a
participant is placed for research purposes may come unstuck when
the talking starts.

Prompts – what are we talking about?

The introductions and the discussion following them last about
twenty minutes in most of the groups I have studied. At some
point the moderator presents a prompt, a pointer to the topics the
researchers want discussed, and the frame may shift from that of a
chat to that of an interview. The prompt may be given in many ways,
by raising a topic, showing a picture, sorting cards, responding to
texts, or even editing video clips (Macgregor and Morrison 1995).
In the study from which I have chosen my first example, our first
prompt was a video of some ads. As with the participants' introductions, the moderator's first 'OK' acts as a cue that enables other
participants to continue the pattern.

```
3.4.1.14
1. Mod:   so you start we're going to move towards
          what the images were for . but it might help
          to start with just what you saw there . what
          sort of images stick in your mind . cause
          I'm sort of interested in that rush of
          images . it is about as much as you would
          see in a commercial break?
2. Joe:   limbless victims
3. Mod:   yeah OK . What else?
```

```
4. Paul: sadness
5. Mod:  what are you thinking of was the sadness .
         that ( )
6. Paul: er . the limbless victims and also the one
         before it . just normal people living their
         lives not like our lives . you know they
         were struggling to live
7. Mod:  OK . so the one before that also seemed sad
8. Joe:  the guy hanging over the side of the bridge
         . why was he hanging over the side of the
         bridge?
9. Mod:  OK . other people?
```

Different groups take the experience of watching TV in a group in different ways, some talking over the ads as they would do at home, some waiting to be given a cue on how to respond. Here the participants respond to the ads only after the moderator asks a direct question, and they respond, not to that question, but to the topic he has posed earlier, 'what sort of images stick in your mind'. The first response is in elliptical form, as if for a list: 'limbless victims'. The moderator acknowledges this, treating it as the sort of response that is wanted, and asks for another, confirming the sense that they are building a list. The next item is also in elliptical form, 'sadness'. This time the moderator asks him to expand, and Paul struggles in several stages, before the moderator acknowledges a complete clause as an answer. So far, the interaction is structured around building a list to be used by the researchers. In turn 8, they stop building a list, as Joe asks why the man in the ad was about to jump off the bridge. Here they are talking, not about the ads as ads, but about the content of the ads as possible topics for talk.

So in this one example we see both the response of the well-behaved research group treating the video as a prompt to provide lists and a more informal response of a group of people leaping by association from one ad to another, and using each as a possible occasion for expression of opinions. The direction from turn to turn is cued in part by the moderator's responses, signalling what does and does not count as an answer. It is also cued by the participants taking up previous turns, either as a list (providing items in the same form) or as association (providing items of a related content). They have figured out what to do with the prompt, even though it is very different from what they usually do with television ads.

Closing – who are you?

Closings of encounters define what the relations in the encounter were, as in the closings of phone conversations (Schegloff and Sacks 1973), the signals for the candidate to leave after a job interview (Goffman 1963: 111), the prescription marking the end of a doctor/patient interview (Heath 1986), the abrupt move from interrogation to closure at the end of a broadcast interview (Bell and van Leeuwen 1994: 101) or a phone-in (see Chapter 9). There is a complicating factor for focus groups: often it is only at the end, as the microphone is turned off, that the researchers find out whom the participants thought they were talking to. In some ways, this may be true even for groups in which participants are informed of the sponsors and aims at the beginning; they remain curious about just what is to be done with this talk.

The closing appears on the topic guide as a set of actions by the moderator, leading to what we called the 'beanspill' and Bloor and his colleagues call the 'debriefing' (Bloor et al. 2001). Like earlier stages, it requires the cooperation of the participants to work; they may contribute to the move towards closing or open up the closing by raising new topics. As with introductions, most go smoothly, but sometimes participants raise unexpected questions. The crucial issue in many closings is just who the moderator represents and what will be done with the findings. At the end of its second session, during the moderator's wind down, the Small Business Owners group that I have been following asks a series of questions:

```
3.4.2.48
    with the information you've got now . what's the
    answer?
    [3 turns deleted]
    how many people have you done up til now?
    [3 turns deleted]
    and every group's different?
    [one turn deleted]
    how did you come about us?
    [18 turns deleted]
```

```
what's it going to be worth this research in the
end . I presume it's going to be worth a lot of
money isn't it?
[1 turn deleted]
where can we read your results about this?
```

These questions were apparently there all along, waiting for some situation in which they could be asked. This last question is one that comes up in almost all of these groups: where will all this talk go? I will consider this issue further in Chapter 4.

Cues in a hybrid genre

Focus groups are inherently unstable, since participants may see them in terms of more familiar kinds of interaction: classrooms, public meetings, market research surveys, talk shows. It may be that the genres we see as more stable are also hybrids, as in the Quality of Life questionnaire studied by Antaki and Rapley (1996), the doctor/patient interview studied by Tannen and Wallat (1987) or ten Have (1991), the general practitioners' examination studied by Roberts and Sarangi (1999), or the travel agency encounters studied by Coupland and Ylänne-McEwen (2000). In all these examples, participants have multiple frames in which the activity could be interpreted, and they try to interpret cues signalling which frame they are in at the moment.

Of course it remains an open issue how the participants interpret these negatives, receipts, collaborative lists, continuers, and closings. In the moderator's introduction, the moderator uses negatives to try to close off alternative frames, such as that of the classroom. But participants can interrupt with explicit questions about the frame. In the participants' introduction, each speaker says where he or she is from, as a routine piece of background data. But they may also raise questions about which form of self-identification is relevant here and modify these introductions later in relation to the issues being talked about. Prompts may be taken as tests or recall, to be answered with lists of elliptical items, or as opportunities for associating topics, to be answered with more extended turns; participants decide which kind of response is required on the basis of the moderator's receipts. At the end, the group may close with social thanks and farewells, as at a party, or may raise questions (as at the beginning) about who this is for and whether it is a representative group. At each stage, the cues and responses do not settle the kind of interaction but make us as analysts aware of alternative frames.

Shifting forums

The surprise, given such a range of forums, and the instability of focus groups as a forum, is that people are willing to put up with the unfamiliar setting, the strangers, the tape recorder, and with ceding control of topic and turn-taking to a moderator whose aims and institutional affiliation may be mysterious. Each person still speaks his or her piece. The apparent robustness of expressions of opinion might seem to be a strength of public opinion research: people will say *something*, even under strange conditions. But few researchers really want to know what anonymous people will say to strangers, after a prompt, in a short interaction with no consequences. They want to know what this remark can tell them about other conversations going on unrecorded, between friends and family, about long-term attitudes, and about possibilities for action. There is no reason to assume an opinion is the same under different constraints, or even if it sounds the same, that it will be interpreted in the same way and have the same sort of effect.

It is not just a matter, as some handbooks suggest, of the moderator firmly setting the right context at the outset. The focus group is not a well-bounded event, and if it were, it would be less valuable as a tool for researching opinion. We have seen participants construct and reconstruct the norms of who, in this group, speaks to whom about what. The kinds of questions that they raise at the closing of focus groups remind us that the form of the discussion is a question of politics as well as one of social science methodology. I will return to these questions in Chapter 11.

4

Institutions of opinion: voice of the people?

It is 15 September 2001. On the lower right-hand corner of the CNN home page is a frame labelled 'Quick Vote'. It asks the question, 'What are your feelings now about Tuesday's terrorist attack?' There are three choices, each with a circle to tick:

- ○ Shock
- ○ Sorrow
- ○ Anger

At the bottom is a link to 'Results', which tells me that the current tally is 26 per cent shocked, 26 per cent sorrowful, and 49 per cent angry.

There are some obvious problems with this survey as an indication of public opinion. The sample is not representative: it includes only those with Internet access who are interested in the news and interested in giving their emotional response. The possible responses are limited to three nouns, the same three feelings set out in the same sequence as they were presented in the news reports ('Americans are shocked and sorrowful today, but tomorrow they will be angry'). The 'Quick Vote' also assumes that participants interpret this question in the same way, no matter who asks or why, and it disregards their strength of feeling, or the differing reasons they might give for it. All the words have potentially variable meanings, and even the 'now' can slip; it does not correspond to the moment of clock time shown on my computer's browser but suggests to the respondent that *now* is different from *then*, that one will go through stages of feelings. Finally, the tally goes nowhere, except back to the people who complete the form; but the first question one might ask in responding is 'What is this for?'

The web editors at CNN could say that the 'Quick Vote' was not intended as a poll; it was just one of a number of interactive features of the web page. But at the same time, there were many examples of more carefully planned and more broadly influential polls that week. A *New York Times* / CBS News poll of 1,216 Americans conducted between 20 and 23 September said that 92 per cent favoured military action against those responsible for the attacks on 11 September, with only 5 per cent opposed, and 3 per cent don't know. The article reporting the poll also drew on quotations from representative Americans. (For other polls, see the *New York Times* web site at www.nytimes.com, *USA Today*–CNN–Gallup at www.cnn.com, or the *Observer* at www.theguardian.co.uk.) The results of these polls did not just go back to those who took them, as a matter of interest, as an interactive feature of a web page. They were reported as news and would be considered by leaders among other factors in their decision to go to war.

These polls after 11 September were not asking people a question they had not previously thought about. Almost everyone talked that week about the events in New York: family members phoned each other, Internet discussion sites were full of comments, petitions circulated around the Internet, and people went to rallies and memorial services, flew flags, sang 'The Battle Hymn of the Republic', made murals and signs, or stood silent at sports events. A poll, as Susan Herbst (1993) points out, is a symbol like these other expressions of opinion, suitable to circulate in mass media. Its authority comes, not from law or from tradition, but from the institutions and practices with which it is associated: CBS and the *New York Times* in this case, and more generally, the whole history of public opinion research techniques. In this chapter, I will consider the way talk gets transformed through research and broadcasting institutions into the terms and figures of mediated public opinion.

Like most key terms in social sciences, *public opinion* has been used with many different definitions or used without defining it at all. In her useful history of the field in the US, Susan Herbst sorts these definitions into four categories:

- aggregative: the collection of individual, anonymous opinions, each treated as equal in value

- majoritarian: the association of 'opinion' with the view held by most respondents
- discursive/consensual: including conceptions of the public will and taken-for-granted agreement
- reification: the projection of an opinion by the media or elite onto an imagined or constructed public (Herbst 1993: 45–7).

Most current conceptions of opinion are based on the idea of aggregation of individuals, the first of these definitions. Much of the press reporting of opinion implicitly takes the second definition, treating it as a sort of on-going referendum in which there are binary choices and the winner takes all. In both these views opinion is something out there, constantly shifting as the public follows events, that can be elicited informally (by talking to a cab-driver or bringing up a topic at a dinner) or more formally and systematically, for instance through polls. Both views are individualistic, cognitive, and aggregative: public opinion is the sum of personal opinions in people's heads.

The two other views that Herbst lists suggest other lines of inquiry. If opinion is a kind of consensus maintained by constant communication, then the strongest opinions may be just those that people don't express, that they don't need to express, and 'the public will' is to be seen (and invoked) in all sorts of formal and informal communication, not just voting. Such a view calls for detailed discourse analysis and ethnography, a project of which this study is a part. Finally, if public opinion is the projection of policy choices of an elite, then we need to look at the role that symbols of public opinion play along with other factors in decision-making. As we will see, a number of sociologists have called for study of how elites construct and respond to opinion in their day-to-day activities. I would not use the term 'reification' only for this construction, as Herbst does, because all these views of opinion, and not just the last, involve making an accountable thing out of an on-going process.

There is, of course, a whole field of academic and applied research devoted to public opinion and how it is shaped; examples of current research may be found in such journals as *Public Opinion*, which was instrumental in shaping the field in the 1940s. But I will argue that if we want to understand why public opinion can be so powerful and yet so weak, we have to go back to the interactions, and

to the ways they are elicited and represented by the institutions that
study public opinion. We may see these institutions more clearly if
we look at them from two points of view, first through the dom-
inant view of opinion as a cognitive and individual phenomenon,
and then through views that see it as social and interactive. We will
find then, not a one-way transformation of tiny bits of opinion into
large and influential measures, but a messier cycle that goes through
representations and representatives, and that always involves messages going both ways, from people to pollsters, but also from polls
to people.

The shaping and reporting of opinion: a cognitive view

Talk obviously plays a large part in interviews, focus groups, and
other qualitative research, but it is also a necessary part of quantitative surveys and polls. One of the founders of public opinion
research, George Gallup (1901–84), often quoted the nineteenth-
century British political theorist James Bryce, who said, for instance,
that 'The best way in which tendencies which are at work in any
community may be discovered is by moving freely among all sorts
and conditions of men and noting how they are affected by the news
and arguments brought from day to day to their knowledge . . .
Talk is the best way of reaching the truth' (Bryce 1888, as quoted
in Gallup and Rae 1940: 31). Gallup says he is following in this
tradition: 'The modern polls rely on interviewers . . . who listen to
voters expressing their attitudes in ordinary conversation' (1940:
31–2). The importance of this grounding in talk is clear later in the
book when Gallup describes 'Meeting the People' in a poll:

At eight o'clock, then, the interviewer approaches a middle-aged man,
dressed in working clothes, who is sitting on the front porch of a house
classified as 'poor.' The interview might go something like this:

Interviewer: I am interviewing people to get their views for the American
Institute of Public Opinion – the Gallup poll. Every day, in every state, we
ask representative people their opinions on questions of national importance. I'd be glad to have your ideas on a few questions. I don't want your
name – just your opinions.
Respondent: I don't believe my opinions are worth much.
Interviewer: That's where you're wrong! In this poll we get the opinions
of wealthy and poor, old and young, men and women, Democrats and

Republicans – we take a cross section of the country. The results of these surveys are published by newspapers throughout the country. You may have seen these reports in your own daily paper.
Respondent: Well, come to think of it, I believe I have.
Interviewer: Do you plan to vote in the next election?   (Gallup and Rae 1940: 113).

And from here the interviewer is off down the clipboard. Gallup clearly believes it is important that to establish the authority of polling, he starts with one interview with all the particularities of a single encounter: the place and time, the introduction, traces of evaluation and attitudes. This specificity and concreteness (even in a fictional example) is his warrant that his organisation is, in Bryce's words, 'moving freely about among all sorts and conditions of men' and reporting what they really said.

I will argue that all expressions of opinion begin in interactions, if not in opinion poll interviews, then in focus groups, dinner-table conversations, or chat at coffee breaks. But these interactions have wider effects only when they become 'public opinion'. They undergo this transformation when they go through institutions such as Gallup's polls, or through meetings, petitions, letters to the editor, focus groups, advertisements, or academic research. These institutions transform the scale and medium of talk, stripping talk of its local, specific character, of all the issues of how and when they said what they said, leaving only numbers.

In the cognitive view of opinion, changes of opinion come down to two key phases – the information going into individuals, and the information coming out. These phases correspond to two vast bodies of academic work, one growing out of studies of propaganda and the other growing out of studies of polling. One body of studies concerns the influence of newspapers and other mass media sources on members of the public; whether researchers are promoting informed citizenship or warning against propaganda, the assumption is that the media do shape opinions. The other body of studies seeks constant refinement in the measurement of opinion.

Cognitive views of opinion: news

The classic *Public Opinion* by Walter Lippmann (1889–1974) focuses on the limitations and distortions of information available

to an American reader of the newspapers. What is so striking about
Lippmann's work, today, is the central role he gives to the shift from
politics based on immediate associations and experience in a local
community, to politics based on mediated images: 'The world we
have to deal with politically is out of reach, out of sight, out of
mind. It has to be explored, reported, and imagined' (Lippmann
1922: 18). So he outlines for himself an agenda in examining the
connections between 'The world outside and the pictures in our
heads':

Those pictures outside which have to do with the behavior of other human
beings, in so far as that behavior crosses ours, we call roughly public affairs.
Those pictures inside the heads of these human beings, the pictures of themselves, of others, of their needs, purposes, and relationships, are their public
opinions. Those pictures which are acted upon by groups of people, or by
individuals acting in the names of groups, are Public Opinion with capital
letters. And so in the chapters which follow we shall inquire first into some
of the reasons why the picture inside so often misleads men in their dealings
with the world outside.   (Lippmann 1922: 18)

Lippmann makes a clear case that citizens can never be very well
informed about the broad range of public affairs; they are necessarily biased in their perception, prone to oversimplification, limited
in their attention span, baffled by the sheer number and speed of
messages. He is less persuasive about what should be done, when he
proposes an expert, unbiased organization to screen and interpret
news – that is, an officially sanctioned institutional version of Walter
Lippmann (he advised successive American presidents and wrote a
magisterial column for *Newsweek* until his death). 'My conclusion
is that public opinions must be organized for the press if they are to
be sound, not by the press as they are today' (1922: 19).

   Lippmann's book is always perceptive and powerfully written; I
feel like taking it out again after each new American election. But his
drastic view of influences on public opinion has two limitations: in
what counts as a public issue and in what counts as influence. The
distinction that he makes between 'public issues' and everything
else seemed clear enough to a member of the American political
elite in the 1920s; public issues included labour unions and foreign
relations but would not include matters of diet, exercise, travel, or
shopping. The distinction is no longer so clear when participants in
our focus groups feel the need to defend their decisions to drive to

work, or eat beef, or go on holiday in Africa. Environmental issues often involve this collapsing of public and private issues; so do issues of gender, sexuality, and consumption. As Michael Schudson (1998) points out, the blurring of the distinction between the private and the political was one of the main shifts in the political discourse of the late twentieth century. And if there is no longer a clearly set apart discourse of 'public issues', the great gap between the real world and perceptions, the gap that so worries Lippmann, is no longer so straightforward. Citizens are, I would imagine, as ill-informed, inattentive, self-interested, and prone to stereotyping today as they were when Lippmann wrote in 1922. But it is harder to see that expert information from the world outside would lead to a democratic consensus on any issue, or even on what the issues are.

Most commentary on public opinion since Lippmann has followed his emphasis on the mass media, assuming that newspapers, and later radio and television, would be the main source of opinions, so there are studies of gatekeeping at news agencies, institutionalized news values, and readership. But people are also influenced by the people they talk to. In another classic study, *Personal Influence: The Part Played by People in the Flow of Mass Communications* (1955), Elihu Katz and Paul Lazarsfeld applied theories of groups and empirical studies of a medium-sized American town to explore the influence of locally influential people. They found, contrary to what one might think reading Lippmann and his followers, that people are more influenced by their contacts with family and friends than by messages from the mass media. This research has had a great influence on advertisers trying to target opinion leaders as a way of carrying along the rest of the community (Schudson 1984). Katz and Lazarsfeld make the key move of locating opinion in interpersonal, as well as mass, communication. But the shaping of opinion is still for them a cognitive process of decision-making, influenced by rather than constituted by social interactions.

Cognitive views of opinion: polls

Critics of polling have to deal with the fact that there are better and worse ways of predicting voting patterns: annoyingly, polls often get it right. The canonical history of public opinion refers constantly to failed predictions and to improvements that led to much better results. Gallup, for instance, devotes a whole chapter to the 1936 *Literary Digest* poll, which drew for its sample on lists of automobile and telephone owners and thus had an unnoticed bias towards middle- and upper-class voters; it predicted a landslide for the Republican challenger Alf Landon, when in the election Franklin Roosevelt won 46 of the 48 states (Gallup and Rae 1940). The *Literary Digest* fiasco becomes the centrepiece of an argument for careful representative sampling rather than large samples. Of course pollsters still make famous mistakes (such as the underestimate of the Tory vote in the 1992 UK general election, or the repeated wrong projections of Florida during broadcasts of the 2000 US presidential election). But many of these announcements could be attributed to journalistic pressures, not polling methods, and the response in each case has been to modify the methods, not to question the concepts.

Polls make a broad and vague disposition into a reportable event. Gallup acknowledges that his polls were paid for by newspapers and praises them for their public-spirited support (Gallup and Rae 1940: viii); as Schudson points out, 'polling questions are still designed not to afford general knowledge of public opinion so much as to generate news' (1998: 224). But Gallup had greater ambitions for his polls; they would complete democracy, by providing the politicians with scientific and up-to-the-minute measures of public opinion on a range of issues, as a guide to decision-making, bypassing the smoke-filled rooms of politicians and the organized campaigns of pressure groups. They would rationalize the collection and effects of public opinion. The same ambition persists in the arguments of those who would like to use the Internet to provide governments with direct access to public opinion (e.g., *The Times* 1999).

The cognitive view of opinion draws on quantitative research methods, such as statistical analysis of surveys, but it is not necessarily limited to such methods. Paul Lazarsfeld, founder of the Office of Radio Research at Columbia University, and a key figure in the US Government's propaganda research during the war, wrote as early as 1944 about the possible weaknesses of 'the straight poll question' and the ways such questions might be complemented by open-ended, qualitative interviews (Lazarsfeld 1944; for background on Lazarsfeld see Morrison 1998). He argued that interviews might be needed to clarify the meaning of an answer, to determine which aspects of an opinion are decisive, and what influenced the opinion, to clarify complex attitude patterns, to interpret motives, and to clarify complex correlations. That is, he fully recognized the kinds of interactional issues raised by social psychologists, sociologists, and discourse analysts (see Chapter 2), but he saw the interactions as distortions in the technique of polling, to be corrected by new techniques, not as a fundamental challenge to the very idea of public opinion.

The critique of public opinion polling is as old as polling itself. The criticism that most concerns us is that first made by the Chicago sociologist Herbert Blumer as early as 1948: 'its current sampling procedure forces a treatment of society as if it were only an aggregation of disparate individuals' (Blumer 1948: 546). Blumer had an explanation for why surveys worked so well in predicting voting (and, though somewhat less well, in predicting purchasing): 'the casting of ballots is distinctly an action of separate individuals wherein a ballot cast by one individual has exactly the same weight as a ballot cast by another individual' (ibid., 547). But this is just what does not happen in the cycle of public opinion, considered sociologically: 'Public opinion gets its form from the social framework in which it moves, and from the social processes in play in that framework . . . the function and role of public opinion is determined by the part it plays in the operation of society' (ibid., 543). This criticism does not just call for improved techniques of public opinion research; it suggests we have to look for public opinion somewhere else.

I am particularly interested in researchers who have studied empirically the interactional situation of surveys. Some of the best critiques are by traditional survey researchers, such as William Belson, researching the interpretation of test questions (Belson 1981). Graham Low has used think-aloud protocols to explore students' interpretations of questionnaire items, and specific problematic constructions (Low 1999). These lines of work have been used to improve survey questions, but they also lead to broader questions about just what survey respondents are doing. In a classic paper, Lucy Suchman and Brigitte Jordan considered the survey situation, and specific questions, through conversation analysis (Suchman and Jordan 1990); for them, there is no quick fix available that will remove the indexicality of the expressions used. Charles Antaki and his colleagues have applied a similar critique to various kinds of surveys (Antaki and Rapley 1996; Houtkoop-Steenstra and Antaki 1997; Antaki et al. 2000), including a 'Quality of Life' survey used to assess the need for social services; in each study, they ask how this institutionalized interaction is reinterpreted in the light of participants' everyday interactional processes. In the most extensive study along these lines, Hanneke Houtkoop-Steenstra (Houtkoop-Steenstra 2000) has analysed 'the living questionnaire' in terms of turn-taking, participant roles, recipient design, and conversational implicature. She makes a point I will raise repeatedly: 'standardization of question wording does not necessarily imply standardization of meaning' (8).

The construction and circulation of opinion: a social view

An alternative to the cognitive, individual, aggregative view of opinion would start with two related criticisms of traditional public opinion research:

- public opinion is interactional, so we need to look at the ways it is constructed at every stage
- public opinion is institutional, so we need to look at the ways it is mediated between stages

Blumer suggests that one way to construct an alternative model is to work backwards, 'That is, we ought to begin with those who have to act on public opinion and move backwards along the lines of the various expressions of public opinion that come to their attention, tracing these expressions backwards through their own various channels' (1948: 549). If we follow Blumer's advice and start with the *effects* of public opinion, we can pursue it through different systems – government, media, interest groups, local associations – without taking for granted the packaged public opinion offered us by the very institutions we wish to study. I will consider five stages, and the ways interaction is involved at every stage:

- decision-makers and agendas – interactions with the people who are supposed to make decisions based on public opinion
- researchers and questions – interactions between researchers and members of the public

- talkers and commonplaces – interactions between members of the public
- audiences and media – representations of arguments and expressions of opinion
- decision-makers and media – governments and institutions do not just respond to public opinion, they can (or think they can) shape the way it is represented

This movement takes us from the people making decisions back to the people expressing opinions, but without assuming the actions and effects all go one way.

Decision-makers and agendas

Like the weather, public opinion may typically be taken for granted, as a vague feeling about what's outside, and research may be needed (like the weather report) only when a great deal is at stake, or when there are conflicting signals (Mary Douglas and Aaron Wildavsky develop this analogy in more detail in relation to risk perception (1982: 68)). In the view offered by James Bryce, George Gallup, Robert Worcester, Philip Gould and others, the ultimate consumer of public opinion is the decision-maker who wants to know 'what the people think' – through an organization that will find out what the people say. But in a social view, the decision-maker can be the start, as well as the end, of the process.

For Blumer, public opinion is to be found in the operation of institutions such as parties, lobby groups, unions, local organizations, through all the contacts that might influence a decision-maker. And in these contacts, individuals are anything but equal: 'views count pretty much on the basis of how the individual judges the "backing" of the views and the implication of the backing' (545). One can devise samples representative of the whole, and one can inquire ever more deeply into the statements of individuals, but real public opinion, for Blumer, is in the operation of these institutions, and in these processes, any given individual may matter a lot or not at all. 'The mere fact that the interviewee either gives or does not give an opinion does not tell you whether he is participating in the formation of public opinion as it is being built up functionally in the society' (546).

Pierre Bourdieu has argued, in an often cited essay, that 'Public opinion does not exist' (1971/ 1993). Like Blumer, he sees opinion as an artefact of the methods of opinion researchers; people are asked to take positions on questions formulated by the researchers, and these results are then aggregated without regard to the different meanings these questions may have for different groups. The kinds of public opinion imagined out there are the constructs of decision-makers' need to know: How will people in this district vote? Who will buy this brand of drink? Which social categories watch this television programme? Why do people drive their cars? How many will recycle glass? How does this university course compare to others? The agenda for any particular research is set by negotiation between the people who want to know and the people who will try to find out, even if (as with broadcasters' audience research, a political campaign focus group, or with an end-of-course evaluation) the people are in the same organization.

Researchers never set out to find public opinion in its ideal form; there are always practical issues of what we have done before, what we already know, what we can do in the time, what will give a clear message. For instance, in the focus-group studies that I will use as material, there was always some negotiation of which groups should be studied, how many groups could be covered and how many times they could meet with the money available, what the topic guide could and could not cover in the time. Do mixed-gender groups work? How and where can we recruit unemployed men? Will young professionals have any incentive to turn up?

With academic research, these negotiations take place among the team in preparing what they hope is a plausible proposal, and with comments from sometimes unfriendly referees; with research commissioned by a government agency, non-governmental organization, or corporation, the negotiation can take place more directly. The horizons of answerable questions, available techniques, accessible publics, and interesting results are all worked out in practical terms, based on the experiences and immediate needs and resources of the research organization and the organization paying for the research. In negotiating what is practical, they give a certain temporary definition to the public. Qualitative research does this just as much as the more familiar and influential quantitative models.

When, say, a local government agency wants to know something about public opinion, such formal, contracted research is not the only channel; it is perhaps a last resort where the usual channels are not giving the information or perspectives they need. A member of the county council may meet representatives of various public interests (unions or pressure groups or non-government organizations), or get letters, calls, faxes, and e-mail, or meet with people who claim to represent the public, or see opinions represented in the media. He or she may pick up a sense of public opinion from informal contacts, outside work, the taxi driver or spouse generalized to represent 'the public'. The question a decision-maker asks of these expressions of opinion is not about the epistemological basis ('how do they know?') but about the political basis (what Blumer calls 'the backing' for an expression). Gallup argued that formal (and expensive) public opinion research should in the future replace all these other channels of influence, which he characterized as 'smoke-filled rooms' and 'pressure groups' (Gallup and Rae 1940). But they haven't.

Researchers and questions

Just as there is a gap between the decision-makers and the researchers that must be bridged in interaction (the meetings that set the agenda), there is a gap between the researchers and the participants representing the public that must be bridged with some form of questions and answers. Bourdieu points out that 'the opinions asked in an opinion survey are not questions which arise spontaneously for the people questioned, and . . . the responses are not interpreted in terms of the problematic actually referred to in their answers by the different categories of respondents' (1993: 154). The most researched questions on education, health, media, or the environment bear little resemblance to the kinds of issues people actually talk about, because the research aims to help policy-makers make a specific decision. One could work on better-formulated questions, starting with broader issues and more colloquial language, with open-ended questions to explore participants' perceptions, and a large part of the practical guidance on surveys is about just such issues. But as Bourdieu says, 'the first imperative in evaluating a poll is to ask what question the different categories of people thought they were answering' (1993: 151).

Besides the issue of what researchers ask the participants, there are also issues of who is being asked. Social science research handbooks provide guidance on sampling (for its relevance to qualitative research, see Becker 1998). But in any research, one must also ask who participants think they are, in what role (of their many possible roles) they are being asked this question. When a telephone market researcher asks me questions about my radio listening, am I representing my age, my gender, my occupation, or some bizarre subculture of Lancashire country music fans? Participants choose their responses accordingly. The problem is not that they fail to represent the group to which they are assigned, but that, once they figure out what they think this group is, they can hardly do anything else but represent it.

The transcript I quoted in Chapter 2 was produced as part of a study done by the Centre for the Study of Environmental Change at Lancaster University for Lancashire County Council (LCC/CSEC) (Macnaghten et al. 1995). In producing the topic guide, the researchers had to rework policy language into the kind of language that might be recognized by participants in the groups. 'Sustainability' is not an issue on which people generally have an opinion; it is part of the language and framework of the Rio Summit, the Brundtland Report, and Local Agenda 21. The first step was to frame the questions, not in terms of sustainability but in terms of participants' feelings about their neighbourhoods, their kids, the changing quality of life. Different groups would have different access to such topics as 'environment' or 'transport' as matters of opinion; some would recognize right away that these were issues for public decision, while others would consider them technical issues. Different groups would have different ideas of who they were talking as (mothers of young children, for instance, decided very soon that motherhood was the aspect of their identities that was of interest to the researchers). And different groups would have different interpretations of just who they were talking to, of what this research was for (they guessed at various points that it was for the Labour Party, news organizations, the national government, or a local company).

The problem is not just that participants' worlds are different from those of the researchers (that is an issue in any social researcher) but that their relevant worlds could be different from group to group. They were asked the same questions, but they answered different questions. So, for instance, each group was asked to say what actions they do because they are thinking of a better future. For some groups, this led to a list of standard environmental activities (recycle paper, don't use hairsprays), more or less as expected, while for others, it led to a display of technical knowledge (about different forms of pollution), or defensive comments about the impossibility of action, or complaints about present unemployment and hopelessness. It is not just the researchers who preformulate what counts as public opinion; participants also have their assumptions about what is a topic and what is not, and researchers will find it very hard to work against these assumptions. And these assumptions may vary between groups; different groups (Youth Training Scheme participants, professionals, retired people, unemployed men) will have different senses of what they can do, or whether they can do anything, to change things.

Groups and commonplaces

Questions are preformulated by researchers and reformulated by participants. They are preformulated in another way too, in that speakers share a range of commonplaces that are available for responses. When a participant in one group says 'we keep hearing about should we be recycling . . . shouldn't be using hairsprays', she doesn't need to elaborate on these issues, because they are just what everyone already knows about.

As I mentioned in Chapter 2, John Shotter has developed from Vico a concept of interaction in which commonplaces are central.

[T]he social processes involved [in a culture], he claims, are based not upon anything pre-established either in people or their surroundings, but in socially shared *identities of feeling* they themselves create in the flow of activity between them. These, he calls 'sensory topics' – 'topics' (Gr. topos = 'place') because they give rise to 'commonplaces', that is, to shared moments in a flow of social activity which afford common reference, and 'sensory' because they are moments in which shared *feelings* for already shared circumstances are created.'   (Shotter 1993: 53)

So, going to the bottle bank, reading the hairspray label to check for CFCs, or going on holiday, and the motivations and practices

involved, are referred to as common experiences that can be signalled with a phrase, without explanation. At the same time, the
reference evokes a shared feeling (as we see in the discussion that
follows) that includes a feeling of doing good as an individual, an
exasperation with the practical difficulties of doing good, a sense of
the smallness of this act, and an annoyance at being told what to do,
all this invoked with a phrase like 'we keep hearing about should
we be recycling'. And similar commonplaces – about doing things
for the children, or responsibility to neighbours – can turn up on
opposite sides of an argument (Myers and Macnaghten 1998).

Commonplaces are just what a lot of public opinion research is
after, not what this particular person said in this situation, but what
anyone could have said. But they pose three problems for social
researchers who draw on talk in some way (and that includes survey
and ethnographic as well as interview and focus group researchers):
silence, reflexivity, and indexicality.

First, if commonplaces are the things we want people to say,
they are just the things that need not be said. Thus there is the odd
silence after the easy question, about whether the environment is
important, or whether people should drive less, or whether they
trust the government. This is the same silence one hears when a
teacher asks what everyone in the class knows so no one will say.
Surveys, interviews, and focus groups have to be crafted to provide
slots in which people can say the obvious – often in response to a
formulation – so that the obvious can be included in reports.

Second, commonplaces give the sense that the participants are
saying back to the institutions just what the institutions have said
to them. The woman just quoted, who thinks we should recycle and
not use hairsprays, goes on to say 'that's the sort of thing individuals
do isn't [it]', repeating back to us the distinction between government, corporate, and individual responsibility that one finds in public information leaflets. The advertising executive Adam Lury raises
the same issue as a problem for evaluating advertising: 'When you
access today's consumer – *what they think, and what they think
you want them to think, are often one and the same*' (Lury 1994:
96). This stumbling over commonplaces is not necessarily proof
of the effectiveness of environmental or advertising campaigns. It
just shows that participants in groups can talk about talk, refer

reflexively to the kind of talk one commonly has, and expect others to recognize it (see Chapter 7).

Third, commonplaces refer to common experiences and feelings, but they do not have a uniform meaning in context. One can say 'we keep hearing about should we be recycling . shouldn't be using <u>hairsprays</u> . that's the sort of thing ind<u>iv</u>iduals do isn't [it]' in all sorts of situations, to support all sorts of arguments. But as we will see in Chapter 6, a phrase can have a different use in each situation: to display one's knowledge of environmental issues, complain about media pressure, or contrast major with trivial issues.

If one grants these problems – that commonplaces don't need to be said, that they repeat what has been said, that they are used in different ways – then one can study such talk as exemplifying the way people talk in groups, not as giving access to internal, distinctive, and characteristic opinions (Myers and Macnaghten 1998). But then one is no longer studying autonomous opinions as a base for policy, or responses to media texts as a measure of the effectiveness of those texts; one is studying a cycle of talk about and in media. I will look more closely at this cycle in Chapters 9, 10, and 11.

Publics and media

As I have already noted, opinion polls were first developed in the US by newspapers, as a way of representing the public back to the readers. In Gallup's example of an interview, it is assumed that most interviewees will know about polls from seeing them in the local newspaper. Of course there were and are many surveys done for private consumption, by advertisers, political parties, government agencies, or other clients. But visible public opinion has a special symbolic importance and, it has sometimes been argued, an influence on wavering members of the public in a 'Bandwagon Effect'. (Gallup and Rae feel it is necessary to rebut such charges (1940: Ch. 20).) Besides polls, media representations of public opinion include letters to the editor, vox pop interviews, phone-in talk shows, photos of crowds or queues, demonstrations and placards, sounds of applause at a speech, even expressions of people in photographs, when they are taken as representative of an audience, a moment, or the feelings of a whole nation.

The LCC/CSEC study that I mentioned earlier resulted in a readable and rather detailed report with a bright cover, available to the public from the council (Macnaghten et al. 1995). But it also resulted in a story in the local *Lancashire Evening Post*, with the headline 'Lancashire Misses Feel-good Factor'. This is an attempt to make the report into news by (1) stressing its local setting, (2) posing the issue in current party-political terms ('the feel-good factor'), and (3) interpreting the results as showing a failure. In the headline, just one comment in the report, based on just one comment in a group, is made into the basis of the whole story. The story is one way of playing the study back to the public as news, as something to talk about.

Representations of public opinion can have their own effects. The overwhelming displays of grief after the death of Diana were played back to viewers, and the fact that everyone shared the emotions, or was assumed to share the emotions, was part of the grief for the grief-stricken or part of the annoyance for those who did not respond in that way (Richards et al. 1999; Walter 1999; Myers 2000b; Turnock 2000). Polls and projections of election votes have been argued to have an effect on the outcome (Herbst 1993). The bestseller list encourages still more people to buy the number one book. Representations of public opinion do not just convey information but provide the background to further actions.

These media effects on the public depend on the ambiguous way that the public is both *they*, a body of people out there whose views and actions can be reported, and *you*, the audience of press and (in particular) broadcast reports. NBC's Tom Brokaw referred on US election night 2000 to the mysterious workings of projections of the final vote of each state, while also reminding viewers 'these decisions are being made by you and they have been made in most of these states . we're just responding to the uh projections as they come in'. Viewers do not just see politicians close up (Meyrowitz 1985), they see themselves, or other people standing in for them as members of 'the public' (see Chapter 10). The final link in this cycle is when people in a crowd, shown as representative of a mass response, see themselves on TV being shown as an example (as with the crowd in Austin celebrating Bush's apparent victory on the night of the 2000 election).

Of course decision-makers do not just wait for the reports from polls or shots of crowds and hope that they are favourable. Since

the nineteenth century political parties have conducted polls to
represent their candidates as winning and their opponents as fail-
ing miserably (Schudson 1998); they have done the same sort of
representation of crowd sizes at rallies (Herbst 1993: Ch. 7). Political aides comment on polls, play down those that go against their
candidate, or find patterns or trajectories in those that seem to support the candidate; scenes with representatives or spokespeople of
groups (farmers, workers, retired people) are presented as standing for broader support. The aim is to reconstruct hypothetical
conversations in which people already support one's candidate or
cause.

Talk and the cycle of public opinion

I have given an overview of some stages of public opinion, but following Blumer's suggestion, I have followed them backwards, not
from news to public opinion to government decision, but from the
agendas of decision-makers, to the questions of researchers, to the
talk of participants, to the representations of opinion in the media.
This reversal of order has the advantage of avoiding the teleological
fallacies that dominate some thinking on public opinion.

We would expect to see that:	Instead we see:
decision-makers in a democratic society follow the aggregated measurements of individual responses to set questions that are institutionalized public opinion	decision-makers draw on many alternative representations of public opinion, including spokespersons and informal encounters
polls and other institutions merely convey these opinions to decision-makers	researchers negotiate a practical approach that serves their needs and projects, issues and responses
proper procedures will deliver original, individual, uninfluenced reports of opinions	participants tailor their responses to what they think interests the researchers or represents themselves as they would wish to be seen
people read the news in order to form opinions and they form opinions in order to influence decisions	people already have a stock of commonplaces
public opinion works as an independent variable, a check on the representations used by political parties and other organizations	policy-makers and organizations try to influence the representation of opinion in the media

Of course it is a simplification to see the processes as going in one direction, or in just this order, from policy-makers to pollsters to public. I have suggested throughout this overview that actors at any stage can try to shape the responses at another stage, and that representations of public opinion can leap from stage to stage. So, for instance, decision-makers may try to gauge public opinion for themselves, cutting out the researchers. Or participants in groups may frame their language and select their topics to have an effect on those they see (rightly or wrongly) as the ultimate audience for this group, not just the participants and researchers who are present. Or, as we saw in the 'Quick Vote', quoted at the beginning of the chapter, you can express your opinion just to have a sort of public opinion reported back to you instantly, without any effect on anyone else.

The cycle of public opinion is very leaky because everyone engaged in it – decision-makers, researchers, research participants, and reporters – is aware of the potentially powerful effects of the magnification of *an* opinion into *public* opinion. And in using and reusing everyday language, they can leap from one stage to another, providing a convincing sound of public opinion without necessarily going through all the machinery to produce it. The original interaction is transformed when a poll question is asked, and the answer is converted into numerical form, and that number is transformed by aggregation, comparison, and correlation, to result in a new statement ('Americans support President'). At the same time, there is always the possibility of enhancing validity by reverting to the vernacular, apparently interactive expression. A political speech draws on phrases from focus groups, a questionnaire is rewritten in more accessible language, people talk about real or hypothetical situations for opinions, and the news makes the abstract representation of public opinion concrete with a single picture or a quote from some anonymous participant. Apparently public opinion, to be effective, cannot be entirely reduced to the quantitative form it has always been given by its leading researchers. It needs to carry in its mediated forms some traces of the situation in which someone speaks out.

Why public opinion still exists

If, as Bourdieu dramatically says, public opinion does not exist and is an artefact of the methods used to study it, why do politicians, researchers, advertisers, journalists, and members of the public continue to act as if it does exist? I would argue that the cognitive, aggregative view of public opinion has become a kind of common sense even to those of us who take a social, interactive view of what actually happens in opinion. It works as common sense because of its consonance with our assumptions about ourselves as subjects, as people who can act, in our roles as audiences for media, consumers of brands, and citizens of a democracy.

Broadcasting, Paddy Scannell (2000) has argued, is addressed as if 'for anyone as someone'. When I hear the radio, I know and appreciate that the voice is speaking at the same time to anyone in the broadcast area who cares to listen, and yet I can also feel it is addressed specifically to me, in my immediate situation. This is obviously true of the great media events that mark important moments in our personal lives, but it is also true of the BBC Radio 1 (pop for young people) DJ taking callers from around the country and producing a sense of a nationally shared event (Montgomery 1985). It is a community of people doing different things (driving vans, cutting hair, studying, getting ready for a date) but sharing this broadcast (compare Sean Hannity in Chapter 9). The cognitive, aggregative view of opinion picks up on this sense of a unique self that is also tied, paradoxically, just anyone. When a market researcher asks me questions, I know that I should respond for myself, in all my particularity and oddity. But I also know that I will be taken as part of a quota of people of a certain type (bald middle-aged PhD joggers?) and that I will be heard only as a potential representative of that group, that is, as anyone.

Advertising also addresses 'anyones' – whoever happens to read, watch, or listen – as 'someones', individuals making entirely individual choices. Advertising practitioners constantly hark back to the face-to-face, one-to-one encounter of the expert salesperson sizing up a customer in a shop (Ogilvy 1983; Hopkins 1995). But the products they sell have to be designed for just anyone in a category of people. They make the link by addressing customers in a way that calls on them to recognize themselves as addressed personally (Williamson 1978; Fowles 1996). Representative democracy has also come to be seen in these individualistic, aggregative terms; that is the view of elections as the US networks report the projections for one state after another and colour in the map behind the anchorman. That is the view underlying mailshots, phone banks, zip-code targeting. The categories of public opinion polls and of elections draw on a social model that we already know as consumers.

The view of public opinion as the sum total of private, individual opinions, elicited in weekly polls and daily focus groups, is not the only possible view. An alternative social view focuses on the processes in which opinion is constructed and represented through institutions of decision-making, research, and reporting. In this view, the way the public is presented to decision-makers is important, but so is the way that the public is represented to the public, in poll reports, crowds, letter campaigns, or symbols such as ribbons. These representations show what counts as an issue, what effect opinion can have, who expresses it, and how it is expressed. In the following chapters I will consider examples both of the ways opinions are constructed in talk and of the way mass media structure and represent opinion. In the final chapter I will address some of the critical questions raised in media representations of public opinion and opinion research, especially the criticisms of focus groups. I have been arguing that representative government as practised in most democratic countries is thoroughly caught up with mediated representations of opinions. Does this make democratic processes more responsive and open, or shallower and more trivial?

5

Topics in interaction: 'Why that now?'

'Hold on, are we still talking about sex?' The not too bright Joey asks this in the second episode of *Friends* after the other characters have developed an elaborate extended metaphor comparing foreplay to the opening act at a rock concert. The joke is that he needed to ask. Unlike classroom lessons, parliamentary debates, or this book, conversation does not come with a gloss to tell us, at any moment, what it is supposed to be about. Yet participants in a conversation usually assume that it is about something and make contributions relevant to this something, even if they seldom name what they are talking about unless there is some confusion, or unless a new person enters the room. But as soon as one looks at a transcript, one can see that this apparent simplicity covers very complex moment-to-moment negotiations by the participants. And most people have had the experience of joining in a conversation only to discover that their contribution is puzzlingly, humorously, or offensively unrelated. Tom Stoppard's plays, the mock interviews of the British comedian Ali G, and some classic routines of the Marx Brothers all rely on this slippage.

In this chapter, I argue that there are problems in any attempt to code this flow of topics in focus groups into the researchers' categories, to make them into discrete opinions. But there is an alternative approach that treats 'topical content (what is talked about) as secondary to topical structure (how topical talk is done and done properly)' (Maynard and Zimmerman 1984: 301n.). Or as Schegloff and Sacks put it, topic is the participants' answer to the question 'Why that now?' (Schegloff and Sacks 1973). Instead of labelling topics, we can study the boundaries of topics, the ways participants, including the moderator,

1. introduce new topics (or treat topics as new)
2. acknowledge or reject them
3. shift, broaden, narrow, or change the topic
4. close the topic as an interactive process, signalled by the participants as well as the moderator
5. reopen topics

Attention to this conversational work will highlight the ambiguity and incompleteness of topic when it is frozen by the analyst at any one point, and the complexity of the ways people interpret and use topics in sequence. It won't make the focus group coder's problem any easier (ten Have 1991: 148–52), but it can make the analysis richer, by challenging or complicating the categories the researcher brings to the data.

The term *topic* has several different specialist meanings within textlinguistics (for an overview see Brown and Yule 1983). But for our purposes we can follow 'the commonsense notion . . . that the "topic" in a conversation is what the conversation is "about"' (Maynard 1980: 263). (One linguistic test is to say before a sentence 'As for X', and see what goes in the slot X (Tomlin et al. 1997).) Though this notion of aboutness seems unproblematic, there would seem to be three basic problems in determining topic for participants in and analysts of conversation: the many meanings of each reference, the multiple names, or lack of any name, for each topic, and the relation of one topic to the next.

Let us take, for example, a turn in which a participant looking at a photo says 'these people . they should be locked up' (3.2.2.27). Such demonstratives as 'these' depend on a kind of pointing for their meaning; they are one example of a class of expressions called *indexicals* that depend for their meaning on the immediate situation. If the concept of indexicality stopped with pronouns, demonstratives, and other words that are obviously tied to the situation (for an overview, see Levinson 1983: Ch. 3), we could still pin down most referents unambiguously (for instance by looking at the picture to which the speaker refers). But Garfinkel (1967) and Sacks (1992) argue that *all* descriptions are tied to the situation in this way: 'descriptions are "indexical" and are to be understood by reference to where and when etc. they occur' (Heritage 1984b: 140).

In this case, the participants are sitting around a pile of photos. But even if we have the photo this man is referring to, we will still need to look at the interaction of the people to decide what 'these people' means here. For instance, does he mean the particular people in the photo, or a category of people that he takes them to represent? For an analyst, there is a question of whether the topic to be coded here is *roads*, *protests*, *clothes*, *citizenship*, or a number of other possibilities. For the participants the question is much simpler: what can they say next? A participant does ask quietly in the background at this point, 'Who are they?' She does not need to ask 'What are we talking about?'; she will find out.

How can we access participants' sense of topic? One problem for analysts is that participants can follow a topic without giving it a name at all. Topics are only named as a metacommentary when there is some problem, pause, newcomer, or distance in time, when for some reason participants step out of the conversation and become analysts themselves:

Jane: Boy, this is really funny, when you think about our conversation we've hit about 12 different topics in the last seven minutes.   (Maynard 1980: 263)

Participants may also name the topic when someone new enters the conversation:

Joe: We were in an automobile discussion.   (Sacks 1992: I.175)

While any utterance might mean all sorts of things, one usually finds out what it means at the moment, for these participants, here, by looking at the next turn. To return to the passage just quoted from Heritage, 'descriptions are "reflexive" in maintaining or altering the sense of the activities and unfolding circumstances in which they occur' (1984b: 140). Participants take each expression as being relevant to what was just said, and as setting up or closing off other possibilities in the next turn. In this case, the immediate next turn is the moderator saying 'one view is that at least they're not apathetic'. This turn does several things (discussed later in the chapter), but on the simplest level his use of 'they' says to M2, and to others present, that the moderator thinks he knows who 'these people' are, and that he and M2 are sharing the same unproblematic reference, and that 'these people' constitute a topic on which there can be differing opinions.

It might seem that the assumption that one turn is relevant to the previous turn (Grice 1989: 28) would keep any conversation on just one topic. But all that is assumed is that one turn is relevant to the previous turn in some way: agreeing or disagreeing, commenting on it, ironicizing it, picking up on one aspect. There is no guide to *how* it will be relevant. When the moderator says 'one view is that at least they're not apathetic', the next speaker could intelligibly refer to 'another view', 'apathy', 'they', the use of 'they' by the moderator, demonstrators, airports, criminal justice, or many other topics. So, as we will see, the topic may shift gradually through the conversation, as each turn relates to the last but offers new possibilities for further development. This kind of shifting topic has been noted in many contexts: for instance meetings (Boden 1994), kids arguing in the street (Goodwin and Goodwin 1990: 97), dinner parties (Tannen 1984), family dinner conversations (Blum-Kulka 1997a), and phone calls home (Drew and Chilton 2000). The conclusion has been that while it is hard to define what conversational topics are, it may be possible to trace where they shift (Schegloff and Sacks 1973; Jefferson 1984a; Button and Casey 1984; Maynard and Zimmerman 1984; Schiffrin 1987; Beach 1990; Goodwin and Goodwin 1990; Button 1991; Hartford and Bardovi-Harlig 1992; Drew and Holt 1998). Or as Maynard (1980) puts it, conversation analysis turns from topic as content to topic as structure.

Many kinds of institutional interaction control topic in one way or another (Levinson 1992). In the classroom a teacher refers to the syllabus:

Elaine: Right. What we're going to start on today is a new topic, and it is called 'organic chemistry'. So can you put that as your main heading please? (Ogburn et al. 1996: 26)

The teacher can cut off talk that is off task. In broadcast news interviews, a topic is announced in a headline:

Next tonight, we turn to one of the hottest political issues of the day, drugs, and examine how politicians are dealing with it. (Clayman 1991: 65)

An interviewer can treat answers as evading the topic (Greatbatch 1988; Harris 1991; Bell and van Leeuwen 1994). In a business meeting, the chair keeps the discussion to agenda items:

TT: Okay I'll start off an – I think m*ost* of you – or a*ll* of you should have a c*opy* of th*is* and I'll kinda give you a bri*ef* idea of s*ome* of the things that has been happening. (Boden 1994: 98; transcription simplified)

The chair of a meeting can cut off a side sequence to return to the agenda (Edelsky 1981), and participants who want to insert comments will try to relate them to the agenda item, however distantly. In more tightly controlled institutional talk, as in a courtroom or parliament, a speaker may be silenced or even ejected for continuing talk that is ruled to be off the topic.

One handbook gives the following definition: 'A focus group is a carefully planned discussion designed to obtain perceptions on a defined area of interest in a permissive, non-threatening environment' (Krueger 1994: 6). As Agar and MacDonald (1995) point out, there is a tension in this definition between the careful planning and the permissive, non-threatening environment. A focus-group project typically begins with a 'topic guide' (Morgan 1988; Krueger 1994; Morgan and Krueger 1998) or a set of 'focusing exercises' (Bloor et al. 2001) that lay out the topics to be discussed, the transitions, and the timings, so that different moderators will produce comparable groups. The moderator's task is to keep the group on topic while also allowing the feeling of open, natural talk. It might seem that there was a danger of stilted, questionnaire-like talk. But as any moderator knows, and as we will see, discussions have a way of getting out of hand, running with astonishing speed and energy far away from the topics of interest to the researchers.

The more worrying constraints on topic may be at the other end of the research process, when the talk is taped and transcribed, and the researcher determines topics again in the form of content analysis. This process can involve many readings and gradual emergence of new and unsuspected topics embedded within the topics planned for the research (for detailed references, see Frankland and Bloor 1999; Bauer 2000). But it always involves a gloss on participants' words that is different from the interpretation that they themselves make as a part of responding to the previous turn. So the bit of transcript quoted earlier about 'these people' might be glossed as 'direct action' or 'local vs. non-local' or 'media images: environment' depending on the researchers' interests, even though these would not be the words or categories used by participants. (In some cases, of course, participants alarm researchers by using the researchers' vocabulary: in our case 'sustainability', 'globalization', 'cosmopolitan', 'risk assessment'.) So we have two views of topic in focus groups, one from the outside that sees the talk spatially, in blocks with labels, and one from the inside that sees the talk sequentially, in terms of momentary openings for one's own intervention.

Opening topics

Focus-group researchers start with a topic guide, but a skilled moderator seldom names the topic in the terms used by the researchers: 'local community', 'sustainability', 'substance abuse', 'nationalism'. As Merton, Fiske, and Kendall say in their classic study, 'There would be little point in using an interview at all, if it simply resolved itself into a series of stock questions put by the interviewer. For this would abandon a distinctive merit of the interview in comparison with the questionnaire: the give and take which helps the interviewee decode and report the meanings which a situation held for him' (1956: 13). Instead, talk on a topic is elicited indirectly through a series of questions that create a context (Krueger 1994: 63–7), such as (in our groups) where people shop, what local organizations they belong to, what they watch on television.

In one of our studies, participants responded to unattributed statements on cards. A new topic was signalled by the moderator pulling out a new card. For instance, the moderator might show a card containing these statements:

- Never underestimate your power as a consumer. You can effect change with what you buy.
- A man is rich by the number of things he can do without.
- As consumers, we are all responsible for the behaviour of the companies we give our money to.

But as the moderator shows the cards, he also steps in to define what makes these statements a topic. In one group, he begins the new topic as if these statements have arisen from their own talk:

```
but since we're talking about consumers all the time .
how about some quotes about consumers' consumption .
which follows from a lot of things people have been
saying
```

Then after the statements, he formulates a question to which they are to respond:

```
now just following on from the consumer thing . first
. this idea of consumer power which seems to make a
difference . I mean we've had a lot of talk about how
consumer demand is actually pushing you know . what
industry produces . this sort of thing . how about
the idea that consumers can use that power to change
that
```

This is at once highly constrained ('just following on from the consumer thing') and apparently open ('how about the idea'); it refers to responses heard in this or other groups ('we've had a lot of talk'), and these are categorized as a known point of view ('this sort of thing'). The group is given a frame in which to read the prompts.

Topics may also be introduced by giving some non-verbal prompt, such as posters (Kitzinger and Farquhar 1999), tape editing exercises (Macgregor and Morrison 1995; Baker and Hinton 1999), visualization games (Rothenberg 1994), ranking exercises, news bulletin exercises, photographic narratives (Bloor et al. 2001), and even site visits. In one study, on ideas of 'Global Citizenship', we used videos, and then a diary exercise, and then a stack of photos of public figures and representative types on cards (for the use of photos as interview prompts, see Meinhof and Galasinski 2000). The participants sorted the pictures into piles, and were then asked to explain why various people belonged with the others in each pile.

```
3.2.2.22
1. Mod:        so maybe you could talk us through
               what piles you have there and why you
               put them the way they did
2. Maureen:    this pile . do you want to speak
3. Dick:       no go on
4. Maureen:    this pile was for caring . it was
```

They gave names to each pile – 'caring', 'they're there just to make money', 'trying to put something right after it's been done' – that then became the basis for further questions.

Acknowledging topics

The topic that the moderator introduces does not become a topic for participants until it is acknowledged and developed. Participants often try out a range of responses, joking, hesitating, or incomplete, until the moderator's receipt suggests they are on the right track.

In 3.5.2.29, the participants have just watched a series of video clips
ending on one about the production of mangetouts (snowpeas) in
Zimbabwe for the Tesco supermarket chain.

3.5.2.29
1. Mod: OK that's it
2. George: the plot thickens
3. Paul: ye:s (2) I thought I saw a light at the
             end of the tunnel and I did . it was a
             bugger with a torch bringing me more
             work
4.   ((laughter))
5. Mod: OK then what were . let's . run through
             while they're fresh in your mind you
             know . what what . sticks in the mind
             there .
6. Ben: that were one hell of a advert for peas
7. Paul: yeah . were they related to those cards
             that we had on the floor?
8. Mod: oh yeah . of course yeah yeah (2)
9. Len: I thought that . uh exploitation /was a
             big issue
10. Adam: /well
             it started it started(   )
11. Mod: the guy at the end?
12. Len: yeah
13. Mod: and what what do you mean . ((lower
             voice)) I thought he might be a
             favourite (with you)
14. Len: cos it was the end like . but
15. Mod: ((laughs))
16. Clark: well I wrote down no I wrote down cheap
             labour early on . exploitation's the
             same thing
17. Len: yeah
18. Clark: I wrote that down / a few minutes ago
19. Len: /I think I think it
             brought on how we're all being exploited
             in one way or another aren't we . day
             to day working

First the moderator gives no cue but simply notes that the video clip
is done (1), and the participants make two jokes, one as if it was a
mystery (2), and another commenting on the task as work (3). The
moderator then gives a more specific cue: 'What sticks in the mind

there?' (5). The first response (6) is another joke, referring ironically to the way that the documentary undercuts the supermarket; this gets no response from the moderator. The second response (7) asks tentatively about the task, whether they are supposed to relate this to the earlier sorting exercise, and the moderator acknowledges this without saying anything that leads to further development.

Only when another participant names an abstract noun ('I thought that . uh exploitation . was a big issue' (9)), does the moderator respond, asking for clarification ('the guy at the end' (11)). He then confirms this as a topic by continuing with a joke: 'what do you mean . I thought he might be a favourite' (13) (suggesting ironically that trade unionists would like this smug middle-class character). And Len responds to this joke with a joke, saying that the video was a favourite because it was the end of the task. Then Clark uses the same word, 'exploitation', translating his first response into the vocabulary the moderator has already accepted: 'I wrote down cheap labour early on, exploitation's the same thing, I wrote that down a few minutes ago.' Len reformulates this comment into a general statement with a tag question ('aren't we').

They have established the topic they call 'exploitation' as an allowable response to the video for this group and have found terms on which they can relate other comments for a discussion that can go on. Sacks notes that naming the topic of conversation is one way of orienting a newcomer and comments: 'the choice of a topic name counts in a variety of ways' (Sacks 1992: I.74). Here the name 'exploitation' tells us not only about the video, but about what they take their group to be for present purposes. By joking and undermining the task at the beginning, they present themselves as resisting, in a playful way, the task this young researcher has set for them. By using this shared terminology ('exploitation'), they present themselves to each other and to the moderator as trade unionists.

Interpreting topics

To the moderator conducting a group, or the analyst coding a transcript, it may seem obvious what the topic is, but as we have seen, the participants wait for cues, often in the form of keywords, to tell them what they are responding to. Even when a topic is proposed and

discussed at length, the participants may maintain different interpretations of what the topic is. Usually these alternative interpretations will leave no trace in the transcript, as participants gradually
realize what the others are talking about, or drop their own interpretation, or the topic moves on, without anyone saying anything. But
in some cases the divergences erupt after several minutes of apparently focused talk. In the following example, the participants are
responding to this prompt from the moderator:

```
I'd like to ask people to think of thirty years time .
into the future . think of when your grandchildren
are . thirty year's time
```

A participant refers to 'this nuclear stuff'; a simple content analysis
of this passage, and others parallel to it, might categorize 'nuclear
stuff' among the kinds of worries the group had about the future.

```
1.5.1.20
1. F1:    will we all be here in 30 years time
2. Mod:   why why why not
3. F1:    all this nuclear stuff . I I don't like
          it I=
4. Mod:        =ok . ok so so so if we think in 30
          years our first thought is are we going
          to be here=
5. F1:               =yes
          yes=
6. Mod:        =is that a serious thought=
```

The moderator formulates this response as 'our first thought is are
we going to be here' (4) and then asks them to continue on what
they take to be this topic. I omit 16 turns in which various people
agree with this worry. The moderator then comes to write the topic
on the flip-chart as 'nuclear anxiety', selecting this visually as the
gist of what they have been saying.

```
1. Mod:  so we'll put that down /as nuclear anxiety
2. F2:                          /like some . crackpot
         might get hold of a
3. F1:   no
4. F2:   bomb and set it off
5. F1:   (that wasn't meaning no)
6. F3:   I mean the sun will collide with the earth
7. F?:   /well it couldn't
8. F3:   /or something
```

```
 9. F1:    no . oh no no . all this nuclear stuff . um
           yeah I just think something could happen
10. F2:    yeah all it needs /is one idiot to start the
           ball rolling
11. F?:                      /something could happen
           yes something could be
12. Mod:   yeah
13. F1:    all this nuclear stuff they are burying now
14. Mod:   right
15. F1:    all this nuclear stuff
16. Mod:   right right
17. F1:    is it going to kill everything off
18.        no
19. Mod:   right
20. F1:    are they going to grow food? I don't know
21. Mod:   it's a worry . right . what else?
```

The issue of 'this nuclear stuff' is named as if it were a single unambiguous issue on which other participants have an opinion. Other
participants categorize the statement: F2 responds to the phrase as
referring to a nuclear holocaust ('some . crackpot might get hold of
a' (2)), and F3 responds to that by raising another threat as in some
way parallel ('the sun will collide with the earth' (6)). F1 tries three
times to correct this interpretation ('no' (3), 'that wasn't meaning
no,' (5) 'no . oh no no' (9)), and finally says, 'all this nuclear stuff they
are burying now' (13). F1 does not take the moderator's 'yeah' and
'right' as indicating understanding; she keeps repeating her meaning
as he responds (15, 17, 20). Finally he gives an evaluation ('it's a
worry' (21)) and moves to a new item on the list.

Why does F1 have such difficulty repairing this misunderstanding? The responses to her statement, from turn to turn, have
taken 'this nuclear stuff' to refer to nuclear weapons. Displays
of opinion on common issues can normally be given in just such
shorthand form (compare the first naming of topics in phone-ins,
Chapter 9). The mechanisms for confirming one is on topic are
so strong that it is hard to show any contribution has misinter-
preted another. The disentangling here of nuclear power and nuclear
weapons requires unpicking of several minutes of conversational
work like faulty knitting. Most participants probably don't try as
hard to unpick the conversation as F1 does here. This suggests that
analysts can not be entirely confident that there is one topic in play,
even when the group seems to be agreeing.

Rejecting topics

Only occasionally are topics explicitly rejected, by the moderator as
not fitting the topic guide, or by the participants as not appropriate
to this group. Usually silence is all that is needed – the participants'
lack of response (which leads to the question being rephrased), or
the moderator's lack of a receipt or elaboration (which leads other
participants to offer other responses). Where they do reject topics,
we can see indications of what they think the proposed topic is. In
3.5.1.48, again with trade unionists, a moderator refers to a previous
comment on the poverty in the Third World:

```
3.5.1.48
1. Mod:    are you saying this this this poverty
           though . staying on a worldwide thing here
           is something that . you know . Britain is
           too wealthy . you know
2. Adam:   yeah
3. Mod:    is that . we're talking about distribution
4. Adam:   (I mean) you can drive down the motorway in
           this world Land Rover Discovery or a
           Mitsubishi Shogun a BMW
5. Ben:    distribution of wealth and then we're
           getting into a heavy subject aren't we
6. Mod:    well I don't want to get in that /aware of
           the time ((laughs))
7. Ben:                                  /no but
           that's that's the argument . that is
           definitely what the argument is isn't it
8. Len:    it is it's like 25,000 pound vehicles
           just flying past you . and that's a lot of
           money
```

The moderator's tentative formulation 'Britain is too wealthy' in
1 offers many possible topics for development (too wealthy compared to what?). In turn 4 Adam offers this list of cars as a
development of what the moderator has said. Then Ben elaborates
the moderator's 'distribution' as 'distribution of wealth'. The 'heavy
subject' of distribution of wealth is for this group of trade unionists
the kind of 'ultra-rich topic' that Sacks describes: 'within cultures
there are topics which are intrinsically rich, in the sense that whatever it is that members of that culture tend to talk about – that is,
whatever themes they talk about – they can talk about via that thing'

(Sacks 1992: I.178; see also I.390). Ultra-rich topics are as much a problem for focus group moderators as ultra-poor topics that mean nothing to participants.

Why does the moderator say 'Well I don't want to get into that [distribution]' when he has just asked them 'is it something about distribution'? He rejects the interpretation of this phrase as distribution within Britain, by acknowledging its richness, 'we haven't got time'. Ben allows him to reject the topic, acknowledging that the moderator does control topic, and again naming it explicitly as a topic ('that is definitely what the argument is'). But instead of dropping it, Len offers a formulation of Ben's turn 4, the list of brands, as 'it's like £25,000 vehicles just flying past you' (8). The discussion of expensive company cars then goes on for another ten turns. When the moderator intervenes again, it is to give up on the topic guide interpretation of 'distribution' as 'a worldwide thing' and move the group on to another exercise.

Of course not all topics are referred to explicitly by participants, as is done here with 'a heavy subject' or 'the argument'. Just as acceptance of a topic is more likely to come in a flurry of competing bids for turns, rejection is likely to come in an awkward silence. But when the moderator or participants do address the current topic directly, we see how it is interpreted in relation to the previous turns, the occasion, and the group; it is not just laid out on a menu like a category for questions on a game show.

Changing topics

We have seen that for each turn there are multiple interpretations of what the topic is, and what counts as the topic depends on what interpretations and phrases are picked up in succeeding turns. Each turn is typically offered as and taken as relevant to a previous turn, what Grice (1989) called the Maxim of Relation. But, as any moderator knows, this assumption of relevance does not guarantee that the conversation stays on the same topic. Each new turn can pick up a different aspect of the previous turn, leading to a stepwise transition (Gail Jefferson's (1984a) term) of topics. In ordinary conversation between friends, it often happens that we arrive by stages far from our starting point (even if we can remember it), without any clear break in the topic. But in focus groups there is someone present, the moderator, whose acknowledged job it is to keep the conversation on topic. And as we have seen, participants monitor and name their own topics, checking that they are acceptable. So there is likely to be more explicit signalling that one's contribution is relevant than one finds in ordinary conversation.

Through such shifts, participants can make connections between what might seem to the researcher and analyst to be quite different topics, but which pass for participants as related. In the next example, the participants have responded to a card directing readers to various environmental actions, including one saying 'you can affect change by what you buy'. One participant has said that a boycott of cars is different from a boycott of tuna.

2.7.31
```
 1. Mod: but what does that affect . or who does that
         affect
 2. M2:  well . it does affect it perhaps quicker
         than
 3. M4:  the company will take more notice of it .
         quicker . in that daily or weekly purchase
         than long term purchase like a car or .
         something
 4. M1:  (count it up) most car companies are
         saying now that 85% of their cars are .
         recyclable /
 5.                      /mm
 6. M1:  but . you know . I mean=
 7. M2:                        =I think with cars
         as well you've got to look at who the
         consumer is . you look at who buys the cars .
         companies buy most of the cars /
 8. M1:                                  /that's right
 9. M2:                                  /they don't
         give a damn . they don't give a damn about
         the environment (1) you know and and
         individuals that may you know . care . you
         know don't affect anything . you know because
         it's the the companies that are putting in
         the orders to the /car
10. M1:          /we're buying diesel cars at the
         moment because they're more economical
11. Mod: right
12. M2:  yeah . you buy whatever suits your /company
```

```
13. M3 :                                    /yeah but
        going on from that . I'm sorry . I slightly
        disagree . because people caring for the
        environment they said right . pollution .
        right let's get diesel cars=
14. M1 :                                =yeah, but now
        they've been proved /to be worse than
15. M3 :                        /that's right the cadmium
        the cadmium in diesel . right . so it's all
        this on . going process of right . I know
        someone who bought one and said I bought
        diesel I'm green
16. Mod: right
17. M3 : now I'm not green . you know . so it goes
        around . I mean . where are you learning
        these facts from . these people . as I said
        before . these people know about them .
        scientists or whatever and they're finding
        these things out . so why aren't they then .
        directing . us as a more aware sort of
        society now to say . right .
18. M2 : they perhaps need to be given the authority
        to direct somebody . to direct somebody
        else . if you like
19. M3 : yeah
20. Mod: right
21. M2 : like . as you were saying . who's going to
        give authority /to do it
22. Mod:                /yeah . yeah yeah
```

A content analyst coding this passage might list the following topics: consumer boycotts, recycling of cars, risks of diesel cars, and the unreliability of scientific information. But we could also start with the points at which participants mark the topic of their turn as related to that of the last turn, when they say 'but you know I mean' (6), or 'I think with cars as well' (7), or 'but going on from that' (13), or 'as you were saying' (21). Or they echo words and forms from the previous turn: 'it affects it perhaps *quicker*' (2) is followed by 'the company will take more notice of it, *quicker*' (3), and 'why aren't *they* then . *directing us*' (17) is followed by '*they* perhaps need to be given authority to *direct somebody*' (18). At each stage the speakers tie in to something from the previous turn, while introducing a new element as in some way related. In doing so, they show they have the sense that they must remain on topic and account for shifts. Most of the shifts are between specific examples, not back to more general claims, to warrants or backing. That could be because it is on the specifics of cases, who has done what, that each participant has something distinctive to offer to the discussion.

For the moderator there is always a practical question of whether to cut off such extended chains. Here he encourages this line of development with back-channel utterances. He says 'right' at three points at which one participant has interrupted another and reached a possible turn transition:

- we're buying diesel cars at the moment because they're more economical (10)
- I know someone who bought one and said I bought diesel I'm green (15)
- they perhaps need to be given the authority to direct somebody . to direct somebody else . if you like (18)

In each case the moderator confirms this new speaker as having the floor, and this contribution as relevant to the researchers' aims. In each case the participants are also making an evaluative statement; the moderator's 'right' acknowledges it has been made (without his agreeing the way M1 or M3 do when they say 'that's right'). The constant stream of back-channels in focus groups confirms the moderator as the audience for this talk, as it confirms to participants that the talk is on topic.

These shifts of topic can challenge the moderator's nominal control of the focus group. One group in our data is particularly adept at derailing the topics: sixth-form (high-school senior) girls, who one imagines practise this technique on their teachers. The moderator is no match for them, as they move from Nelson Mandela (whom the moderator has mentioned as a possible 'citizen of the world') to Martin Luther King to a mobile phone commercial about Martin Luther King to other commercials for that brand (One to One).

3.3.2.9
1. Hilary: like at first it was for himself
              because of the way he was treated when
              he was in prison . but there is .
              what's that man called that Ian Wright
              has that one to one with

```
 2. F:          someone gave me a book about it in
                town
 3. Hilary:     Martin Luther King
 4. Mod:        right yeah . I saw that last night
                yeah . yeah
 5. Roseanne:   I haven't seen that one yet
 6. Mod:        have you seen that . One to One
 7. Hilary:     it's quite good
 8. Mod:        yeah: . Martin Luther King
 9. Roseanne:   I do like the One to Ones actually
10. Hilary:     they're good aren't they
11. Helen:      what are they?
12. Roseanne:   you know Kate Moss's Elvis=
13. Helen:                              =oh yeah
                yeah oh I always watch them
14. Danielle:   I ate that one ((sound of crisp
                packet, laughter))
15. Si-F:       anyway ((laughter))
```

Here there are at least two side conversations (about Hare Krishna (2) and about crisps (14)), while the main conversation, the one encouraged by the moderator, shifts by steps from global citizenship to One to One ads. After one recovers from one's horror that Martin Luther King is remembered mainly for his appearance with a famous footballer in a thirty-second mobile phone ad, one can see this discussion as an indication of what their associations are, what they take as a plausible link: not to other global citizens (the researchers' interests) but to other figures who have appeared in these ads. This work shows what links appear as shared and obvious to the participants – not always those that would occur to researchers.

Closing a topic

It has often been noted in studies of institutional discourse that the participant who closes a topic has an element of control (for references, see Chapter 2, p. 34). Blum-Kulka makes the same point about a less obviously institutionalized setting, parental control in dinner table conversation. But she also notes that 'It is a general feature of this talk that regardless of the general thematic frame, topics as a rule are suspended rather than formally closed'

(Blum-Kulka 1997a: 64). In focus groups, the moderator can determine when a topic is to be closed, just by stepping in and introducing a new topic. These interventions are typically signalled with such discourse markers as 'okay', 'so', and 'now'.

These conventions would seem to lead to an asymmetrical interaction, with the moderator firmly in control. But a close look shows that topic closure is usually collaborative. Before the moderator steps in, participants typically signal their willingness for a topic to come to a close, using minimal responses (Maynard 1980), and jokes and laughter (Jefferson 1984b). They also use commonplaces, or as Drew and Holt show in their data, figures of speech (Drew and Holt 1998). Since the moderator's intervention typically follows such signals, moderators seem to be drawing on some of the same expectations as they would have in everyday conversation. But instead of the usual closing pattern, as in, say, telephone conversations (Hopper 1992; Schegloff and Sacks 1973) in which participants check each other's willingness to close, we have the moderator stepping in.

The following examples illustrate the way topics close with minimal responses (2.2.51), jokes and laughter (2.1.50), and commonplaces (2.2.48):

<u>2.2.51</u>

```
     1. M1:   so looking at the whales, why is a
              progressive nation like Norway . way in
              advance of places like Britain with
              regards its responsibilities and its
              social responsibilities . why is it
              still going out there and blowing whales
              up out the water=
     2. M2:                         =why doesn't it say
              scare Japan?
→    3. M3:   um
→    4. M4:   um um =
     5. M5:         =well why Norway /(on what xxx)
     6. M6:                          /stopping buying
              prawns stopping whaling what's the
              connection there =
     7. Mod:                      =( xxx ) could I could
              I focus . before we leave this one could
              I focus on . . .
```

```
2.1.50
    1. F1:   no you only give them the information so
             that they can do something about
             it . you're not actually ringing up and
             saying that's their sheep in their river
             are /you
    2. F2:        /no - no
    3.            (3)
    4. F2:   (I'd think) well - somebody else has
             seen / it!
→   5.                   /((laughter 3 seconds))
    6. F1:               /(it's not) reporting
    7. F1I:  say hey look at that dead sheep!
→   8.       ((Laughter F1 and F2 ten seconds))
    9. Mod:  ok (2) right - so

2.2.48
→   1. M:    so that second last one is the - in
             theory spot on /
    2. Mod:              /great great but
             (involves a lot of skepticism)
→   3. M:    but in practice =
    4. Mod:                   =could I move on to
             some other kinds of suggestions for
             action
```

In each case, the moderator gives a receipt ('OK', 'right') or refers explicitly to a new topic, suggesting his control. But in each case this move follows turns by participants that allow possible closure. Minimal responses suggest a participant has nothing further to contribute on the topic (they are part of the pre-sequence for closings in one-to-one conversations (Schegloff and Sacks 1973)). Commonplaces and jokes rely on implicit shared understandings. And laughter is in many cases shared around the table; it overcomes attempts to speak next and ends with a pause (Jefferson et al. 1987). The moderators most often break in when the group has first signalled the end of a topic this way.

Reopening topics

The participants do occasionally reopen a topic that the moderator has closed (Schegloff and Sacks 1973; Hartford and Bardovi-Harlig 1992; ten Have 1999a: Ch. 2), but in these cases the participants acknowledge the control of the moderator:

```
2.5.45
   1. M1:    what's got better=
   2. Mod:                      =has anything got
             better . yeah=
   3. M2:                   =not a lot
→  4. M3:    can I say something a little=
   5. Mod:                            =yes
             please go on=
   6. M3:                  =about the safety
             problem . . .
2.6.8
→  1. F1:    can I just interrupt?
   2. Mod:   yes . go ahead
   3. F1:    don't you find that interesting this
             . out of us group . three people here
             who the children suffer with asthma
```

The participants request permission, acknowledging the moderator's role ('can I say something a little', 'can I just interrupt'), in a
mitigated form, and also state explicitly the relation of their topic
to previous topics ('about the safety problem', 'don't you find that
interesting this'). Clearly they see a shared imperative to talk on
the topic that overrides even the moderator's signal that the topic is
closed.

Participants sometimes reopen topics long after they have passed,
but this usually happens in moments when the focus group rules are
suspended, such as during a break, or after final 'beanspill' in which
the moderators explain the funding and purpose of their project.
Here, as the moderator explains the study at the end, two participants refer back to comments made earlier, one jokingly (referring
to the British supermarket chain Tesco) and the other seriously.

```
3.5.2.63
   1. Mod:    so . I think actually/
   2. Ben:                      /so you don't work
              for Tesco after all /(so that's a total
              loss)((laughs))
   3. Mod:                     /no no there was
              there's no final / (pay-off I'm afraid)
   4. Clark:                   /well I was thinking
              about your question about the wrapping .
              eh . all all last week I was thinking
              about it . and I was thinking about the
              old-fashioned shops where you used to
              get all this stuff
```

```
 5. M:       yeah?
 6. Clark:   and they'd just wrap it in a piece of
             paper and you slung the paper away /
 7. Ben:                                        /and
             you can't buy /
 8. Clark:                  /now you get boxes and cans
             and tins and /
 9. Ben:     /and you can't buy one of anything now
             can you
10. Clark:   no (you can't buy)
11. Ben:     you can't go in and say can I have . one
             of them screws
12. Clark:   yeah
```

The discussion continues with other participants raising other examples of packaging. Ben's joking response (2) is the sort of closing comment that usually occurs at this point. Clark's intervention (4) is marked as following from a previous discussion, not what was just said: 'well I was thinking about your question about the wrapping'. This discussion develops without any intervention from the moderator. Finally, after six more turns, the moderator refocuses the discussion from commodity packaging to the researchers' issue of their environmental actions.

```
Mod:   actually what you were saying [Ben] about uh:
       you know it's not clear how people can get
       anything out of it you know . doing something
Ben:   yeah
Mod:   actually reflects a lot of what people
       said . . .
```

So participants treat it as the moderator's role to introduce topics, and even when participants introduce a topic, it is in a special slot, such as closing, marked off from the focus group proper, and it remains open to the interviewer to formulate what this topic means.

Why do topics matter?

I have said that we need to look at *how* people say things in opinion research, as well as *what* they say. Topic is central for this project because it is the intersection between the study of how people talk (which is what interests conversation analysts and linguists) and what they talk about (which is what interests just about everybody else). The 'aboutness' of talk and texts is an issue, in different ways, for social scientists, researchers, and participants in focus groups, and analysts of talk in institutions more generally.

Most approaches to topic in social sciences involve replacing participants' words ('Land Rover Discovery or a Mitsubishi Shogun a BMW') with the analysts' more abstract vocabulary ('cars' or 'wealth' or 'consumption' or 'mobility'). Conversation analysts reject the imposition of analysts' categories involved in such coding, and we have seen in this chapter how problematic analysts' categories can be. While the analyst is trying to put 'Land Rover Discovery' in one category or another, the moderator and participants are also trying to categorize it, but their question is not 'under what sociological concept does this instance belong?' but 'what can come next'? Something does come next, and that operates as the topic for them, and as an interpretation of what the previous turn was about for practical purposes. Any coding that relies on the analysts' categories is likely to miss these processes, and thus to miss links that matter to these people (for instance, the ambiguity of the relation of these Land Rovers to 'distribution of wealth').

In focus groups, the topic guide gives the structure to the session, the guarantee of usable results and of common ground that will make the groups comparable. But as we have seen, the moderator does not entirely control how topics develop. The moderator recognizes and acknowledges some responses as being on topic, and the participants name candidate issues that might be relevant to this topic and respond to cues from the narrator and other participants. The occasional challenges to relevance, and responses to these challenges, from both moderators and participants, show that all the parties take for granted the need to stay on topic. Topics are closed collaboratively, with the moderator often responding to cues from participants. The smooth taking up and development of topics in a group discussion over two hours is the result of skilful moderation, yes, but also of work by the participants. It is hard to see this work because participants in conversations do not, in general, treat the selection of topic as something problematic, something worth commenting on explicitly; that happens only when the usual patterns break down.

The development, linking, and closing of topics are processes through which participants define their relationships to each other. Two people meeting for the first time at a party, on a plane, or in an experiment (Maynard and Zimmerman 1984) may search for shared topics in their work or study, places, acquaintanceships, or experiences. There is little of this kind of personal talk in focus groups. What brings them together is not a shared goal or shared views, but the ability to recognize a topic from a given reference in the same way and confirm that recognition. Sometimes the reference works and is picked up as a topic by others, and sometimes it doesn't. Surprisingly, participants in these groups do not play it safe, do not refer only to such entities as 'anyone' would recognize, topics they share only by virtue of being 'contemporaries' (Maynard and Zimmerman 1984). They try out references that might be known to, or have a specific meaning for, the people here, at this moment in the talk: 'this nuclear stuff', 'Land Rover Discovery', 'the One to Ones', 'whales', 'the wrapping', 'Sellafield'. Because of this mutual exploration, the development of topics can be part of the process by which a collection of strangers becomes a group (Myers 2000a).

The treatment of topics in these discussions can tell us about focus groups and the institutions of opinion of which they are a part. I have noted that constraints on topic play a crucial role in defining the institutional nature of interactions in parliamentary debates, business meetings, classroom lessons, or appointments with the physician. The striking feature of a focus group, in contrast to, say, a dinner party, is that participants do not have to generate topics; the moderator does that for them. But they are still left with the considerable tasks of interpreting, elaborating, and linking turns, making dynamic talk out of the moderator's list, and making this talk useful, or what they think will be useful. If participants needed to learn new rules for dealing with topics in focus groups, then conversations would be stilted, a set of interviews with individuals. But focus groups rely on routines that participants already have for talking in groups, routines that were learned from other conversations outside the institutions of marketing, education, or politics. We will see a similar crossing over in each of the next three chapters; focus groups work only because they are a hybrid of institutional constraints and everyday routines.

6

Agreeing and disagreeing: maintaining sociable argument

In a Monty Python sketch a man knocks on a door and says 'I came here for an argument.' A man sitting at a desk in the room says 'No you didn't.' 'Yes I did.' And they are off on an argument about what constitutes an argument. Disagreement is essential to a pub conversation about football teams, talk over coffee after a movie, or speculation about an election. Some institutional interactions are built around disagreements: not only Prime Minister's Question Time and courtroom litigation, but also television talk shows (Tolson 2001), radio phone-ins (see Chapter 9), vox pop interviews (see Chapter 10), academic seminars, and children's games (Goodwin 1990). In all these settings, even in the Monty Python sketch, there are conventions governing how and when one can disagree, and the forms used for disagreement.

Disagreement has a bad name: heated or unresolvable arguments are often seen as a kind of failure of the friends, host, diplomat, counsellor, or family. But Deborah Schiffrin pointed out in a classic paper ('Jewish argument as sociability', 1984), arguments among friends can be a form of sociability, not the breakdown of civility. The term 'sociable' as used here goes back to an essay (first published in 1910) by Georg Simmel, who argued that a theory of society needed to consider the centrality of a 'play form of association', a 'social game', apart from economic and political interests (Simmel 1949). Later this interest on social play, on passing the time in a pleasurable way, was taken up by Gregory Bateson (1972) and Erving Goffman (1974). In linguistics, the idea of sociability underpins Schiffrin's analysis of the arguments between family members and close friends in the interviews she had conducted for a sociolinguistic study, Shoshana Blum-Kulka's study of sociability in family dinner table talk (Blum-Kulka 1997a), and Suzanne Eggins and Diana Slade's analysis of a group of friends (Eggins and Slade 1997). In 'sociable argument', Schiffrin says, 'speakers repeatedly disagree, remain nonaligned with each other, and compete with each other for interactional goods. Yet they do so in a nonserious way, and in ways which actually display their solidarity and protect their intimacy' (Schiffrin 1984: 311). Schiffrin cautiously applies her claim only to 'Jewish argument', as a feature of the particular culture she was studying, but after many other studies of such exchanges, we can appropriate the old slogan for Levy's rye bread and say that 'You don't have to be Jewish to enjoy arguing.'

Though disagreement is often essential to interaction, it is hard to do. One of the most fundamental and well-attested patterns in conversation is a preference for agreement in the second turn of an adjacency pair. That is, when one person asks a question, makes an assertion, or performs some other conversational action, a response that is to be taken as agreeing will typically be immediate and unmarked, while a response to be taken as disagreeing will typically be delayed, prefaced, or modified. Sacks put it in the characteristically sweeping and informal fashion of his lectures: 'You know perfectly well that zillions of things work that way – a next turn (e.g. answer) is in "agreement" with the preference of the prior (e.g. question)' (1987: 57). (Sacks's statement itself indicates what the preferred response of his listeners is to be.) One type of adjacency pair that shows this preference for agreement is an assessment, an evaluative statement, and the second evaluative statement that typically follows it (Pomerantz 1984). Charles Goodwin and Marjorie Goodwin point out that taking seriously Pomerantz's analysis of assessments would lead us to change our interpretation of qualitative data: 'Assessments reveal not just neutral objects in the world, but an alignment taken up toward phenomena by a particular actor' (1992: 166).

Evaluative statements, and responses agreeing with them, make up much of a typical focus group transcript. But if participants in focus groups always agreed, the technique would be useless for most purposes; the researchers would learn only the opinion of the most eager or insistent member of the group, and all the others would be lost in misleading and polite nodding. The patterns turn out to be more complex than that. First, the moderator encourages disagreement, in the introduction and in later interventions. And while participants do show a preference for agreement, they also have ways of marking and presenting disagreement. One of these devices is to use the moderator, to present the comment to him or her rather than to the other participants. They may speak as devil's advocate, marking their contribution as a necessary balance to those of other participants. Another device is the construction of another person, not present, to whom views can be attributed, without the participant necessarily standing up for these views themselves. With such complex devices in play, an analyst of focus-group transcripts must see any particular statement in relation to previous turns, to see what the participant is doing with it.

Encouraging disagreement

Deborah Schiffrin quotes one of her interviewees saying to her, after she as interviewer has raised the issue of marrying outside one's group, 'Oh you: want to start a fight here' (1990: 253). This is meant as a joke; she was not deliberately provoking conflict, just getting a recording of informal talk for a sociolinguistic study. But moderators and interviewers may try to encourage disagreement, if not 'start a fight'. In a handbook for focus-group researchers, Morgan and Krueger (1993: 7) say that a good introduction to a focus group will explicitly encourage expression of disagreement (as we saw in the introduction quoted in Chapter 3, pp. 58–60). The moderator may come prepared with prompts that Krueger calls 'challengers': 'Successful challengers can sometimes bring to the surface opposing points of view that may remain undisclosed with other strategies' (1998: 46). More subtly, the moderator can also invite opposing views, note disagreement when it is not marked by the participants, reformulate turns to present them as opposing, introduce opposing views from outside the discussion ('some would say'), or directly invite opposing views.

Moderators are typically prepared with a range of stock phrases intended to encourage further discussion while not directing it too heavily:

```
2.3.27
Mod:      no no I can see your point but (2) (any)
          other reactions? how does anyone else feel
          about that ( xxx )
```

```
3.7.1.27
Mod:        You were shaking your head there Robert
Robert:     I can't see Tesco's producing that
```

When participants don't disagree, the moderator may attribute a different opinion to others outside the group. Here the participants have referred to 'eco-warriors' and the moderator is prompting other views of the roads protesters.

```
3.5.2.32
Mod:        I mean some people have called them eco
            double u something else
```

More subtly, the moderator can license differences of opinion by commenting on them as differences, often with the names of the participants, making the ownership of the opinions a topic:

```
2.6.49
Mod:        this is quite a live issue down here then
2.4.20
Mod:        ok - we've got a difference of opinion
            that's all right - now um
3.7.1.22
1. Mod:     So you're the opposite of [Rachel] really?
1. Sam:     Yeah, absolutely
```

In the first and second of these examples (2.6.49 and 2.4.20), the moderator is commenting on a difference that has just emerged; in the third (3.7.1.22), he is labelling a view as 'opposite'. Often the moderator notes difference this way as a prelude to moving on to another topic (see Chapter 5). Like the opening remarks, these responses set up a situation in which differences are expected and can remain unresolved, without any threat to the on-going discussion or the face of participants.

In Example 2.7.19, the group has been agreeing on the need for business to clean up its processes, and on its evasion of its responsibilities, and the moderator makes a general probe for different views.

```
2.7.19
1.    M1:    . . . you know if they start getting too
             restless up there, the people that have
             got the money . will pull the rug (2.0)
             you know
2.→   Mod:   um . what do other people feel on this?
             I mean =
```

```
3.     M2:              = well you can be you can be as
                    green minded as you like . but if it
                    actually affects you in a business where
                    you have to use certain products for
                    your business to survive . then I'm
                    afraid that goes out the window
                    ((laughs))
```

In turn 1, M1 has made an extended assertion about corporations
and environmental damage and has offered the other participants
a chance to disagree, with a 2-second pause. Then his 'you know'
recycles the assertion, presenting it as a statement of a generally
known truth (Schiffrin 1987: 276), but this does not prompt either
agreement or disagreement. Finally the moderator explicitly calls
for a comment (2); his 'I mean' suggests he will go on to back up
his question with a restatement of what it is they are responding
to. At that point M2 interrupts (3); his statement is in the form for
dispreferred responses ('well') and is addressed to an impersonal
'you', not to M1. But it is presented as an explicit disagreement
and it characterizes a stance like that of M1: 'you can be as green
minded as you like . but'. The moderator's intervention between 1
and 3 seems to give a target for M2 to disagree without directly
addressing M1.

Agreeing

As we would expect from the findings of conversation analysis, the
typical form of exchanges between participants is that when someone says something, others agree. Here Anna and Sally are talking
about an ad for the International Red Cross that features people
injured by land mines.

3.1.1.34
```
1. Mod:    mm . so do you think that advert is aimed
           at a particular kind of person . or was
           trying to appeal to you in a particular
           kind of way in terms of . getting its
           message across?
2. Anna:   I think it's aimed at parents /really
3. F:                                   /yeah . mmm
4. Anna:   because as a parent you see that mum there
           . with . do you kn-
```

```
5. Sally: yeah
6. Anna:  and she's lost a leg and she has a /baby
7. Sally:                                    /baby
8. Anna:  and you think I'd hate to be in that
          / situation . having children to look
          after
9. Sally: /situation . yeah.
```

Sally chimes in with agreement in turns 5, 7, and 9, echoing 'baby' from Anna in 7 and 'situation' in 9 (they actually say these overlapped words simultaneously). But these are not heard as interruptions; they are carefully timed to support Anna. In 3 the overlap comes after a turn marked as an assessment ('I think'). In turn 5 it comes as Anna ends with the tag 'do you know'. They are constructing collaboratively the plight of the mother. Then as the same passage continues, the pattern turns around, with Sally now developing a view, using reported thought as Anna did in 8 above (see Chapter 7). Now Anna overlaps in the same way as Sally had, and at the same pace, formulating Sally's turn and echoing her tag question in 4.

```
10. Sally: you know and I thought God . you know that
           little boy couldn't play football/
11. Anna:                                  /yeah
12. Sally: what if it were Dan /do you know what I
           mean?
13. Anna:                      /you just (bring it
           to) your own children don't you?
14. Sally: you do don't you you you know (6)
```

The long silence at the end comes as the moderator writes something; the participants seem to be performing this, not to each other, but for him. This contrasts with the very fast pace of the previous talk; such agreement comes quickly, and is a matter of quick signals and echoes.

The preference for agreement is shown by the fact that it comes first in the turn, without delay or modification, sometimes even interrupting. If there is any further comment, agreement typically comes first in the turn, as a concession, followed by the disagreement. One of the key findings of Pomerantz (1984) is that second assessments do not just repeat the first assessment (as we saw in the previous example) but typically elaborate or upgrade it. We can see all these

patterns in the following example, in which the group has been talking about dog mess on the Downs:

```
1.2.6.6
  1.     Mod:  yeah so so . so it's not just a problem
               on the streets/
  2.     F1:                /oh no / no it's
  3.     Mod:                       /locally it's a=
  4.     F2:                                 = yeah
  5.     F1:   and in the parks as well . they're not
               so bad =
  6.→    F2:           =parks are better=
  7.     F1:                        =but better
               the parks are better . but they still
               could be=
  8.→    F3:            =the Downs are particularly
               bad actually . now you've said that
               it's almost as if the owners think . ah
               . you know=
  9.     F1:                 =yeah=
 10.     F3:                      =long grass . leave
               it /but it's
 11.     F1:   /that's right
```

The sequence Pomerantz described is illustrated here in turns 5, 6,
7, and 8, where the participants are contrasting dog mess in parks
and on the Downs (an open, hilly area outside the town):

parks . . . they're not so bad [assessment][
parks are better [upgraded]
the parks are better but [agreement and then disagreement]
the Downs are particularly bad [agreement elaborated]

In turn 8, F3 presents her turn as elaborating on turn 7 ('now you've
said that') and offers a hypothetical reported thought version of
what the dog-walkers are thinking (see Chapter 7). F1 agrees before
she has even heard the thought to be reported. Again the constant
agreement leads to intertwined, collaborative construction.

Disagreeing with other participants

The observation of preferred (agreement) and dispreferred (disagreement) second turns does not imply that people will always agree, but

that when there is disagreement, it will typically be delayed, or will
be presented in the form of weak agreement followed by disagreement, or will have markers of dispreferred turns, hedges, questions,
concessions, attributions, and devices of repair.

An example of the markers of a dispreferred turn can be seen
in 2.5.10, where they are discussing whether parents are forced to
abandon public transit because of the shopping that they carry:

```
2.5.10
      1. F1:   to stick them in the car is so much
               quicker and so much cheaper =
→     2. F2:                           = well
               I disagree with /you
      3. Mod:                 /(I tell you what) .
               I think yeah actually this issue
               about possessions and materialism is
               a quite interesting one . . .
```

This is obviously a direct, explicitly marked disagreement. But the
disagreement is prefaced with 'well'. In fact it comes so quickly
in response to the first turn, overlapping it, that it is more like a
response to criticism than to an assessment. F2 seems to have heard
this opinion as a direct attack on people like her (she has said one
doesn't need a car).

In contrast to this explicit 'I disagree', many instances of apparent disagreement are presented as extensions or rephrasing of the
previous turn. In the next example, M2 disagrees in turn 3 with one
aspect of the statement (wind farms shouldn't be in Shoreham) but
puts it in a form in which they can agree on the underlying principle
(wind farms shouldn't be located in residential neighbourhoods) by
recategorizing the site as 'derelict' rather than 'residential'. "

```
2.7.15
1.     M1: but it's not it's not for residential
           areas /
2.     M2: /nah nah
3.     M1: although I don't live by where the wind
           farm was going to be . I would object if
           I lived here . I would object to it .
           yes - should be in non-residential
           areas - and pipe it into the national
           grid /(and I think)
```

```
4. →   M2:          /but if you see what's . if you see
                    what's over there at the moment . I mean
                    it's . it's like a derelict site anyway .
                    so I mean something's (1.0) I would
                    would have said is better than . than
                    nothing
```

M2's use of 'I mean' (twice) marks transitions between three parts
of his statement (Schiffrin 1987): from what 'you see' there now,
to his evaluation ('it's like a derelict site anyway'), to a familiar
saying or commonplace ('something's . . . better than nothing'). The
commonplace is offered, though, with two interpolated markers that
it is just his view ('so I mean' and 'I would have said'). A potential
disagreement is positioned both as his view and as reflecting a shared
consensus.

Another way to imply shared agreement within disagreement is
to present one's opinion in the form of a question, as in turn 5 in
the following example: "

```
3.9.1.29
        1. Penny:  but it's usually poverty isn't it
                   that brings them over here
        2. Jack:   yeah come and exploit the um . UK
                   system
        3. M:      well we don't have /(rights xxx)
        4. Penny:                    /well not
                   necessarily . the Asians are are
                   are mainly self-sufficient . the
                   Asians don't . exploit our uh
                   social services (1)
   →    5. James:  but do we have a do we have a
                   right to impose our culture on
                   other people . I don't think we
                   do
        6. Mod:    um . um
        7. Pam:    well if you're talking about
                   civil liberties then yes we do
                   because /I mean
        8. James:          /the . the laws of the
                   land I think wherever you're
                   going you have to comply with
                   them . I think /that's
        9. Mod:                   /but that's
                   separate from customs isn't /it?
       10. Den:                               /yeah
```

Jack presents himself as agreeing with Penny (2), but she disagrees
with him (4). James presents his question as a new topic ('a right to
impose our culture'), but his 'but' implies that (5) is a direct response
to (4). He poses his question as an open one, but also answers it for
himself (8). Pam frames an alternative interpretation of the topic,
'if you're talking about civil liberties' (7). Her alternative, elliptical answer to Jeff's question ('yes we do') comes only after this
extensive preface. There is a complex exchange about just what is
at issue in the argument: 'our culture', 'civil liberty', 'laws of the
land', 'customs'; such wordings allow the participants to present
the two sides of the disagreement as in fact covering different
areas.

One very common pattern both in everyday talk and in these
focus groups is a turn in which weak agreement leads to disagreement, that is, a preliminary concession (Pomerantz 1984). In the
following example, the participants disagree about the candour of
the nuclear reprocessing industry.

```
2.3.28
1. F:   I think they don't admit that the when /
2. M:                                        /they
        they
3. F:   they've had problems . they seem to / . they
        do cover them up
4. M:                                   /no they
        don't like to admit little problems when they
        know they'll be blown up into big ones/
5. F:                                        /you
        know like the the
6. M:   but on the other hand I'm not saying that
        /(xxx)
7. F:   /like the houses where the dust was very high
        in radioactivity . . .
```

Here F says 'they don't admit that the when they've had problems',
and M responds echoing this statement 'no they don't like to admit
little problems'. M goes on to say 'when they know they'll be blown
up into big ones', that is, modifying what he took F to mean. But as F
continues he makes another concession 'but on the other hand . . .'.
The transcripts are full of the kinds of phrases that mark this concession structure, such as 'no . . . but' (as we see in this example),
'yes, but', and 'having said that'. Kotthoff (1993) has noted the

crucial role concessions play in extended sequences of disagreement between pairs of speakers. Here, with a relatively large group, the concessions seem to work in a different way, acknowledging the previous speaker, and thus showing one is on topic, while raising possible disagreements.

Because these devices for dispreferred turns are so conventional, the moderator may take any delay or modification in dyadic conversation as an indication of disagreement. In the following example, the *well* used by M1 in 2 and by M2 in 4 precedes a qualification on the agreement with the moderator's formulation:

```
2.4.11
1. Mod:  so so er . so the important thing is to have
         green spaces which are close to the cities
         is that right (1.0) is that=
2. M1:                            =er well yeah .
         yeah=
3. Mod:  =so you've got the difference . you've got
         the urban and then=
4. M2:                          =well  . I would argue
         for green spaces in cities too
```

The moderator offers a formulation of the previous discussion and asks 'is that right'. When there is no response, he begins to repeat or rephrase the question ('is that'). The beginning of M1's turn ('er well yeah') (2) would indicate a dispreferred response. But M1 goes on to repeat the 'yeah'. The moderator does not seem to take this 'yeah' as indicating agreement, though; he takes M1's 'well' as a preface to a disagreement and reformulates his summary before continuing. This suggests that any hesitation or modification will be taken as a possible preface to disagreement. In his second formulation (3), the moderator starts to put it in terms of some alternative possibilities ('you've got the urban and then'). But M2 now interrupts (4) to disagree explicitly (marked by 'well' and 'I would argue'), disagreeing not with what the moderator has just said ('you've got the urban') but what he said earlier and seems to be about to say ('to have green spaces which are close to the cities'). By saying 'I would argue', M2 treats it as an arguable topic, not as the repair of an error. By saying 'green spaces in cities too', M2 explicitly marks this as an alternative to, not a part of, the moderator's formulation. The result is an addition to or extension of the view first formulated by the moderator, without a direct disagreement with that view.

In some cases disagreement is handled using mechanisms of
repair. Logically, these are different ways of responding to a difference between participants. To treat it as disagreement focuses
on differences between positions, while the treatment of apparent
disagreement by repair presents it in a less face-threatening light,
attributing the difference to some miscommunication. In Example
2.7.51 a participant questions whether Greenpeace is the same as
the Green Party. I present a long passage because the persistence of
the attempts at repair is itself of interest:

2.7.51

```
      1. M1:  I think they blew it when they went
              political . because I would see them
              as wasting my money on trying to
              become an MP . when they've got no
              chance of becoming an MP . you know
              and I think that's where
→     2. M2:  what's that Friends of the Earth?
      3. M1:  Greenpeace=
      4. M             =Greenpeace=
      5. M:                      =Greenpeace
      6. M1:  /(xx give me)
→     7. M2:  /have they gone political?
      8. M1:  oh . yeah / (that's right)
      9. M2:             /I don't know that
     10. M1:  on the ((low pitch)) on the last
              Euro elections . you know . huge
              campaign . they spent millions
              . well . they've got to get that
              money from somewhere=
     11. Mod:                  =right=
     12. M1:                        =and
              they've obviously got that from
              us=
     13. Mod:    =right=
     14. M1:           =you know and if they're
              going to blow it=
→    15. M2:             = what Greenpeace
              /have (turn)
     16. M1:             /but they've lost their
              deposits all over the place
     17. Mod: right
→    18. M2:  do you mean the Green Party . or
              Greenpeace?
     19.      (3)
```

```
20. M1: well . Greenpeace . Greenpeace
        effectively funds
21. M2: /uh
22. M1: /the Green /
23. M2:         /uh/
24. M1:              /Party . you know=
25. M2:                             =uh
26. M1: it's a spin off isn't it? (2) from
        Greenpeace=
27. M2:           =no . no . not
        necessarily . no
28. M1: well they're I think /
29. M2:                      /they're in the
        same school but I don't I don't
        think they fund each other=
30. M1:                          =(I'm
        not sure about that)
```

Here M2 asks questions four times (2, 7, 15, 18), pointing with
increasing explicitness to the error of M1. Then M1 makes a statement about Greenpeace with a tag question (24) and M2 does not
respond with assent (25). M1 then puts it as a direct question ('it's
a spin-off isn't it?' (26)) and only then does M2 explicitly disagree.
Through the exchange M2 maintains the possibility of miscommunication rather than disagreement; his 'I don't know that' can mean
either that he doesn't know or he disagrees. And when he does finally
disagree directly he hedges ('not necessarily'), makes a concession
('they're in the same school'), and hedges again ('I don't think').
This example may seem to be different from the other examples of
disagreement that I have discussed, since M2 presents it as a simple
error of fact (the international campaign organization Greenpeace is
not in fact financially linked to the UK Green Party). But in this and
other cases of repair, the repair links to larger areas of disagreement
(here, about the political effectiveness of Greenpeace) and does not
just check on the communication of information.

Participants in focus groups draw on many of the devices used in
everyday conversation: responses showing agreement are unmarked,
and responses showing disagreement are marked with delay and particles like *well*. They use devices such as reformulations, questions,
concessions, echoes, and repair that present disagreement against
a background of possible consensus and shared knowledge. This
means analysts considering the range of disagreement in a group
should look not just at explicit disagreements, which may be rare,

but also at the conversational prefaces and devices that mark even apparent disagreement as a possible challenge.

Disagreeing with the prompts

We have seen that the moderators of these groups offer various verbal and visual prompts intended to encourage discussion. These texts, and the moderators' own formulations, seem to have a special status as positions without persons and are treated as occasions for talk, not as turns that get responses; in semantic terminology, the quoted statements are mentioned, not used (see Chapter 7). So in contrast to the muted and modified disagreements we have seen between participants, disagreements with the statements on the cards can be presented emphatically. Participants say things like 'I disagree with that' and 'it's wrong, isn't it' and even 'load of bollocks' in the first turn after being shown a card or video clip. In our data, they never respond to another participant this baldly (though they do in some other focus group studies (Kitzinger 1998: 203)). Statements by the moderator can be treated with the same abruptness when they are taken as prompts within the conventions of the focus group, not as the views of that person.

The contrast between bald response to the prompt and mitigated response to other participants can be seen in Example 2.1.20. They are responding to a statement on a card: 'Every time we use electricity, gas, coal, or central heating in our homes, we are damaging our other home, the Earth.' They have just been told this statement came from a UK government campaign.

```
2.1.20
      1. Mod:   so so if they say that to you . what
                would you think?
→     2. F1:    >load of bollocks<
      3. Mod:   ((laughs))    yeah do we have any
                agreement there . or .
      4.        ((3 seconds laughter))
→     5. F2:    I don't know . I might look up .
                from the point of view . if they are
                saying the resources are going down
                . and we're going to put your costs
                u::p . I mean . they could get more
                money . from pro- promoting a view
                like that
      6. Mod:   right
```

After the laughter of the group (4), F2 expresses agreement with
the statement on the card, and by implication disagreement with
F1's comment ('load of bollocks'). F2 does hedge, beginning with 'I
don't know' and 'I might', mitigating her threat to the face of F1.
(The use of 'from the point of view' signals an attribution, which I
will discuss later.) These devices are what we would expect from the
literature on conversational politeness (Brown and Levinson 1987)
when someone has to disagree with another person who is actually
there, not just with a statement on a card.

Using the moderator

The patterns illustrated so far suggest that the moderator sets up and
promotes possible disagreements and heads off premature agreement, while participants use devices from everyday conversation to
avoid direct disagreement. But participants do not just respond to
the moderator's prompts and other participants' assessments. They
also draw on the presence of the moderator as a resource through
whom they can express disagreement in a much more direct form
than they would immediately after the turn of another participant.
The moderator can serve as an audience, as a sort of buffer by his
or her presence; participants acknowledge the moderator, the tape
recorder, and the wider use of their talk, by playing devil's advocate,
attributing opinions, and accounting for disagreement.

Participants sometimes address direct disagreements to the moderator, as if he or she were chair of a meeting. The effect is that the
two participants' turns parallel each other, juxtaposed with each
other, without the second turn being presented as a response to the
first:

2.7.8
```
      1. F1:   don't you find that interesting this
              . out of us group . three people
              here who the children suffer with
              asthma
→     2. F2:   I was just going to say . that at
              Christmas I was diagnosed with
              asthma and it seems to be such a .
              you know everyone I speak to .
              someone within that that family has
              got asthma
```

```
     3. Mod:  right
     4. F2:   and years ago asthma was unheard of
              - when I was a kid/
     5. F3:                   /can I just (xxx)
     6.       ((laughter))
     7. Mod:  yeah go ahead
→    8. F3:   when I was a baby I was born with a
              heavy fluid on my lung . and I had
              bronchitis and that left me with a
              very weak chest . and the doctor
              said I was an asthmatic, and the
              doctor said um (1) that I would
              grow out of it by the time I was
              seven and I did and . there's your
              proof /
     9. F:         /that it's not all /
    10. F1:                           /but . . .
```

F2 addresses the moderator to ask for the floor (1) and notes the recent increase in the number of children with asthma. F3 then also addresses the moderator (5) and offers a turn disagreeing about the significance of this increase (8). F3 parallels the end of the turn of F2, displaying the relevance of her contribution to the previous turn by repeating 'when I was a kid' (4) as 'when I was a baby' (8). There is no direct indication that her turn is disagreeing with the previous one until she says 'and . there's your proof', which suggests she is engaged in an argument, not just a narrative.

Even 'there's your proof' is not necessarily a statement of disagreement with F2 (depending on what it's a proof of). But when another participant continues this statement with 'that it's not all' (9), she is interpreting F3's comment as direct disagreement with F2; the explanation implied for the increase in asthma cases may not be the right one. F3 addresses the moderator, not F1, presenting the new view as parallel to rather than contradictory to the previous view. Then when F1 interrupts to respond to this, her turn is marked as adversative ('but'), signalling that she does take (8) as disagreeing with her. This way of addressing the moderator to disagree (as in some chaired meetings) is less apparent in the transcript than it is in the few groups for which we have videotapes, where participants may look steadily towards the moderator and orient their bodies towards him, even where their words might seem to be addressed to another participant.

Constructing others

Even when the moderator does not intervene and is not directly addressed, the participants still adapt their interaction to his or her presence and what they take to be the aim of the focus group. The participants themselves ensure that as a group they provide a usable range of opinions, by playing devil's advocate, attributing views to others not present, and accounting for disagreement. These moves show their orientation to making the group work in terms of what they have been told is its purpose, to display opinions.

One way in which participants can display opinions is by attributing a particular view to some particular person or group rather than presenting it as their own. We saw in the passage I quoted in Chapter 2 that a man introduced a dissenting view on the railway and Sellafield by saying 'there is one school of thought', a possible view, implying that it needs to be presented alongside any others. There is a similar sort of speaking for others when a group of women talk about the case of Louise Woodward, a British nanny working in the US who was charged with murdering the child for whom she was caring. The moderator is asking why participants haven't put her picture in one of the piles.

```
3.1.2.36
     1. Mod:   . . . is there another reason why
               she's . doesn't belong there?
→    2. Gail:  some people would say she's not a
               victim . I mean in the case of
               the diseased boy
     3. Mod:   right
     4. Gail:  he's a victim . it's nothing to
               do with his
     5. F:     it's not his fault
     6. Gail:  not saying that it is her fault .
               but people would view her . it as
               . there's a possibility that it
               is her fault . therefore she's
               not a victim
```

Gail offers a view in turn 2 of what 'some people would say'. And lest this be taken as an indirect way of giving her own opinion, when other participants clearly disagree, she says in turn 6 that she is 'not saying that it is her fault . but people would view her . . .'. This example suggests that speaking for others (Schiffrin 1993) fits within the analysis of 'footing' described by Goffman (Goffman 1981; Levinson 1988; Antaki, C. et al. 1996, see my discussion in Chapter 2). The participant signals that she is not the principal, the person whose views these words represent, but the unappointed spokesperson for these so far unrepresented views, carrying their words without necessarily agreeing.

A frequent pattern once discussions have got going is that some of the more vocal participants present themselves as devil's advocates, deliberately presenting their view as different from that of other participants, as an addition to what the group has presented so far.

3.5.1.45
```
    1. Mod:     Far East, Asians etc, do you
               think they should have the
               rights to, you know, do you
               think that's part of the=
    2. Clark:                      =I
               don't think they should have the
               right . but obviously they do do
    3. Mod:    they do . obviously they are
               doing
→   4. Ben:    but I mean playing devil's
               advocate . what do you say to
               companies that are providing
               jobs and income to people that
               are working for what we'd call
               slave labour . . .
```

The footing in turn 4 is complex. Ben presents himself as devil's advocate and then challenges the others ('you') with a rhetorical question. And yet he also represents himself and his trade union colleagues as the 'we' who are involved in a campaign against such practices, and whose efforts could have counterproductive effects. Rather than play down disagreement as we might expect in every-day conversation, the devil's advocate makes it explicit. But in doing so, he or she also shifts the terms in which the opinion is offered, as if it were something that has to be part of the record, and that could encourage further argument. These moves suggest 'sociable argument' in that they include what Schiffrin (1984) calls a 'prefer-ence for disagreement' as indicated by the unmitigated form in these examples. In some groups, there is clearly an element of playfulness in the back and forth.

In fact Ben in the previous example is not just voicing an opposing position; he is speaking for another group (girls working in Third World factories making footballs) that isn't otherwise represented here. Speaking for others is a way of accounting for differences in opinions, by referring to interests associated with given groups. The fact of disagreement needs to be explained and legitimated, in focus groups as well as in academic controversies (Gilbert and Mulkay 1984). In the example just given, the opposing view can be explained in terms of the employment needs of workers in developing countries. In other groups, various participants speak for farmers, unmarried mothers, Israelis, residents of Sellafield, gypsies, old people. Why do participants need to explain in this way? The accounts make sense as addressed to an observer who is the audience for opinions, rather than to other participants. The situation of the focus group constructs participants in this role as bearers of representative views; that is how they are addressed in the moderator's introduction, and that is how they treat each other's contributions.

Disagreement and the analysis of opinions

As we saw in Chapter 1, Michael Billig takes two-sided, contradictory argument as the basis, not only of rhetoric but of thinking (1987), and this applies as well to focus groups. Bloor and his colleagues make a distinction between a group interview, in which the same questions are asked of each participant, and a focus group: 'In group interviews the interviewer seeks answers, in focus groups the facilitator seeks group interaction' (Bloor et al. 2001). Processes of agreement and disagreement in groups are central to the very idea of focus groups. The moderator encourages disagreement among the group in his or her introduction, in eliciting further comments, and in making disagreement a topic. Participants manage disagreements by using typical conversational devices for dispreferred second assessments, by making concessions and treating them against a background of shared opinions, and by using the moderator as an audience and attributing views or playing the devil's advocate. In all these processes participants act as if their purpose as a group was to display opinions, in contrast to discussions in other settings, such as a pub or a meeting, where the main purpose might be passing time, arriving at a decision, or getting to know each other. If researchers pay attention to these processes, instead of trying to reduce or eliminate them, they can gain practical insights into aspects of their research. They can learn more about (1) the *variation* between groups, (2) the role of the *moderator* in any one group, and (3) the effects of taking single statements out of the *flow* of talk. And beyond these immediate features of discourse, close attention to these exchanges can tell us something about (4) what kinds of utterances the participants think count as *opinions*.

   1. *Variation between groups*. Moderators of focus-group projects try to elicit similar kinds of discussions across groups with very different participants: men and women, younger and older, working class and professionals. But moderators also know that each session feels different, in those moments about ten minutes after the start when they take off, or in that moment just after all the participants have left and the moderator is winding down. Groups differ especially in the scope they allow for disagreement and the style with which it is performed. There may be too many factors to say whether the variation between groups was due to gender, age, size of community, the specific mix of this group, or some unnoticed difference. But the difference in styles of disagreement will have a strong effect on what the group feels like and may provide a basis for looking at further interactional differences.

   2. *Moderator*. A commercial client unfamiliar with focus-group research or an academic reading a study based on focus groups might reasonably be concerned about the intervention of the moderator. As we saw in Chapter 5, the moderator necessarily, if sometimes indirectly, leads the participants, opening and closing topics and signalling whether a contribution is on or off topic. This may seem more problematic than the work done in a survey in which all interviewers are carefully trained to use exactly the same words and make the same limited responses (see Chapter 4). But if focus-group researchers attend to interactions, and not just to isolated statements from their transcripts, they can account for the moderator's interventions in a way that is not usually done in surveys (or for that matter, in other forms of data-gathering). If we take focus groups

as another kind of talk, we can apply our knowledge of how people interact, to see how the constraints we have considered might shape the talk turn to turn. The apparent artificiality of the situation – the moderator's intervention, the topic guide, the time limit, the tape recorder – stops being a weakness for which we apologize and starts being a feature we can use to begin our analysis of what the participants are doing.

3. *Flow and sequence.* We saw in the last chapter how previous turns could inform the participant's sense of what they are talking about in any excerpted turn. Detailed analysis of agreement and disagreement also has lessons for qualitative analysis of transcripts, the typical coding and quoting that reduce the thousand or so pages of transcript to usable resources for publication. For instance, if participants routinely upgrade the strength of agreement when agreeing in the second turn, then the strong wording of a statement may have more to do with its position in a sequence than with the speaker's depth of commitment. If participants use concessions as a form of disagreement, then the first part of a statement may be only a prelude to the main issue that they intend to emphasize. Participants can define consensus positions and excluded devil's advocate positions in the ways they address each other and the moderator; it is surely misrepresentation to take these unproblematically as statements of their own opinion, but it may also be a mistake to separate the speaker completely from these stances.

4. *What are opinions?* A close look at the processes in these groups can take us beyond questions of focus-group research methods to the more basic social questions with which this book is concerned:

- How are opinions treated in a way different from the treatment of offers of knowledge, experience, or jokes?
- When is the expression of opinions appropriate and when is it not?
- Who is entitled to offer opinions?

In particular, the last section of this chapter raises these issues, as participants attribute statements to others or speak as devil's advocate. We see then that opinions are taken to go with social interests (such as people in Sellafield) and individual experience (one's own experience of asthma), that they are imagined in opposing pairs ('on the other hand'), or they are on a continuum, so that a participant can pose a more extreme version of a view already given as a new and useful contribution to the range of the discussion. What comes across most strongly is that participants resent the idea that their own opinions can be taken for granted, read off from their group identity. Other people may have fixed opinions because of where they live or what they do for a living or how old they are, but *we*, talking right now, are open to see what happens in the next turn.

7

Representing speech: other voices, other places

Institutions of opinion promise to deliver 'the voices of the people' (Gallup and Rae 1940), letting the young parent, the unemployed plasterer, the company director, the retired nurse speak for themselves. Now imagine a poll in which respondents could, at any moment, answer for someone else, so the company director says what a young single mother might say on this issue, or the nurse speaks for a poor person in another country. All the careful sampling and standardization would go out the window. And yet, as we saw in Chapter 6, participants in interviews and focus groups can and do speak for others, attributing opinions to other people, telling stories, enacting voices. Analysts and readers may pay little attention to these shifts, just because they are so much a part of everyday talk. But they are crucial to understanding what opinions are doing. Participants can use other voices, not to evade giving their own opinion, but to make an opinion rhetorically effective, in all its complexities, relations, and ambivalences. In *Frame Analysis*, Erving Goffman notes our attachment to 'the basic notion that in daily life the individual ordinarily speaks for himself, speaks, as it were, in his "own" character. However, when one examines speech, especially the informal variety, this traditional view proves inadequate' (1974: 512). Goffman shows that there are many ways of shifting to another character: a change of clothes (taking off a tie), a movement (posing like a fashion model), a position (taking a seat at a meeting). One of the most common shifts is the reporting in one context of words that have been said or thought in another.

Here Robert is suggesting that he and others might be at fault when they holiday in Third World countries.

```
3.8.1.40
Robert:      . . . so somebody once said to me on
             holiday you're holidaying on some other
             people's misery . they pay those low wages
```

Robert presents a view in terms of what someone else said to him in another time and another place; these words are brought into this new context, the focus group, so that for a moment, other participants hear as he did this view and the implied criticism. In this example the shift is to some other, unspecified time and place ('somebody once said to me'); Robert was the hearer in the reported context and is the speaker in the reporting context. But as we will see, there are many possible variations in who is reported, and how much of the reported utterance is conveyed. (In this chapter I will use bold font to indicate words that may be interpreted as reported speech. The boundaries of what is reported are often unclear. (Here I take 'they pay those low wages' as said in Robert's own voice, because he had used this phrase earlier, before the quotation.)

Participants don't just repeat words that were actually said; they may also invent words and speaking voices that enable them to dramatize indirectly their own stance:

```
3.7.1.59
Amy:         I just don't think you should say oh . it's
             nothing to do with me . that kind of
             everyone going well never mind . someone
             will deal with it . that kind of attitude
Steve:       yes that's a scandalous attitude
```

Amy expresses her view by ironic quotation, not of something said, here or elsewhere, but of something somebody *could* say. She shows that she is quoting directly, even if hypothetically, by saying 'oh' (which, as we will see, is a common a way of signalling a quotation).

Participants use reported speech to map part of the landscape of opinions, providing grid references for what they say. Other opinions ('that kind of attitude') have to be possible for one's own opinion to be an opinion at all, opinions from other participants in the discussion, from people in other situations, or perhaps from their own dramatized dilemmas of uncertainty (Billig 1987; Billig et al. 1988; Shotter 1993). In this chapter, I outline some of the uses of reported speech in opinion discussions, by linking them to a view of reported speech as demonstration, as doing and not just telling, and by showing how these uses shift some of the components of speech events that I discussed in Chapter 3.

Forms and functions of reported speech

Different aspects of reported speech have emerged as it has been studied in literature, in general corpora (computer collections of language use), in conversation, and in specific speech events. The earliest analyses were devoted to written texts and in particular to literature (Leech and Short 1981; Banfield 1982; Bakhtin 1986; Volosinov 1986; Short 1988; Semino et al. 1997; Short et al. 1998; Semino et al. 1999). This body of work by some of the major stylisticians has been useful in pointing out the cline between direct speech ('He said "I'm going now"') and indirect speech ('He said that he was going then'), the relations between syntactic transformations and deictic cues (such as 'now' and 'then'), the subtle articulations of point of view of the reporting writer and reported speaker, and the occurrence of reports of hypothetical speech, all of which are relevant to my analysis. As we will see, these taxonomies can be applied to social as well as literary issues.

A much wider range of lexical and grammatical forms in signalling represented speech has emerged as linguists have turned from literary examples to surveys of large corpora containing computer-readable texts from many written and spoken genres, such as COBUILD (Thompson 1996: 506), CANCODE (Carter and McCarthy 1995; McCarthy 1998: Ch. 8), the British National Corpus (Leech 2000), and a corpus of phone conversations and radio phone-ins at the University of Konstanz (Gunthner 1999; Klewitz and Couper-Kuhlen 1999). Corpus-based descriptions have found, for instance, that:

- A quotation may be signalled by 'like', goes', or 'gets', as well as by some form of 'says' (McCarthy 1998: 158, 164), or that there may be no markers at all (Yule et al. 1992)
- Discourse markers such as 'oh', 'well', and 'God', are often included in reports (McCarthy 1998: 159), even in indirect speech and reports of thought (Holt 1996).
- Prosodic cues such as variations in pitch, volume, pace, and rhythm may indicate stretches of reported speech in

conversation, but the signalled boundaries do not always coincide exactly with those of the words to be taken as reported (see the particularly insightful transcriptions and analyses in Gunthner 1999; and Klewitz and Couper-Kuhlen 1999).

- Everyday talk and news reports can use complex hybrids of direct and indirect reports (Slembrouck 1992; Caldas-Coulthard 1994; Semino et al. 1999; Slembrouck 1999; Mitchell 1998: 211–14) that had been thought to be the province of literary texts such as the novels of Jane Austen.

These studies of forms of reported speech tell us that we are looking in our focus group transcripts for rather varied lexical and prosodic cues that can have a range of interpretations.

To understand how reported speech works in focus groups, or any other particular genre, we also need analyses that take reporting as a part of interaction, as Volosinov put it, 'to take the phenomenon of reported speech and postulate it as a problem from a sociological orientation' (1986). A wide range of researchers, not all sociologists, have taken up this challenge to consider why people use reported speech in talk in a variety of settings (reviewed in Baynham and Slembrouck 1999), including college students' talk about race (Buttny 1998; Buttny and Williams 2000; Buttny 1999), children's arguments and play (Goodwin 1990), teacher and students in an adult maths class (Baynham 1996; Baynham 1999), conversations among school pupils (Maybin 1997; 1999), or among co-workers (Holt 1999), a psychiatric interview (Ravatsos and Berkenkotter 1999), research interviews (Schiffrin 1993; 1996), radio news (Mitchell 1998), and courtroom testimony (Philips 1993; Jacquemet 1996; Matoesian 2000), as well as the function we might expect from literary studies, everyday storytelling (Mitchell-Kiernan 1972; Tannen 1989; Johnstone 1993; Shuman 1993). What links many of these interactional uses of reported speech is that they are rhetorical, that is, the participants assume the existence of opposing views and use reported speech to dramatise, shift, or reinforce a view, or to bring out the tensions between views.

Any particular use of reported speech can have apparently opposite functions; for instance, in the first example I quoted the reporting speaker identifies his own view with that of the accusation reported ('you're holidaying on some other people's misery'), while in the second the speaker distances herself from the apathetic view reported ('never mind someone will deal with it'). Clark and Gerrig (1990), in a key account of reported speech, argue that this sort of apparent contradiction can be understood if we see quotation as a kind of demonstration, a non-serious depiction of the words of another. This approach is useful to me in dividing two aspects of quotation that I will address in each of the main functions I discuss:

(1) *detachment*: The reported speech is separated from what the speaker says for himself or herself, and is in this sense 'non-serious'. Their example is someone demonstrating the tennis serve of John McEnroe, without being John McEnroe or even playing tennis. This aspect emphasizes the juxtaposition of two different roles, reported and reporting speaker.

(2) *direct experience*: The report is a depiction of what is said, rather than a description, so it can carry an immediacy, an indexical connection to the original setting. Their use of the word 'depiction' suggests that demonstrations and quotations *do* rather than *tell*, as the imitator of John McEnroe's serve might convey perhaps the way he lifts his arm or shifts his weight. This aspect emphasizes the way those in the reporting context respond to the act in the reported context.

Of course speaker and situation both shift in any quotation (even in self-quotation and in reference to something just said), and there are elements of direct experience and of detachment in each of the examples I will give. But I will argue that quotations may have different functions when the emphasis is on detachment, on the one hand, or direct experience, on the other.

Because of these shifts, quotation is always (in Clark's and Gerrig's terms) both 'partial', in that some aspects of the depiction are to be disregarded, and 'selective', in that only some aspects of the reported phenomenon are depicted. In the examples I have quoted, 'on holiday you're holidaying on some other people's misery' is partial in that the speaker does not try to convey the speaker's accent or intonation; it is selective in that these words, of all those the speaker could have said, are chosen to represent the whole conversation, and many other conversations. Because the speaker's use of quotation is always partial and selective, listeners must also be partial and selective in their interpretations, deciding what alternative voices are proposed, what aspects of this report are immediately relevant, and what aspects must be ignored. In view of all this complexity, it is perhaps surprising that people talking nearly always identify reported speech and seem to understand what it is doing.

Functions of reported speech and thought

While categories of reported speech based on form can be clearly differentiated (Semino et al. 1997; McCarthy 1998), categories of function, as for any human activity, necessarily blur, double, and multiply. It may be useful, then, to return to some of the components of speech events (Hymes 1972) that I used to introduce forums of opinion in Chapter 3. I will focus on four of his eight components:

- Situation: reported speech shifts to another time or place
- Participants: reported speech enables participants to take on multiple roles, as speakers, hearers, or overhearers
- Acts: reported speech can give different words for the same meaning, or give the same words a different meaning
- Key: reported speech can cue a shift in interpretation, like an indication of modality, more or less of a claim to factuality

As one might expect, the categories are not exclusive – an utterance can have more than one function and interpretation; a shift that focuses attention on setting may also raise issues of participants. And they are not exhaustive. There are other possible components: one could consider the importance of Ends (e.g., in transcription of parliamentary debates (Slembrouck 1992)), or of Instrumentalities (e.g., the use in court of read out vs. audio-recorded speech (Matoesian 2000), spoken vs. e-mail discussion of medical treatment (Hamilton 1998)). The shifts in one activity type could be divided up in different ways (e.g. Thompson 1996), and there are certainly other functions in other activity types (e.g. Baynham 1996; Hall et al. 1999). But these four categories, each divided into two contrasting effects, can provide a basis for exploring the range of functions we find in focus groups, and for relating these functions to the ways participants display opinions.

Table 1 *Functions of reported speech*

	direct experience (depiction)	**detachment** (non-serious speech)
situation	intensifying an event *She says, 'Are you in the van?'*	typifying an encounter *I'd be asked, 'Well do you need it?'*
participants	enlisting overhearers *'You must be bored out of your mind'/ 'Lady of leisure' they get*	speaking for others *They say 'you live in town'*
acts	formulating the gist *'The responsibility is shared'./ 'It's not my fault'.*	mentioning the wording *They'll have to do something about that. / 'They'.*
key	offering evidence *People say to me, 'Well, there's fish as Lostock'*	enacting hypothetical speech *'Right there you are, that's signed out to you'*

Situation: intensifying an event

In reported speech, the scene shifts from here and now to a village street or office or beach where the reported interaction is set, at some past (or as we will see, future) time. We saw this in the example in Chapter 2, when Lynne uses 'oh:' to convey a sudden realization as reported thought. Here Patrick is responding to the moderator's questions about whether they take global communications links for granted.

```
3.4.1.38
1. Mod:   yeah you go on holiday regularly so you're
          aware of that
2. Pat:   I've got me mobile ((laughter)) everywhere
          I go
3. M:     yeah
4. Pat:   I'll give you an example I was by a pool in
          Majorca last year and daughter rings me up
5. M:     yeah
6. Pat:   all right I was sitting by the pool she
          thought I was . by the van ((laughter)) and
          she is talking away for about five minutes
          and I am nattering away to her it's as
          clear as a bell
7. M:     yeah
8. Pat:   and she says uh . are you in the van? I
          said no I am in Majorca . oh my Go:d she
          says I'm on me boyfriend's phone slammed
```

```
                the phone down . ((laughter)) you know I
                mean . it was so: . all right we were
                thousands of miles away . whatever
 9. Mod:        mm
10. M:          yeah
11. Pat:        but it was so close isn't it . years years
                ago it didn't happen you know . you'd link
                up here link up there and
12. M:          yeah
13. Pat:        it took you ten minutes to get through
14. M:          that's right yeah
15. Pat:        the whole world's /shrunk
16. Mod:                         /do other people have
                that that feeling that it affects their
                lives as it does [Patrick's] . does
                it . . .
```

The story starts with a clear indication of a place and time: 'I was by a pool in Majorca.' The story is signalled by a discourse marker ('all right') and a shift to present tense. The first report of the talk ('she is talking away for about five minutes and I am nattering away to her') is not a quotation, but a description of the action without a depiction of its content, what Semino, Short, and Culpeper (1997) call a Narrative Report of Voice; 'nattering' suggests that the content of the talk is not relevant to the story. The shift to direct reported speech is indicated by reporting verbs ('she says', 'I said'). Holt (1996) notes that in conversation these are often repeated redundantly, giving a kind of rhythm to the reported exchange. McCarthy (1998: 166) shows in a corpus study that the anomalous use of present tense ('she says') is typical. The shift to reported speech is also indicated by the question, the shift in pronouns from 'I' to 'you', the reference to 'me boyfriend's', and the use of 'oh my God', with stress on 'oh'. There are also prosodic cues: the words 'oh my Go:d she says I'm on me boyfriend's phone slammed the phone down' are higher pitched, louder, and faster, this style continuing beyond the end of the quotation to the end of the story (Klewitz and Couper-Kuhlen 1999 note a similar continuation of a cue beyond the end of the reported speech). Patrick then continues to show he told this story for a reason: he compares this call to calls made in the past (11, 13) and gives the gist as 'the whole world's shrunk'. The moderator then asks if other participants have 'that feeling that it affects their lives as it does Patrick's', confirming that the story as dramatized

supports a specific point of view on globalization. Since reported
speech can evoke a particular setting and scene, it can prepare for
a possible admission of tension or change in one's opinion; we will
see some examples in later sections.

Situation: typifying a repeated event

A common use of reported speech in the focus group transcripts is to
present some utterance as happening again and again: not 'then they
said this', but 'this is what they always say'. Where *intensification*
(discussed in the last section) dramatizes a response at the time, the
typicality of the remarks stresses the on-going tension between the
points of view, not identified as persons but embodied as voices.

```
2.7.35
1 F1:    but also . if you have got a car sitting
         outside the door you feel you should use it
         ((laughter)) whereas I'm sure if I
2 F2:    (use mine enough I'd) I'd be asked . well do
         you really need it ((laughter)) and you think
         oh . yes I do . you know . it's like taking .
         if you're used to having a car and . then
         it's . someone says oh no . you don't need
         that
3 Mod:   yeah . how about this idea that
4 F2:    how do you justify it
```

One marker of the typicality here is the use of *you* as a general pro-
noun. So the 'you' in 'do you really need it' is used by the (typified)
quoted person to refer to the quoting speaker, but the 'you' in 'you
have got a car' or 'you feel' or 'you think' is a more general reference
that potentially includes the others in the group (on this ambiguity,
see Sacks 1992: I.348–53). F1 offers a justification of her driving a
car and then begins to qualify it (1). F2 presents the same tension
in what seems to be a constructed dialogue (2); on closer observation it is a composite with the kind of question she would be asked
('do you really need it') and then her response as reported thought
('oh yes I do') (see McCarthy 1998: 164 on the passive of 'ask' as
a reporting verb). Though 'oh yes I do' is a reported thought, the
interjection 'oh' marks it as if it were spoken. Then she repeats the
same sort of remark made to her, not as a question but as a statement, with the 'oh no' making this typical speech seem to respond

to the reported thought. The moderator cuts in to change the topic ('yeah. how about'), but F2 continues; she has not yet given a summary question ('how do you justify it') as the gist that shows how this dialogue applies rhetorically to the current topic. The reported speech follows a statement about a daily choice, whether or not to drive, and it represents an on-going and unresolved tension, rather than a specific place or time.

Typification in any setting calls on the other participants to recognize from one phrase that this is just what people always say (note the use, for instance, in the complaints reported by Coates (2000)). Matoesian and Coldren (2002) give a striking example of the miscommunication that results when such a typification used by a participant is not recognized by the moderator. The moderator then challenges the participant to say just who said that, implying that they invented the comment, when apparently they typified it. In focus groups typification has a particular function, because the norms of the speech event call on participants to speak, by implication, not from their specific experience but for a group. Reported speech can enact an on-going, shared, and recognizable contradiction or dilemma, such as between driving or not driving to market, escaping or not escaping from emotional ties at work.

Participants: hearers and overhearers

Reported speech complicates the participation roles of an event, the kinds of footing (see Chapter 2), by adding new layers of speakers and hearers in the reporting context. If I report words said to me in a story told to other people, I am involving an overhearing audience that wasn't present when these words were said and asking this audience to share my response as the hearer in the reported context, drawing on the way reported speech can give those in my new audience the direct experience of my response of shock or delight or unease or whatever. Buttny (Buttny 1997; Buttny and Williams 2000) has given striking accounts of how reported speech can be used in talking about race on campus to invoke the solidarity of the current group in response to some utterance elsewhere that is now interpreted as racist or oversensitive. Hamilton (1998) says that participants in an on-line discussion group for survivors of bone marrow transplants used direct reported speech for the utterances of doctors, and indirect speech for themselves, when they wanted to dramatize the difficulties posed by these doctors and overcome by the patients; the effect is that the other members of the discussion group become sympathetic overhearers to these private incidents. Similarly, Klewitz and Couper-Kuhlen show how people telling stories may mark the reported speech of authority figures prosodically (for instance with higher volume or pitch), while leaving their own words unmarked (1999).

Clark and Gerrig note that, 'when speakers demonstrate only a snippet of an event, they tacitly assume that their addressees share the right background to interpret it the same way they do' (1990: 793). (The same assumption was made in recognizing topics, in Chapter 5.) In the focus groups, the participants quickly pick up on the invitations to share and display the correct interpretation, contributing their own reports. Here a group of mothers is commenting on an attitude expressed towards them:

```
1.3.21
  1. F1:   I think something that has changed now . is
           it's not acceptable now I think in society
           for a woman to stay at home with the
           children [mm] I think a woman . at home
           with the children is very pressurized to go
           to work [yeah] do you feel that? ((xx))
  2. F2:   I feel terrible
  3. F1:   thirty years ago my or whoever's mum thirty
           years ago . it was nothing to stay at home
           with the children it was expected
  4. F:    yeah
  5. F1:   it was expected of them
  6. F:    mm
  7. F1:   to stay at home and put the meal on the
           table
  8. F:    yeah
  9. F1:   more or less . it's not now . I think /
 10. F3:                                          /it's
           . do you not work . do you not work
 11. F1:   women are pressurized to go back to work
 12. F2:   yeah
 13. F4:   when I (packed) working . there's something
           wrong with me
 14. F:    yeah
```

```
15. F:    God what do you do all day ((laughter))
          what do you do all day (xxx) you must be
          bored out of your mind
16. F2:   lady of leisure they get (xxx)
17. F:    yeah yeah
18. F1:   I think that bit's changed
19. F:    that bit's harder
20. F1:   'cause you have to . ask for
21. F:    you're looked down upon . because you are
          not working . 'cause you're at home
22. F:    as though you've got no brains
```

F1 makes a generalization about the changed attitude towards
women whose work is at home and invites others to respond: 'do you
feel that?' (1). After she says 'now' (9), F3 overlaps with reported
speech enacting the attitudes F1 has described (10), in which the
'you' is not F1 in particular but any woman hearing it. The shift to
reported speech is indicated by a rise in pitch and an almost inaudi-
ble 'it's' (Yule et al. 1992 comment on forms of 'to be' as reporting
verbs). F1 repeats the same idea as a statement, not reported speech
(11). Others join in with similar remarks, the reported speech indicated very subtly by (a) the interjections ('God'), (b) the way the
unidentifiable speaker picks up on the use of questions by F3, and
(c) F2's use of the tag 'they get' (16). A more complex example
is the remark 'there's something wrong with me' (13), which cannot be taken as direct reported speech, or the speaker's own speech
(despite the 'me'), but only as a summary of the attitudes of others, presented ironically (see Clark and Gerrig 1990 on such hybrid
forms). In these examples, the group works together to enlist each
other as overhearers, and to recognize that the response is shared
(see Coates 1996 on such collaboration).

Participants: speaking for another

We saw in Chapters 2 and 6 how a speaker can distance himself
or herself from a stance on such issues without a direct threat to
the face of the reporting speaker, by attributing it vaguely ('there
is one school of thought'). Speaking for others (Schiffrin 1993) is
a way of managing the discussion of controversial opinions with a
group of strangers. In our groups, such controversial topics might

include nuclear power, road building, immigration, or government
restrictions on meat due to BSE.

While reported voices may support one's argument, they may also
be offered in contrast to one's own, in tension with it and equally
valid. Here the group is talking about contrasting ways of life in
Britain and in developing countries, and Dan speaks for a Yorkshire farmer to whom he talked when he was at his second home in
Whitby.

```
3.8.2.20
  1. Mod:   . . . in this day and age people often do
            know how other people live
  2. M:     /and not not
  3. Dan:   but some people prefer that . I mean I had
            a drink with some farmers up in in Whitby
            way
  4. Mod:   mm
  5. Dan:   and they say oh you live in the town and
            you have your eight-hours day . well we
            have our eight-hour day but it takes us
            twelve hours to do it
  6. Mod:   ((laughs))
  7. Dan:   . and that's a philosophy on life . and
            it's relative to where we are .
  8. Mod:   yeah
  9. Dan:   I can live twelve-hour days when I'm up
            the:re
 10. M:     yeah
 11. Dan:   and when I'm down here the pressure of
            everything around you
 12. Mod:   you couldn't do it
```

Dan, the teacher, contrasts his shorter hours, with more pressure, to
the longer hours with less stressful work of the farmers. The farmer
is quoted in direct speech; 'you' is the teacher from the city, and 'we'
is the farmers. The time when he 'had a drink' is a particular event in
the past, but this is something 'they say', in the present tense, because
it represents an on-going 'philosophy on life', as Dan sums it up. The
moderator takes the gist of this dramatization as a comment on the
stressful life of the teacher ('you couldn't do it'), but in relation to
previous turns, it is a comment on how one is to deal with ideas of
quality of life different from one's own. Reported speech can be a
way of presenting a potentially face-threatening topic in a way that
detaches it from one's own stance.

We saw in Chapter 6 that the participants treat the focus group as a particular kind of event, one in which a range of views must be presented, and in which each view comes with a possible contrast. One implication of all this speaking for another is that researchers must be careful about taking bits of such elaborate processes of interaction out of their context and simply saying Dan says farmers work hard. The assertion is made in a reported voice to make a point that is clear only in the context of the previous turns, and with these listeners.

Acts: new words for the same meaning

Volosinov, in an often-quoted definition, says that 'Reported speech is speech within speech, utterance within utterance, and at the same time also speech about speech, utterance about utterance' (1986: 118). We have seen so far, in the categories of setting, factuality, and positioning, various ways that speakers may use speech *within* speech, what Volosinov calls 'retorting' (1986: 118). But speakers also set out reported speech as something to talk *about*, what Volosinov calls 'commenting'. There are two broad ways of doing this (and here I shift from Volosinov's terminology to that of more recent discourse analysis): *formulations* give what is offered as the same meaning in other words ('you're saying that . . .'), while *mentions* take the same words but talk about them, as words, instead of using them with their usual meaning ('*talk* is a four letter word'). So a formulation is concerned with conveying the direct experience of what was said, that is, offering a different version that can stand in for it while conveying its full force. A mention, on the other hand, is another of the uses of reported speech in terms of detachment, the temporary suspension of what Clark and Gerrig (1990) call 'serious speech'.

A number of researchers have noted that formulations are associated with powerful participants in asymmetrical interactions; police interrogators (Fairclough 1992: 157–8), the teacher in an adult education classroom (Baynham 1996), or the interviewer on a news programme (Thornborrow 2002: Ch. 5). Moderators use formulations routinely to focus participants' attention on some topic that might otherwise pass by, to model responses, or to move them on to a different form of discussion; learning to use them is part of the training, like learning to use back-channel utterances (such as 'okay' or 'uh-huh'). But participants can also formulate utterances this way. In our studies, participants were presented with short statements, pictures, or video clips for comment. Often they didn't say what they thought of the statement in their words but formulated it ironically in a way that implied a criticism of the statement or its source.

```
2.2.31
1. Mod:  and the third one . the responsibility for
         our environment is shared . it is not a
         duty for government alone . any comments on
         those? why would they say things like that?
2. M1:   What the UK Government . it's not my fault.
3.       ((laughter))
4. M2:   just stating the obvious
```

The reported speech 'it's not my fault' (2) is a formulation of the government's words 'the responsibility for our environment is shared' (1). The laughter in the next turn and the comment in 4 suggest that participants take the formulation as an ironic equivalent, what the government would say if they could say it, made more effective by the way the long and impersonal statement by the government is rephrased into a very short and personal disclaimer. The formulation thus implies something about the kind of act in the original government statement – that it was evasive.

The same sort of ironic formulation can be made of a visual text. Here, for instance, a group of men are giving their response to a recruitment advertisement that shows Special Constables as caring public-spirited citizens:

```
3.7.1.34
1. Mod:   anybody attracted?
2. Jim:   are you a copper?
3. Steve: no . I'm sorry but they're dubious ads/
4. Sam:                                        /not
          for the social stigma . no
5. Alan:  shop your mates
6. Steve: yeah
7.        ((laughter))
```

Steve and Sam give their evaluations directly, but Jim and Alan offer (2) and (5) as possible formulations of what the ad is saying with its high-minded call to community service. Again, the comic effect of the formulation comes from the shift from the language and style of the ad ('would you care to help') to the kind of colloquial language associated with gangs ('copper', 'shop your mates'). The shift of register in their formulations shows the gulf between the ad and its effect.

Acts: new meanings for the same words

Formulation, in the previous section, uses different words for the same (underlying) meaning. Reported speech can also take the same words and give them a different meaning. One way of doing this is by mentioning rather than using a word. The distinction between use and mention is much discussed by philosophers of language: one *uses* a word to refer to the world, but *mentions* a word to refer to the word itself, as when linguists put it in italics as a citation form (as I have done in this sentence) (Goffman 1974: 316; Lyons 1977: 7). One might think mention was the province of linguists, philosophers, language teachers with their definitions, and academics with their scare quotes, but we find it frequently in everyday talk. When a child says 'give me a cookie' and a parent says 'please', the parent is mentioning, not using, the word, expecting the child to recognize it as a reminder of what he or she should say, not a real request from the parent. We also find mentions in focus groups, in echoes of slogans, parodies of magazine headlines, or mockery of the styles of the powerful, condescending, or apathetic.

   In discussion of an ad for Coke, Jim refers to an advertisement that he takes as common currency (though it hadn't been shown in more than twenty years).

```
3.7.1.28
Jim:      when she's letting off the cannon and then
          it shows this sort of I'd like to teach the
          world to sing type group of kids .
```

'I'd like to teach the world to sing' is mentioned, not used; the 'I' refers not to the speaker, but to the singers in the 1971 Coke ad 'Hillside' that had young adults of many nationalities singing these words (Myers 1999: 55). The whole phrase is here treated as an adjective to evoke this particular image of an intercultural group of kids, and in doing so, to remind us that this image is a kind of cliché.

Participants can ironicize their own words in this way too. In the next example, one of the participants has said, 'it won't last twenty years the drugs problem. something will be done about it'. The moderator gives a formulation of this turn (1), and the participants mention his use of 'they' (2, 3, 4).

```
1.3.1.19
1. Mod: this . can I mention something that .
        you've said you've said this with
        reference to a lot of things . you said
        . that they'll have to do something
        about that=
2. F1:              =they
3. F2:   they
4. F3:   notice the they    ((laughter))
5. F1:   the people up there that are supposed to
         be doing it ((laughs))
6. Mod: you said it sort of about the youth
        clubs and things . you said it about the
        beaches and you said it about the drugs
```

The moderator does not stress the word 'they' in any way, and it is not a word from the participant's turn he is formulating, but three of the participants repeat it and there is laughter of recognition. Then F1 offers her own formulation of what has just been said, 'the people up there that are supposed to be doing it' (5). The moderator then responds (6) in a way that acknowledges the topic is now the words in which they presented their opinions.

Mention is implicitly ironic; indeed Sperber and Wilson (1981) develop a theory of irony as a form of mention. Mention is a way of saying words while detaching oneself completely from them, holding them up to scrutiny, implicitly acknowledging the arguable nature of what is discussed. The function parallels those of reported speech in typifying and speaking for other voices. Each involves using reported speech to separate the quoted words from the quoting speaker and the immediate situation.

Key: offering evidence

Goffman and Hymes use the word 'key,' following Bateson (1972), to suggest, for instance, the difference between a 'playful' and a 'real' enactment of the same event (see Chapter 3). 'Key is introduced to provide for the tone, manner, or spirit in which an act is done. It corresponds roughly to modality among grammatical categories' (Goffman 1974: 62). Reported speech shifts key when it suggests the categorical modality of events that surely happened, or, as we will see in the next section, the hypothetical modality of 'might' or 'could' (on modality, see Stubbs 1996: Ch. 8).

Almost all reported speech serves to provide evidence; it can do this because of the sense of 'direct experience' arising from the depiction, the conveying of how it was said as well as what was said. Elizabeth Holt (1996) has noted this as a primary function of reported speech in conversation, and has analysed how a single utterance in reported speech can convey a number of aspects of the utterance and situation compactly and economically. Marco Jacquemet (1996) shows how a prosecution witness, in an Italian trial of people accused of being involved with organized crime, uses reported speech when telling a story to show how deeply he was involved with those he is accusing. He says he had to teach a 'godson' in prison the exact technique of decapitation by practising on rabbits: 'See, the head must be cut off like this. all right . . . no, let me see' (1996: 137). Jacquemet comments that 'the reported situation . . . produces an effect of referentiality, which brings people to assume that the entire story actually took place in the "real world"' (1996: 144).

Sometimes speakers present a quotation to support a potentially controversial remark (rather as an academic might do in a journal article). These instances of evidence need not draw on an authority figure (compare the examples in Chapter 8); they are often vaguely attributed to 'people' or 'the newspapers' or 'they', and indeed may work better for their vagueness (see Thompson 1996: 510).

```
3.4.2.35
1. Jim:        female hormone . oestrogen . which is
               going into the water and it's making the
               male fish turn into females ((over
               talking)) but you don't see that
2. Patrick:    but we never had fish did we?
3. Andrew:     no there weren't fish before I mean
4. Jim:        no that's true
5. Patrick:    you know . we didn't have . I know
               people say to me well there's fish at
```

```
                    the Lostock now and it's 40 years since
                    there was fish at the Lostock
  6. M:             yeah
  7. M:             yeah
  8. Patrick:       you know . they've never seen it . so to
                    some degree it must be a lot cleaner .
                    it must be a lot cleaner . we've already
                    got pollution in a different sense
  9. Andrew:        we've seen that in our lifetime haven't
                    we . that clean-up
 10. M:             yes
```

Here there is a disagreement; to paraphrase, Jim has said that the oestrogen in the water is affecting the fish, while Patrick and Andrew are saying the very existence of fish in these rivers in an industrial region is evidence of the environment getting better. Patrick links these two points of view, by repeating what he has just said (5), and then presenting it as something people in the neighborhood tell him about a particular stream, the Lostock. This then gets a series of 'yeah's' from all around, and then he goes on to qualify this improvement ('so to some degree it must be a lot cleaner') and distinguish it from the 'pollution in a different sense' that Jim has talked about. The attribution of words and acts to others provides a basis for mediating a disagreement, outside the opinions of the people present. It is a shift in key, to a heightened modality in which one is speaking of experienced facts, not just personal impressions.

Key: enacting hypothetical speech

As key can shift up to heightened claims for evidence, it can also be shifted down (in Goffman's (1974) terms) from some primary reality towards fiction, play, rehearsal, or parody. Many of the instances of reported speech in the focus groups involve utterances that have not been made but could be made or should be made or could not have been made: they are in the future, or potential, or conditional, or impossible. Semino, Short, and Wynne (1999) find that reports of hypothetical speech are common in newspapers, and they give a taxonomy of this hypotheticality based on possible worlds theory, as expressing the speaker's knowledge, sense of obligation, wish, or prediction. In their data, drawn from written texts, such reports are usually in indirect speech, while in the focus groups they are always

direct reports of speech, thought, or writing, for reasons we will
see. Amy Shuman (1993) notes how the junior-high-school pupils
she studied use hypothetical reports in stories of past fights or predictions of future fights; Richard Buttny (1997) finds hypothetical
reports frequently in his corpus of students' discussions of race; and
Philip Mitchell (1998) finds similar uses in radio news reporting.
All three link the usefulness of such hypothetical reports to the way
reported speech can be detached from the current speaker and situation.

In the following example, the speaker is imagining a system he
would like to see, but one that he denies ever existed. He has been
describing a scheme for helping old people around the council house
estate.

1.4.1.24
```
 1. Barry:   and I know they get these people if
             they've been to court they give them
             community work so they're expecting them
             to do it . but you should be able to go
             . somewhere at on that council should be
             there if you want to cut your grass and
             you can't afford that (xx) or a
             lawnmower . or the edge trimmers . where
             you should be able to go on that estate
             and your council should say right there
             you are . that's signed out for you .
             cut your fucking lawn . hand it back .
             at least they're tidy aren't they
 2. Mod:     yeah yeah
 3. Barry:   at least you're given the option
 4. Mod:     so what the council should what should
             actually um . look after people
 5. Jack:    no others sh
 6. Mod:     who can't do it themselves
 7. Barry:   yeah
 8. Mod:     is that what you're saying
 9. Jack:    no no but listen
10. Barry:   those who want to look after themselves
             people can do it themselves they should
             give them the the stuff to do . you know
             here's a Flymo for the day
11. M2:      yeah but they did that they did that
12. Barry:   well I never fucking seen it
```

```
13. M2:      the estate caretaker came round Callan
             Street to lend you tools for to cut your
             grass . right? didn't they? but somebody
             abused it somebody abused it by stealing
             the bloody strimmer the grass strimmer
```

Here, as with the uses for typicality, reported speech emphasizes the ordinariness and repetitiveness of the action that goes with the utterance, handing over the mower. The routineness is captured in the way 'the council', though an impersonal bureaucracy, is given in its utterance an interjection and an obscenity. In turns 4 and 6, the moderator formulates what Barry has said as a way of looking after those on the estate who can't look after themselves, but Barry repeats it in turn 10 as a story of people who can and do look after themselves and others, the unemployed men cutting grass. Jack says that in fact such a system had been in operation (11), but Barry insists (emphatically) that he has not seen it (12). His example was hypothetical, offered as a suggestion for improving things; somehow it would diminish his contribution to have it be merely a description of an exchange that used to happen.

Hypothetical reported speech, since it does not report anything that has actually been said, shows the rhetorical usefulness of detachment. In that, it is like the uses of reported speech for typification, speaking for another, and mentioning (Myers 2000d).

Reported speech and opinions

One of the striking features across these examples of reported speech is the way participants signal how the utterance just reported is to fit in the on-going discussion: 'as though you've got no brains', 'how do you justify it?', 'it's relative to where you are'. These gists, pointing up the intended effect, suggest that in focus group discussions, participants seldom use reported speech just for a good story, humour, or economy, though it can have all these effects; they use it rhetorically. I have argued in my taxonomy that the rhetorical uses of reported speech can be seen in terms of shifts of frame, and more specifically of shifts in some of the components of speech events.

- First, *situation* is always shifted, even if one is quoting words said in the same place moments before; the act of reporting separates here and now from there and then. This is crucial because it provides an economical way of showing that views are embedded in a particular experience. References to typical rather than specific situations are also common because they call on hearers to recognize the repeated pattern.

- *Participant roles* can be opened up or complicated by reported speech. Participants can be made into overhearers of interactions for which they were not present, and speakers can speak for people that are not present and stances that have no representative in the group.
- The *act* of speaking can be transformed, so that participants focus on the way it was said, as well as what was said. Participants can link an elaborate message to a short formulation of what it 'really means'. Or they can focus attention on the language of institutions, moderators, or their own discussion, by mentioning it rather than using it.
- Shifts of *key* are most obvious when participants suspend the assumption of factuality and offer hypothetical reports of what people might say, didn't say, or couldn't possibly say, as a way of voicing what is repressed or taken for granted. But there is also a shift in key when they offer a report as evidence to support an argument.

The use of reported speech poses a narrow and a broader issue for any elicitation of opinions. I have already noted the danger of quoting turns out of their context; when a report quotes what someone said in a focus group or interview, the quoted subject could themselves be reporting speech in one way or another: typifying, speaking for another, ironicizing, detaching themselves from these words. And as my examples have shown, it is rather a subtle matter determining where these shifts occur; transcripts may come with quotation marks (inserted by the transcriber) but in actual speech the signals are more subtle. And the same issues apply to surveys: each respondent must decide who they are speaking as, who they are speaking for, what sort of person says (or hears) these sorts of things (Houtkoop-Steenstra 2000). But in surveys, all these shifts are lost when the researcher ticks the box; in interviews and focus groups, traces remain in the transcripts, if only in an 'oh'.

These complex uses of reported speech challenge not only the standard view of opinions but also the simplified view of public discourse that goes with them, in which each person speaks for themselves. John Shotter argues that people 'must see themselves, not in physical space, but as surrounded by a morally textured landscape of "opportunities for action" made differentially available to them' (1993: 162). Reported speech offers a telescopic view of this morally textured landscape. Whenever participants say anything, they are aware of competing voices outside the room, voices from other times, and even voices inside their heads. They are aware that to speak at all is to position oneself morally, to judge and be judged – not a comfortable act in a room full of friendly strangers. And whatever their politics, participants are aware of some differences in opportunities for action; there are those who would have something to say who can't speak here, and those who do speak (governments, companies, advertisements) but can't be trusted. In the next chapter we will see that participants, while undermining the stability of any one statement of opinion, are also looking for relevant authority and expertise on issues that matter to them most. But they don't always find this authority where we might expect it.

8

Questioning expertise: Who says?

We have seen in Chapter 7 that participants in focus groups offer a range of voices besides their own present voice: those of officials, parents, colleagues, passers-by, figures made up for the occasion, and their own earlier or hypothetical or interior selves. These voices may be echoed, answered, or mocked, presented as sources of information, or brought in to dramatize a story. In this chapter I consider a specific way of invoking another voice: the way participants talk about or talk as experts. For instance, a woman in one group refers to what 'they say':

```
I think we have to be awfully careful about these
short term things . when they say we've suddenly got
to stop using everything.
```

I will come back to the context later; what is important here is that she both refers to an authority and questions it. In this chapter I will consider ways participants in focus groups talk *about* experts – the 'they' here – as indefinite, interrelated, inconclusive, and interested. Then I will consider ways in which participants talk *as* experts, by talking to experts they trust, seeing for themselves, or sharing memories. Finally I will consider an extended passage in which participants argue over which experts to believe.

Though issues on which people invoke expertise – largely those concerning risks – are a small subset of what one might discuss in other situations (at a dinner, or talking to one's children, or in court), they are crucial to our project of understanding opinions. Life and death choices, and expert advice on these choices, are just the topics on which one can't let everyone have their own opinion. There can be too much at stake, not just in the dangers (of unhealthy food, side effects of medical treatments, or climate changes) but in the investments in identities (as caring, rational, or sceptical). I noted in Chapter 6 that participants in focus groups tend to be cautious about confronting other participants. But we find in discussions of risk and expertise (*not* in discussions of politics, morality, or even football), the most explicit and persistent disagreements anywhere in our data. I will argue that this is because such topics raise in acute form the on-going issue of entitlement to speak.

Understanding expertise

We could contrast two views of the role of expertise: one that sees experts as speaking for authorized knowledge, and one that sees them in terms of relationships and trust. The Royal Society in the UK and the National Academy of Sciences in the US, along with other national scientific institutions have responded to such issues as hazards of nuclear power plants by urging greater efforts to promote the Public Understanding of Science and, in particular, a greater understanding of statistics and probabilities (e.g., Royal Society of London 1985; 1992). They assume a deficit model in which the public simply lacks the required knowledge, or the understanding of scientific methods, that would enable them to assess risks rationally and understand expert assessments. Polls that ask the public to assess their trust in various categories of experts *in general* (e.g., Worcester 2000) make the same assumption that people take – or leave – knowledge or advice because of its source.

A contrasting view of these issues sees trust in expertise as a matter of a relationship between the advice giver and the advice receiver: it is contingent, open to questioning and revision, and dependent on a cultural sense of natural and social order (Douglas and Wildavsky 1982). The sociologist Ulrich Beck (1992; 1995) argues that we have entered a new phase of 'reflexive modernity' in which new risks and new awareness of risks have meant people do not just rely on experts but question and challenge them. For Beck, struggles over who is to be believed, and how knowledge is to be used, are as central to the period of reflexive modernity as struggles over working hours and pay were to an earlier period.

If one poses an arbitrarily chosen question to a motley panel of scientific experts – say, 'Is formaldehyde poisonous?' – one will be given fifteen answers from five scientists, all of them garnished with various qualifications – if, that is, the persons questioned are good at what they do; otherwise, two or three superficially unambiguous replies. This is neither by chance nor accident. It represents the state of science at the end of the twentieth century.   (Beck 1995: 119).

Public challenges to technocratic authority are for Beck an essential part of the democratic response to new risks.

Brian Wynne (1995; 1996a; 1996b; 2001) questions the simple opposition of expert and lay knowledges. People do not just trust experts or reject them; they draw on evaluations embedded in their own cultures and everyday practices: sheep farmers know about sheep, fishers know about fish, diabetics know about their own physiology. Lay criteria for judgment of science involve questions such as the following (summarized from Wynne 1996b: 38):

- Does it work?
- Do the claims pay attention to other knowledges?
- Is the form in which claims are made recognizable?
- Are the claims open to criticism?
- What are the institutional affiliations of the people making the claims?
- How is this case like others they have experienced?

We will see in the focus groups that people faced with expert advice do refer to situated evaluations like these, and to their relationships to the expert, rather than to general procedures of validation.

As we will see claims to expertise in the focus groups, we will also see claims to ignorance. Mike Michael (1996) has argued that lay 'ignorance' is also constructed for particular purposes, and in different forms. He draws on interviews about risks of radon gas in the home and identifies different ways interviewees refer to their ignorance: one can claim unfamiliarity with the area (I've never heard of radon), one can relate it to one's mental constitution (I never could do maths), one can treat it as division of labour (I can't do maths, but I know about ventilation), or one can take ignorance as a deliberate choice (I object to life being reduced to statistics). These different ways of formulating ignorance imply different relations between one's own knowledge and scientific expertise: one's knowledge is dominated by it, complementary to it, or superior to it. And for Michael, these formulations are resources for self-presentation, not just reflections of what one in fact is: 'The resources upon which people draw reflect and mediate their broader social identities: the sheep-farmers, the electricians, the secretary will have at their disposal a variety of representations of themselves as particular sorts of persons' (1996: 122). We will see in the focus-group discussions the ways that participants can offer different representations of themselves in relation to different issues and different conversational dynamics (compare the devices used on the Internet in Richardson 2003).

Wynne's and Michael's comments on the ways people talk about expertise and ignorance help us understand the curiously ambivalent treatment of experts of all sorts on talk shows and in other mass media genres. Livingstone and Lunt (1994: 93–132) show how experts as guests on one UK public affairs discussion programme (*Kilroy*) are placed in relation to everyday experience of those in the studio audience and the claims of people who have experienced a problem directly: 'The programme . . . invites the audience to ask whether the experts are credible, helpful to ordinary people, comprehensible, trustworthy, attractive, in tune with ordinary experience, and so forth. Broadly speaking, the viewers are thus invited to identify with the studio audience and to be critical of the experts' (Livingstone and Lunt 1994: 117). Their account of this scepticism sounds much like Wynne's summary of the criteria lay groups use to evaluate scientific claims – except that Wynne's sheep-farmers do not (perhaps fortunately) evaluate the attractiveness of the Ministry of Agriculture's scientists.

We can see the evaluation of experts and the assertion of identities by claiming expertise in discussions of a wide range of topics. We find neither scepticism nor blanket, universal scepticism; instead, we find complex interactions about just what can be offered as an expert opinion and when it can be offered.

Talking about experts

One approach to finding out how people respond to the claims of experts is to ask them, in a survey, to rate their levels of trust. For instance, surveys by the leading UK polling organization MORI show a gradual decline in trust in almost all institutions (Worcester 2000), and one study shows that the public trusts scientists in universities more than those in government or industry (Durant and Bauer 1997; May and Pitts 2000; see the methodological comments in Pidgeon et al. 2003). But these responses to set questions do not reflect the ways people talk about experts in interaction and the ways they use such talk to display opinions and construct identities. If I am asked if I trust doctors, in general, I might ask which ones? about what? and why am I telling you? If we look more closely at the ways people talk about experts, we find they are typically represented as indefinite, interrelated, inconclusive, and interested.

We can see all these features in the example with which I started the chapter. Alice is talking about a statement on a card urging that people act to reduce environmental damage. She refers to a programme she has seen on TV which claimed that 'environment-friendly' washing powders turn out to cause other environmental problems.

2.3.43
```
 1. Alice:   . . . because . if you're not careful you
             get short term research which says oh this
             is a marvellous new invention it's gonna .
             solve the world's problems
 2. Mod:     right
 3. Alice:   six months later they do some more
             research and say ((faster)) that was the
             worst thing we could possibly do because
             that was worse than what we were doing
             before
 4. Mod:     okay so
 5. Alice:   as we learn more they often find that the
             research is very limited . and only proved
             the point they were trying to make
 6. Mod:     right
 7. Alice:   > advertising being very cynical
             advertising <
 8. Mod:     yeah?
 9. Alice:   or: quite simply because they only did
             some research or not /
10. Mod:                             / right . right
11. Alice:   a wide enough scope of research to
             actually cover every eventuality
```

```
12. Mod:      right . so does that mean we don't . do
              anything / (until the research is done)
13. Alice:              / no but I think we have to be
              awfully careful about these . short term
              things when they say we've suddenly got to
              stop using everything
14. Mod:      right right
15. Alice:    it's like the (report) when they said cot
              . cot deaths were caused by uh mattresses
16. Andrea:   that's right
17. Alice:    and then suddenly they say /
18.                                      /((others
              overlap))
19. Alice:    no it was actually down to people who
              smoke so what if ( xxx ) baby has a cot
              death
```

Indefinite: 'they say'

References in focus groups to expert authority are both vague and flexible, the opposite of academic references intended to trace all claims to named and accredited sources. In the last example, 'they' are represented with hypothetical reported speech (see Ch. 7): 'oh this is a marvellous new invention' (1). The alternative view (3) is apparently put by the same 'they'. And in 13 'they' are the sum of all expert advice: 'they say we've got to stop using everything'. Such vague reference is common in other groups (as we will see in later examples) and is seldom challenged.

Interrelated: 'it's like'

Not only are experts generalized; expert advice on one issue may be evaluated in terms of the effectiveness or relevance of past advice on another issue. In turn 15 Alice says, of research on phosphate pollution,

```
it's like the (report) when they said cot . cot
deaths were caused by uh mattresses
```

From the point of view of the experts, of course, the issue of phosphates is nothing at all like the issue of cot deaths. But there is, as Brian Wynne has pointed out, an 'overspill' from one case to another, in this case, from past failures to report releases of radioactivity to present predictions on radiation from Chernobyl (1996a: 38), in Alice's case, from a change of advice on cot death to possible changes of advice on other issues. One issue that shows this tendency to overspill is the BSE epidemic that was an issue during our focus groups in Britain in the 1990s. We did not ask our participants directly about BSE, but the issue came up all the time, in discussing mangetouts, or global warming, or chemical pollution. And it could overspill to other issues, as participants paralleled risks of BSE with smoking, vaccination, or salmonella in eggs (for a more complex view of this overspill, see Petts et al. 2001).

Inconclusive: 'Who do you believe?'

Alice says 'I think we have to be awfully careful about these . short-term things when they say . . .' (13). Experts can also be seen to be divided, and any one case inconclusive on grounds of expertise alone (see Dunwoody and Griffin 1993: 28). These divisions are nearly always presented as irresolvable polar opposites: on the one hand and on the other hand, one day and then the next day. The advice is also put in extreme terms ('stop using everything'), a kind of formulation speakers typically used in anticipation of disputes (Pomerantz 1986), but here attributed to the 'they' as a vague and impossible injunction. And there seems to be no need for speakers to account for the differences on a rational basis, in terms of frameworks, perspectives, or methods (epidemiologists vs. physiologists, field vs. laboratory studies, different statistical methods); all these aspects of different approaches are left in a black box. We will see the conflict of experts in a later example.

Interested: 'who's paid for that?'

These differences between experts are never explained in terms of different approaches or even of different institutional frameworks; where participants are forced to account for them, they do so in terms of immediate interests. Alice suggests that the researchers for environmentally friendly products 'only proved the point they were trying to make' (5), did research only for their advertising (7), or the research was limited in scope (11). Participants in other groups also trace the problem, nearly always, to money: 'well I always think well who's paid for that' (2.1.19). Often such an assertion serves

as a commonplace that closes the topic, as we will see in a later
example.

When do participants talk about experts?

Let's look in more detail at one passage with the kinds of commonplaces I have been discussing (indefinite, interrelated, inconclusive,
interested), to see *how* and *when* a participant invokes them, in
relation to the moderator's questioning.

```
1.4.2.24
 1. Mod:    ok . so so this is um . what shall I call
            it . um (2) I'll call it evidence alright
            . so how do we know whether things and at
            the moment we we don't have knowledge .
            ((slowly, writing)) no knowledge . yeah?
 2. Barry:  yeah
 3. Mod:    a::nd . that is because the what the news
            media waits till something happens
 4. Barry:  well if you get one just for argument's
            sake if you get one professor in
            Manchester University . he'll say that
            won't affect us . and yet you'll get
            another one . say . at the other end of
            the country . say Birmingham or London .
            and he'll say . well that's bad for you
 5. Mod:    right
 6. Barry:  so I mean . they must they must know .
            themselves . they must you know what I
            mean?
 7. Mod:    so do you do you think when when one
            professor will say one thing another
            professor will say the other
            thing=
 8. Barry:      =well who do you believe?
 9. Mod:    well . who would you believe?
10. Barry:  well you got two totally opposed different
            things
11. Mod:    yeah
12. Barry:  so you've got to take a choice then of
            what you think
13. Mod:    yeah yeah
14.         ((two people talking at once))/
15. Mod:                              /why why why
            would these experts be camouflaging
```

The way Barry invokes experts is similar to many passages in other groups, in that he seems to be responding to a challenge, generalizing, calling on other participants, and offering an opening to shift the floor to someone else.

Responding to a challenge: dispreferred turns. Barry begins with *well*, a marker that he is presenting a dispreferred turn, not a direct answer to the question and not agreement with the statement

```
well if you get one just for argument's sake
```

The moderator has formulated the group's explanation of why the news media doesn't tell us about the environment: he has played their view back to them, in his own words. The 'well' of line 4 suggests a qualification. In terms of our larger questions about scientific expertise, it suggests that the participants give such responses when they are pressed, challenged, required to comment on other people's priorities or justify their own, or account for their lack of information.

Generalizing: pronouns and tense. Barry attributes the view to a generic *you*.

```
well if you get one just for argument's sake if you
get one
```

The 'you' poses a general, repeated event: all these statements are in the present tense. This is generalization at the level of commonplaces and proverbs, as in 'If at first you don't succeed, try try again.' Barry is expressing, not a technical disagreement or a bias on a particular issue, but a general tendency of authorities to disagree.

Interacting: questions. Note the difference between lines 8 and 9.

```
well who do you believe
well who would you believe
```

The first question is rhetorical, but the moderator turns it back on Barry as a real question. (A moderator, like a psychiatrist, is trained to answer a question with another question.) The function of the rhetorical question seems to be to present the statement as inviting agreement, involving the other participants (even though they are not speaking in this passage). This suggests that these statements about contradictory experts are presented as part of a shared common sense about such experts.

Shifting: so. Barry begins turn 6 with 'so'. Like the other features I have been discussing, *so* can have many uses – it can suggest logical causation, or sequence, or a conclusion (Schiffrin 1987). In these transcripts, it often marks a summary or a shift of topic, especially when the moderator uses it (see Chapter 5). Barry uses this 'so' with several other indications of finality: 'I mean', and repetition, and the question. One interpretation is that he has already made a potentially final remark, but is prodded to go on by the moderator's 'right' (5). The moderator himself uses *so* here (7). This echoes Barry's *so*, but can be heard as asking for a conclusion, a causal link. Finally in turn 12, Barry uses *so* again. I interpret this as suggesting that Barry is shifting from example to summary, and signals that others may take the floor, but the moderator intervenes to push him further, to make him comment on how he responds to this disagreement as a problem.

Repeating. Barry repeats his insistence that one must take one's own choice (10/12). Tannen (1989) suggests one function of such repetition is in bounding an episode of talk. Here the problem is that the moderator breaks the usual pattern and doesn't offer the supportive agreement; the most he usually gives is a 'yeah' or 'okay' as a continuer. In terms of our larger questions, this suggests that Barry expects the account of expert disagreement to be accepted and acceptable. When it is not, he recycles his previous turn.

To summarize the examples so far: experts' reported testimony may be taken up as common knowledge, or rejected as impractical, unworldly, out of touch, or interested. They may be quoted as authorities, but that is only one way they are used; they can also be invoked to close off a topic, link topics, ironicize a stance, present a dilemma, draw in other participants, or move the discussion on to other, more resolvable topics.

Talking as experts

The experts that are relevant in talk are not necessarily just doctors, scientists, or officials. Participants in group discussions routinely offer themselves and others as having expertise that is relevant to a particular topic at this moment. The difference between these claims to expertise and those of scientists and professionals is that the professional identities are permanent and externally certified, while the identities offered in conversation are provisional (other participants can take them up or not) and multiple (the same person can take on different identities in different parts of the conversation).

The flexibility of identities in conversation has been pointed out by various discourse analysts and conversation analysts, such as ten Have (1991) looking at a doctor's shifts of role, Malone (1997) looking at shifting footing in a group of graduate students, and Holmes, Stubbe, and Vine looking at small talk and work talk between colleagues (Holmes et al. 1999; Holmes 2000). Antaki, Condor, and Levine (1996) using conversational data from the London-Lund Corpus, show how the same participant (a medical student practising in a hospital) can take on contrasting roles as expert or novice at different points in the conversation; what matters, they say, is how other participants draw on the offered identities. Here I will consider passages that show how participants present provisional identities on the basis of what they have (1) heard from other experts, (2) seen for themselves, or (3) remembered as a group. I will argue that there is a complex interplay between different kinds of self-presentation – as informed or sceptical, involved or detached, having special knowledge or being like everyone else.

Talking to experts

We have seen that references to scientific experts, media, and government tend to be general: 'they say'. On the other hand, local professionals with whom one has face-to-face, informal contact may be invoked as sources of practical, hands-on knowledge. For instance, in this discussion of restrictions on the consumption of meat after BSE was discovered, Alan draws on the authority of a meat inspector, someone we might otherwise expect to be grouped with the discredited experts.

```
3.5.2.40
1. Mod:   OK . OK . Alan . Alan
2. Adam:  /I want to come back in here
3. M:     /you should have the choice=
4. M:                              = /(xxx)
5. Adam:                            /I had a
          conversation two or three weeks ago with a
```

```
        chap that is a meat inspector and we had a
        long in-depth chat and he said . the
        majority of cases of people having been
        made ill from meat is due to poor cooking .
        people that have it medium rare . and he
        says it causes . is it E coli?
6. Ben:  yeah . but it doesn't cause BSE . cooking
        ((laughs))
7. Adam: no . not BSE but because they get ill off
        beef . it causes scu/( xxx )
8. Ben:                      /well it's like the
        curry argument isn't it . you go for a
        curry and you're violently ill that night .
        it's the Indian curry house . it isn't the
        eighteen pints of lager you had earlier .
        it's the curry house .
9.       ((laughter))
```

Why is this meat inspector treated as an authority worth considering, when this same group mocks scientists and government officials? Adam talked to him, and in reporting this talk, not available to others, claims entitlement to speak in this conversation. The report is in his own voice, not that of the meat inspector; he pauses to check 'is it E coli?', separating himself, as someone who isn't quite sure of the technical term, from the authority. Ben does not challenge this entitlement (6), the claim that Adam knows something the rest don't, but he contributes his own bit of technical knowledge (prions, the infective agent of BSE, are not killed by cooking). Adam begins to acknowledge this distinction and restate his point (7). Ben interrupts him to present an analogy, 'it's like' (8). The analogy seems to raise questions about any account of causes, since people, like the drinker going for a curry, are biased in their use of accounts: they believe what suits them. This can be heard as supporting Adam's, and the meat inspector's, point that there is more danger posed by the familiar problem of undercooking, the fault of the consumer, than by the new and mysterious threat of BSE/CJD.

Such local experts are not usually treated as self-interested or contradictory; they are granted their authority in their domain (for a study of similar claims to expertise in an Internet news group, see Richardson 2001). A source need not be a professional to be invoked in this way; it could be a resident of an affected place, a parent or coach of an affected child, an official at a local plant, a surfer against sewage. This kind of interchange reconstructs a basis for authority based on experts one can know, talk to, and perhaps discount.

Seeing for oneself

Deference to local experts can be used to display that one is well informed and concerned. But when one is justifying personal decisions about eating or other everyday practices, deference to distant experts can be taken by others as a gullible openness to 'the scares'. In Example 3.7.2.50, Donna contrasts this gullibility with her own experience, both as a gardener and as a tourist who has seen for herself the fields in which strawberries are grown.

```
3.7.2.50
1. Alan:    have you got have you got a problem with
            org actually I don't have a problem with
            org with . inorganic food I mean, I try
            and buy free range eggs and stuff/
2. Donna:                               /yeah I
            try to do my bi:t but
3. Alan:                                    /but
            that's a moral thing for animal but I have
            no problem with with chemically processed
            food and /this idea of radiated food and
4. Donna:              /no I have a problem with food .
            yeah I do . I do
5. Amy:     you can taste it . so different
6. Mod:     and uh
7. Donna:   I am complete um now . even more because
            well not I haven't been totally influenced
            by the scares but I mean . from a health
            point of view I have been very conscious
            of things like that
            /for those reasons
8. Amy:     /you can always taste it on the food as
            well
9. Donna:   I don't know whether I can taste it or not
            but I just feel conscious that . well I
            grew my own kind of strawberries and
            things like that over the summer and
            ((laughs)) it was like a rea:l strawberry
            /you know . you can tell the difference
            between the . you know
```

```
10. Alan:                    /it does taste different yeah
                        it does taste different
11. Mod:    if you're a gardener yeah
12. Donna:  the stuff you buy in Tesco's . Spanish
            strawberries that can I just say . that
            I've been I've seen those fields where
            they're grown ((laughs))and they're in a
            place called Huelva which is like .
            heavily polluted it's like the equivalent
            of Ellesmere Port
13.         ((laughter))
14. Donna:  and then there's a field in the middle .
            you know and . those sort of things are
            being . grown there and you know just
            mass-produced and put into Tesco you can
            get strawberries in . December you know
            and . things like that and I just think
            hang on a minute this is/
15. Alan:                              /but they're
            they're obviously imported from the
            southern hemisphere/
16. Mod:                      /why doesn't it why
            does it bother you /[Alan] about the
            chemicals
17. Donna:                /no no they're not . it's Spain
```

Participants present their own claims to expertise incrementally and as needed. Donna only offers her own experience as a gardener (9) after Alan has challenged the need for organic foods (3) and Amy has said that taste is the issue (5, 8), while Donna is saying the issue is one of health. Alan concedes the difference in taste (10), and the moderator picks up on Donna's characterization of herself as a gardener (11). She begins her account of seeing the Spanish fields with the kind of pre-request one finds before stories: 'can I just say' (12). Her presentation is in multiple parts that repeat her main point when there is no audible response from others: 'I've seen where they're grown . . . it's polluted . . . it's like Ellesmere Port . . . there's a field in the middle and these things are grown there . . . they are mass-produced and put into Tesco'. She then re-enacts in reported speech her thoughts: 'hang on a minute this is' (14). The use of reported speech suggests that the response, the incongruity of these fruits in this industrialized landscape, needs to be dramatized as well as asserted. That is why Alan's quibble about the off-season strawberries being from the southern hemisphere (15) matters here, and why she responds instantly to it (17), even though the moderator has referred Alan back to turn 3. She has made an issue – and a brief story – of her personal witnessing.

Collective memory

Claims based on talking to an expert and seeing for oneself are specific to one person. Claims based on memory can be shared with others. In this example, which follows directly on the example of the meat inspector, the moderator is trying to close the topic after the curry house and beer comment and the laughter that followed it.

```
3.5.2.41
 1. Mod:      OK . on that on that note / we gotta move
              on
 2. Len:                              / if there was
              no truth in it we wouldn't have big meat
              mountains would we that . carcasses full
              of you know big warehouses full of
              carcasses
 3. Ben:      give people the choice
 4. Len:      would we really (2)
 5. Mod:      OK . I mean /
 6. George:              /at the end of the day
              they're using every tiny morsel of meat
              you know . they don't throw anything away
              do they=
 7. Ben:                  =the old days a butcher's knife
              took it off the bone . if that couldn't
              get it off the bone / it was left
 8. Tom:                          /everything's ground down
              and used isn't it
 9. Ben:      it's blasted with high power water
              /( xxx )
10. Len:      /somebody said to me like . you always
              give a dog a bone and you don't see
              many mad dogs running around do you
              ((laughs))
11. Ben:      you haven't met mine
12. Mod:      there's a couple in here actually(walking
              around)
```

```
13. M:       you've met the dogs have you
14. Mod:     yeah
15. Ben:     we never used this . crap did we . if the
             butcher's knife wouldn't take it off the
             bone it was left on it/
16. Les:                           /that's right .
             that's right
17. Ben:                          /I used to get a
             bone . >I had German Shepherds< get a
             bone and you could make a meal out of
             what the butcher used to give you . um
             you know if you wanted to . um that's
             right now they're blasted off . the
             spinal cords /chopped up
18. Paul:                  /you go and buy a sheet of
             lamb ribs to make a lamb stew, you can't
             nowadays . you know
19. Ben:     right
20. Paul:    I can remember going off down to the
             butcher's shop
21. Ben:     yeah
22. Paul:    my mum sent me down for a sheet of ribs .
             pork ribs
23. Ben:     yeah
24. Paul:    and there was meat left on between the
             bones
25. Ben:     it's blasted off
```

What unifies this is not a set of positions on BSE, but a style of interaction in which all participants join in to show that the memory is
shared. Each picks up some aspect of the last turn and develops it:
'they're using every tiny morsel of meat' (6), followed by 'the old
days . . . it was left' (7), and 'everything's ground down' (8), and
so on. This joint effort contrasts with the kind of personal expertise offered by the meat inspector or the tourist seeing for herself in
Spain; here the proof that these methods are used is the way the others join in (six of the eight participants). The form of each utterance,
as well as its content, assumes agreement, with lots of tag questions:
'would we' (2, 4), 'do they' (6), 'isn't it' (8). They agree, but what
exactly they are agreeing to is left fluid and ambiguous. They are
not asked to agree on an issue, but to share a memory (Middleton
and Edwards 1990).

   Any of these turns could be quoted in a report on this group to
give an individual opinion on BSE: 'give people the choice', or 'we

never used this crap before'. Such a quotation would be misleading; as the discussion develops, the same participant might seem to take different positions. It is Len who reopens the topic (2) when the moderator has closed it, so he might be taken as insisting on the seriousness of the issue after Ben's joke. But he also makes the joke in (10) about mad dogs, not meant as a serious argument, but another shift of key that defuses conflict. Ben says 'give people the choice', but in (15) he joins in with accounts of the dangers of modern methods of stripping bones. It's Ben who shifts the topic from methods of stripping meat to a contrast of now and 'the old days' (7). These recollections are not presented as opinions, as detachable statements on issues; they are part of an on-going patter.

Talking to someone, seeing for oneself, and sharing memories all seem to be persuasive ways of claiming some special right to speak on a topic. In these short examples we can see only that these claims are offered and, at least for one turn, accepted in some way. To see how the interaction develops, and how these claims for oneself intersect with other attributions of expertise, we need to look at a longer stretch of interaction.

Challenging claims

In the example that follows, two participants develop, collaboratively, a kind of shared, commonsense agreement. Then their view is challenged directly, and the group works out opposing positions without resolving them. The final positions are not there in their initial contributions but are developed in interaction, as they assess the various kinds of expertise put in play.

```
3.4.2.42
1. Mod:        could I go back to the issue about the
               media influence . um on the one hand
               you're saying that in the case of BSE it
               had enormous influence and I think
               [Andrew] was saying it was a bad
               influence . but do people do you feel
               like you personally were influenced say
               in the BSE case
2. Andrew:     yeah
3. Mod:        or in global warming or indeed that
               you're influenced by . what the media
               tells you
```

 4. Andrew: well to me to me the BSE scare was just
               another one in a long run of you know .
               what with <u>eggs</u> and all sorts of
 5. Jeff: yeah eggs chickens
 6. M: (xxx) that's what I've seen
 7. Andrew: in the end well I <u>lis</u>tened to what had
               to be said and read it in the papers as
               <u>well</u> and then decided that . you know .
               what is it what did somebody say
               there's more chance of winning the
               lottery a dozen <u>times</u> in your life than
               having something than getting BSE
 8. Jeff: I mean when you think about it like
               smoking you have the choice/
 9. Andrew: /yeah I
               know/
10. Jeff: /this latest
               thing they've come in about selling
               beef on the bone
11. Andrew: yeah <u>oh</u> well yeah
12. Jeff: which they say <u>real</u>ly isn't legal what
               they've done
13. Andrew: yeah
14. Jeff: it hasn't been through the Commons .
               /eh
15. Andrew: /yeah
16. Patrick: it's . it's a knee-jerk reaction
17. Michael: but don't you <u>think</u> there's something
               wrong they won't let you d<u>o</u> that . or
               they wouldn't <u>do</u> that
18. Jeff: (1) <u>may</u>be . I mean they come up
               /possibly
19. Michael: /perhaps it was . /no one
20. Andrew: /it was <u>tiny</u>
21. Jeff: here again the <u>sci</u>entists . the
               <u>sci</u>entists are sat in the little .
               ivory towers deciding . they're on 30
               40 50 thousand a year . and they've got
               to come up with something . if they
               don't come up with anything what the
               bloody hell is <u>he</u> doing all this time
               sat in there
22. Michael: /if you
23. Jeff: /well <u>may</u>be we'll have to do more tests
24. Michael: but if you had young children . don't
               you think you've to look after . <u>them</u>
               as well?

```
25. Jim:       you've got to be /realistic
26. Michael:                    /you you got to think
               like you know I'm not going to feed my
               children hamburgers
27. Jim:       no well
28. Michael:   in case there is a chance that they're
               gonna be getting BSE
29.            ((lots of over talking))
```

I will focus on three issues: the ways participants present themselves as rational, the challenge to this rationality, and the response to this challenge.

Thinking rationally

The moderator puts the participants in an awkward position; if they admit media influence, they could show themselves to be gullible, while if they deny it, they could show themselves to be ignorant. Andrew's 'well' (4) signals a dispreferred turn, one that rejects both alternatives. Instead, he presents himself as someone who listens and decides. He does this in a rather complex way. First he categorizes the BSE issue as 'just another one in a long run of you know', and two other participants join in to confirm this categorization. When he does state his opinion, he gives an extreme case 'there's more chance of winning the lottery a dozen times in your life . . .' This is one version of the reasonable person. Michael offers a different version in (24) based on responsibility for others.

Challenging rationality

Andrew has attributed his formulation to 'what did somebody say'. Jeff also refers to experts in general form: 'this latest thing they've come in with' (10). Not only is the 'they' often left undefined, its apparent referent can shift without that causing any problems for other participants. Jeff first refers to 'they' as the government, which is responsible for 'this latest thing'. But in (12), 'they' can also be the legal experts or campaigners who question the legality of this process. Michael does not try to disentangle this, but picks up 'they' (17) as a generalized authority that lets you do things or does things itself. In response, after a pause, Jeff begins to say 'they come up' (18), and later says it is 'the scientists' (21) who come up with or don't come up with findings. Then Jeff uses reported speech to attribute a view of these scientists to their employers (the reported speech signalled by 'what the bloody hell' as much as by anything else). Turn 23 is also in reported speech, and the 'we' can be read as the scientists talking back.

In the view Jeff is dramatizing here, the definitive expert advice is always postponed. Each of the uses of *they* seems to be anaphoric, to link back cohesively to previous references, and yet they are not necessarily referring to the same thing. What comes across from this slippage is the sense that these experts are 'them', not 'us'. In Jeff's description, they are 'sat' (science is non-physical, relaxed work) 'in the little ivory towers' (science is removed from the real world), and they are 'deciding' something (they are regulators as well as researchers), 'they're on 30 40 50 thousand a year' (about twice or three times what Jeff probably makes), and 'they've got to come up with something' (this life is only possible if the researchers find something dangerous). Like the commonplace 'who's paid for that', this implicit explanation in terms of immediate interests puts all claims, expert and lay, on the same level.

Responding to the challenge

Why is there the overlapping talk at (29), so much that it could not even be transcribed? It may help to go back to the one second of silence before Jeff's turn 18. He has been challenged directly and in a face-threatening way that is rare for focus groups. But the challenge is not unmitigated. Michael has phrased it as a rhetorical question 'but don't you think there's something wrong'. He then puts the question as 'but if you had young children'. This puts it as a hypothetical case, instead of claiming special status for those who actually have young children. Then he uses direct reported thought to dramatize this view:

```
you you got to think like you know I'm not going to
feed my children hamburgers
```

It is this challenge that leads to the overlapping talk. This could be heard, not just as another way of thinking of risk, but as a kind of accusation, that those who challenge the experts are not properly concerned with dangers to children.

The disagreement in turns 17–18 seems clear enough. But as we have seen in other passages, there are many possible views being offered here, with different kinds of authority. What participants can say depends on the opportunities they are given in the flow of talk; what they are taken as saying depends on what the next participant says, or how the moderator formulates it. There is no one source of authority that will settle the matter.

Experts and entitlement

It seems to be characteristic of these discussions that such risk issues cannot be settled permanently and unanimously by anything anyone says. They can invoke experts, but experts are open to challenge just for being experts, for being cut off from common experience, disagreeing, or serving their own interests. It might be more productive to think of the arguments offered as claims to entitlement, rather like the claims to the floor made when participants tell stories. Others fall silent when someone has something relevant to offer that only they can offer, from their own conversation, experience, or memory. But participants always acknowledge or evaluate these claims, taking them provisionally, moment to moment. The evaluations are treated as merely individual, or as shared by the whole group. As soon as the speaker raises issues of general opinion, he or she is open to interruption.

So how will these people take the claims of scientists? Experts can come across as participants who do not allow their claims to be evaluated, who expect their opinions to finish the matter, regardless of their practical experience, the placement of their claim in the talk, their timing, or their relation to the group. It may be this communicative demand, as much as any epistemological privilege, that is being resisted in the widespread scepticism about experts shown in surveys.

Seeing expertise as an entitlement to speak in a particular context has implications for researchers' categorization of participants. These studies have often taken identities as given: sheep-farmer, local resident, apprentice in a plant, mother. But here we see participants offering identities different from those they are assigned in the research methodology: publicist speaking as a gardener, unemployed man evaluating professors, shop steward voicing a meat inspector, bike dealer speaking as a hypothetical father. In talk, they are what they claim to be and are taken to be at the moment, on the basis of their self-presentation to these people. As we have seen in other chapters, opinions do not follow from identities but are part of the interactional construction of identities.

We see in this chapter, and in many other studies, a broad scepticism of institutional, mediated, distant claims to knowledge. The 'they' that is treated so dismissively is a voice participants hear through the media and hear as one voice. We might expect from their openness to the claims of participants in the focus group that they would withdraw into a smaller world in which they trusted only the local experts with whom they share lived experience. But that is not the case, because their response to expertise is not a matter of simple alienation from authority, it is a matter of looking for appropriate conversational entitlement to make a claim here and now. And as we will see in the next chapter, the voices they hear in broadcasting can be intertwined in complex ways with their lived experience.

9

Radio phone-ins: mediated sociable argument

The discussions that I have been analysing in Chapters 5–8 took place upstairs in a pub, in a hotel conference centre, or in a rented living room. However powerful the utterance of a participant in a focus group, it stays in that room. Opinions that reach out beyond the immediate setting have to be mediated in some way. And the media are full of opinions. Niklas Luhmann notes, in his lectures on media,

> A considerable part of the material for press, radio, and television comes about because the media are reflected in themselves and they treat this in turn as an event. People might be asked for their opinions, or they might impose them. But these are always events which would not take place at all were there no mass media.   (Luhmann 2000)

Of course most of these opinions are from public figures, as in the interviews I referred to in Chapter 2. But there are also events in which individual members of the public call or are called on to give their opinions – polls, talk shows, formal debates, letters to the editor, Internet discussion lists. In this chapter I focus on sociable argument in phone-ins; in the next I look at vox pops in terms of categorization and constitution of a category of 'public opinion.'

Radio programmes that involve listeners phoning a host and talking live on air, often interspersed with talk from the host, studio interviews, or music, are a staple of many US stations, and a smaller, though symbolically important, part of UK radio output. Three aspects of phone-ins need to be explained in any analysis:

1) Phone-ins are entertaining. Even I, who avoid them when I am listening to the radio for pleasure rather than for research, must admit to a fascination with the voices, the unpredictable turns, and the tensions with the host.

2) Phone-ins are hard to do. In almost any broadcast one hears various glitches, with no caller on the line, or the wrong caller, or callers who go into bizarre private monologues or apparently irrelevant associations. Clearly it takes work to make a series of calls from different places fit together.

3) Phone-ins make sense. Despite the diversity of voices and difficulties of production, the broadcast comes across, in real time, as a single multi-stranded cord of opinion. They make sense because the audience and producers share a sense of what is going on here. I come to this shared sense of what opinions are in the last section of this chapter.

I will argue that phone-ins make sense if we see in them a kind of sociable argument. As Schiffrin defines it (in a passage quoted in Chapter 6), sociable argument is where 'speakers repeatedly disagree, remain nonaligned with each other, and compete with each other for interactional goods. Yet they do so in a nonserious way, and in ways which actually display their solidarity and protect their intimacy' (Schiffrin 1984: 311). The usefulness of Schiffrin's suggestion is that it focuses our attention on how stances are taken and developed within a set of conventions that allow participants to bring out arguments, contain them, share them, and give them meaning (without, as we will see, persuading anyone). And it focuses our attention on the pleasure in the interaction for its own sake.

The definition of sociable argument would not seem to include anonymous strangers, such as those in the audience of a phone-in. In this chapter, I will argue that listeners to phone-ins can have a kind of para-social interaction (Horton and Wohl 1956) with the host and callers, rather than just an audience/performer relation. The term 'para-social' was used by Horton and Wohl to describe the audience's involvement with broadcast personae, the characters of various programmes. This involvement is not the simplistic relation imagined by critics of broadcasting, who claim that viewers of soap operas and talk shows confuse television fiction with reality. Instead, it is a genuinely social involvement that allows listeners to explore new roles, complement their existing roles, and play these roles back into their everyday lives (Handelsman 2002).

Two aspects of broadcast form make this para-social interaction possible. One is the regularity of the relationship, the recurrence of the broadcast at predictable intervals in the listener's life, what

Scannell calls the *dailiness* of broadcasting (1996: 149). The involvement works because the broadcast persona is set up to leave room for the audience member; as one commentary on Horton and Wohl puts it:

The persona creates the illusion or intimation of intimacy with great care, since the relationship is one-sided in the extreme. He or she does this by maintaining patter, a flow of small talk, giving the impression that he or she is responding to, and sustaining, the input of an invisible interlocutor – for example, by continually referring to and addressing the home audience as a party to the telecast.   (Handelsman 2002: 139–40)

The concept of para-social interaction applies particularly well to phone-ins, which come at regular times, usually when listeners will be alone, and allow listeners in on one-to-one conversations in which the callers are repeatedly referred to as typical members of the audience. In the way listeners at home eavesdrop, a phone-in is more intimate than a talk show, which takes place entirely within the bounds of the studio. I will suggest that the style of phone-in argument and the enjoyment of it (for those who do enjoy such arguments) are more like the style and enjoyment one finds in a familiar dinner-table rant than in, say, a televised election debate or even a soap opera. For one thing, there is the pleasure of individual, placeable voices.

I noted in Chapter 2 the rich literature on the structure of broadcast political interviews. The application of conversation analysis that is most relevant here is Ian Hutchby's book-length study of a London phone-in programme (1996), which provides the basis for much of my analysis in this chapter. But Hutchby focuses on what he calls 'confrontation talk', and a similar approach to 'deliberate dispute' is taken by Karen Adams (1999) and by Joanna Thornborrow's (2002) chapter on phone-in questions and answers. Thornborrow shows clearly the asymmetry of host and caller: hosts can question callers without themselves being questioned, try out possible stances without taking a stance themselves, formulate what the caller has said, challenge the caller, and in the last resort, hang up. Callers can do none of this. My focus is different from that of Hutchby or Thornborrow; I grant that confrontation is going on, but I will argue that it is not all that is going on. Host and callers (and producers and listeners) have to cooperate to produce a discussion of the kind recognizable as a phone-in.

When I look at phone-ins as sociable arguments, and as para-social interactions, I am arguing that they may be more like everyday face-to-face interactions than we might, at first hearing, think they are. To make this argument, I will be looking at some of the same features we have already analysed in focus groups: frames, encounters, topic shifts, disagreements, the use of reported speech and commonplaces. Then I will look at the ways participants talk about opinion, using different definitions but always presenting opinion as out there, already happening in the world of the listener.

Phone-ins

I have collected instances of radio phone-ins in the UK and US to show a wide range within the genre: host as facilitator vs. host as provocateur, local vs. national audiences, public service vs. commercial broadcasters, open topic vs. single topic, and from short (half an hour once a week) to long (three hours daily). As we will see, the examples also show a range of different host personalities. My examples have in common these features:

- the host speaks to the caller on the phone one-to-one
- guests are allowed multiple turns
- topics are at least nominally focused on public issues, though the scope and nature of these issues is open to negotatiation

These features do not constitute a definition of the genre (which in some variations can include a third party to the conversation, only single turns per caller (Thornborrow 2002), and personal issues). But they are typical of a central core of such programmes and help distinguish this genre from others, such as advice programmes or games.

We might group my examples under the following headings (details in the list of data at the beginning of the book):

- *Any Answers* (and its summer-schedule replacement *Straw Poll*) are broadcast on BBC4, a national public service station; they are outgrowths of *Any Questions*, a series that has been running on the BBC since 1948, in which a carefully balanced panel of four public figures is sent to a location somewhere in Britain (a village hall, a local theatre, a school auditorium) and answers questions posed by the audience for forty-five minutes. *Any Answers*, broadcast the next day, is a half-hour studio programme presenting comments from the listening audience on the previous day's broadcast, following up about half a dozen of the topics discussed by the panel members. These comments used to be written; they may now be phoned in or sent by e-mail. Jonathan Dimbleby, a distinguished British broadcaster (perhaps best known for a famous interview with Prince Charles), usually moderates both *Any Questions* and *Any Answers*.

- BBC Radio Lancashire and BBC Radio Wales both have an hour-long *Lunch-time phone-in*, as do many of the BBC local radio stations. In contrast to the US, where local radio came before national networks, local radio began in the UK only in 1967 and did not really develop its full range until the 1980s; these programmes stress both their local base (otherwise they would duplicate the national BBC stations) and their public service remit (otherwise they would duplicate the local commercial stations). Programmes typically have some local experts to kick off an announced topic ('Are demonstrations effective?', 'Should the liquor licensing laws be changed?') and then invite comments from listeners.

- *Pete Price* on Magic 999 is an example of a long-running late-night phone-in on local commercial radio. The host and his opinions and personality are much more central in this format than in that of the BBC local radio phone-ins, the conversations are more relaxed, the topics are open to whatever might interest the listeners, and the programme is much longer than those on the BBC – four hours from 10 pm to 2 am four nights a week.

- My two examples of US radio phone-ins are intended as complete opposites. Sean Hannity is one of the right-wing commentators who dominate US radio and are influential in Republican party politics; his programme, syndicated from WABC in New York, plays at a large station in nearly every radio market in the US for three hours from 3 pm Eastern Time (1 pm Pacific Time, so it must not be live in all time zones). Peter Werbe is one of a tiny minority of self-described liberal commentators, and his show *Night Call* runs late on Sunday night on one terrestrial station, WRIF in Detroit. Both are available streaming live and archived on the Internet (which is why I can listen to them).

In analysing these programmes, I argue that callers collaborate in producing a smooth and apparently coherent sequence, and that this sequence makes sense as sociable argument (between host and caller or between callers) available for para-social interaction (between broadcast voices and listeners). I argue that opinion is used in the conversations in several contradictory ways, and that it serves as a resource in these discussions, a shared ground that allows for commonality between participants.

Collaborating

Modelling the encounter

In Chapter 1, I noted the puzzle of how it is that people confronted by a survey researcher or a vox pop interviewer know exactly what is wanted of them, what constitutes a usable opinion. This is not a puzzle with phone-ins, because the hosts always begin by modelling the kind of interaction they expect. In my collection of examples, there are two ways of starting a programme, with the host animating a number of possible responses to the topic without giving his or her own view, or voicing his or her own opinion in such an extreme form that it invites a response. Here is the opening of a BBC Radio Lancashire phone-in with Brett Davison:

BBCRL 26/2/03
BD: yes hello good afternoon . welcome to the midweek
    edition of the lunchtime phone-in with myself .
    Brett Davison . some people argue that travel
    broadens the mind . but is it right that a
    child's one chance at education . is disrupted .
    in order that parents can sun themselves on a
    Spanish beach . we want your views please oh one
    two five four . five eight three five eight three
    . eh tell us the decision . you've taken in the
    past . call and . and have your say is it right
    will it work . the fine system that is being uh
    talked about . all that and all your thoughts .
    please . you can text us . as ever on oh double

```
      seven eight six . two oh one . nine double five .
      > tell us if you ever played truant as well< .
      it is a big problem . eh across the UK . uh
      should parents be punished . if they encourage
      this . perhaps you don't think it's truancy . at
      all . uh would you take your child out of school
      . for a holiday . ((faster)) they do say travel .
      broadens the mind . I'm interested to hear your
      opinions please on this . the midweek edition of
      the lunchtime phone-in
```

This opening identifies the programme, identifies the issue, and identifies people who are entitled to have opinions on it. The programme is 'the' *Lunchtime Phone-in*. Scannell argues that 'dailiness' is the 'unifying structure' of radio and television broadcasting (Scannell 1996), and all these programmes refer frequently to their time slot, and to the way that slot (such as 'drive time' or 'late night') might fit into the listeners' daily schedule. The host introduces himself only by name, as somebody already known to listeners. The basic format for introducing the topic is the dramatization of a difference between two possible responses that could lead a listener to call. For instance Davison uses a commonplace ('travel broadens the mind') and an opposing commonplace ('a child's one chance at education'), and then gives a phone number. As he goes on, he gives two more possible openings for talk and gives the text number, then two more, as parent or truant or parent again, and then the opening commonplace again. Throughout we hear him animating other voices, shifting pace for the commonplaces, shifting pitch and volume as he suggests you might have played truant, imitating the emphatic objection of one who doesn't think such absence is truancy.

On *Night Call*, the invitation to call is given by the announcer (AN), which is followed by Peter Werbe launching into a topic:

Night Call 24/8/03
```
      ((phone bells ringing))
AN:   one oh one W R I F Detroit presents . Night Call
      . the rif's phone in talk show . with Peter Werbe
      . to express your opinion call three one three .
      two nine eight . W R I F . now . here's the host
      of Night Call . Peter Werbe
```

```
PW:   thank you very much . well well we uh what-
      survived the great blackout of two thousand three
      . a:nd I guess most of us have survived . so: big
      . right? that computer virus . some of you . when
      I talk to you I say ((faster)) you have . uh
      Internet access and you say . kinda guiltily . or
      almost shamefacedly . no: I'm I'm not . or I'm
      going to . I tell you . if you can stay off the
      Internet . do it . it is a theft of time and a
      theft of money
```

In contrast to Davison's rapid animation of many views on one topic, Werbe has a long introduction ranging over many topics; it is his personal tone and stance that holds them together. Then he comes to his invitation to call:

```
PW:   if if this was- and I'm surprised the British
      government has lasted- but if this was most
      European countries . these guys would be out of
      here . they would get a vote of no confidence .
      either because of their abject stupidity . or
      their blatant lies . so wh- what is it . you know
      you can call up at three one three . two nine
      eight . W R I F . and tell me . do you think
      these were blatant lies o:r- or just absolute
      stupidity . now real quickly and I'll get to your
      phone calls . we can talk about . u:m the gas
      prices . at a dollar eighty now we can talk about
      the the virus . and what effect it's had on your
      computers . um gay marriage . any reason not to
      allow it . and what a good reason is not because
      you don't like it or because you um you don't' um
      you know you don't like gays or . ((change to
      stupid voice)) did you ever think about what they
      do ((end stupid voice))and I mean stop thinking
      about it . that'll get you you know um good way .
      down the road
```

As he lists a range of possible issues on which people might call, he states opinions intended to be provocative (or having that effect). When he animates possible alternative views with reported speech ('did you ever think about what they do'), it is to display them as unacceptable. This aggressive stance on every possible issue might seem to close down discussion. But Werbe gets his callers, and it is by no means the case that they all agree with him. His aside as he elaborates ('real quickly and I'll get to your phone calls') reminds us that the calls, not his monologue, are the reason for the programme.

Both ways of generating opinions, Davison's on the BBC and Werbe's on WRIF, contrast with what we saw moderators doing in focus group introductions (Chapter 4). A moderator characterizes in general terms what the space of opinions is like: everyone has one, the moderator has none, all are welcome, all should be heard. Phone-in hosts instead animate specific stances to show that usable opinions are personal, they represent different voices and personalities, and they are opposed to some other opinion, of an imaginary caller or of the host.

Opening the encounter

The beginning of the phone call on a phone-in is an odd hybrid of what we expect of broadcast interviews (Clayman and Heritage 2002; Bell and van Leeuwen 1994) and what we expect of phone calls (Schegloff 1968; Hopper 1992; Sacks 1992). Thornborrow (2002) notes these opening turns are multifunctional, giving the caller's name and place, signalling the line is open, giving a summons and response, exchanging greetings, setting up the slot for a question from the caller. The calls are both sociable, affirming the informal and intimate relation of caller and host, and para-social, bringing listeners in.

The BBC local radio phone-ins have very similar brief introductions to each new speaker. Here Brett Davison sets aside an expert in the studio to introduce George. The expert has been presented in terms of her position in local government; George is presented only in terms of a geographical location. George takes the host's 'hello' as only a signal that the line is open; he does not respond to the greeting.

BBCRL: 26/2/03
```
BD: Viv just stay with us for a moment . Viv . Clark
    is head teacher of Brindle Gregson Lane Primary
    School . because George has called us in Burnley
    . hello George what would you like to say
G:  the reason I I rang up is because .
```

This minimal form of opening is the most common on all the BBC programmes; the caller is given a place, a greeting, and a cue, and launches immediately into naming an issue. We find a much more elaborate opening on the US programmes; on *Sean Hannity*, callers are always identified by first name and the regional affiliate on which they hear the programme, and the greetings may be followed with extensive talk about the place and any possible links between host and caller.

<u>Sean Hannity 9/9/03</u>

```
SH:  all this nonsense and all this talk about
     bringing Yassar Arafat back is just asinine . in
     my view . ah alright to the phones we go . we
     stay on Long Island our home base . Heather . is
     next Heather where on Long Island are you that's
     my home . town
H:   hi I'm out in Lyndenhurst
SH:  oh I used to be out there with you . my sister
     lived out there for a while too . you doin' all
     right out there?
H:   absolutely . me and my two-year-old listen to ya'
     all the time
SH:  uh . w- . thank you . I hope she understands
     everything I'm saying
H:   I'm tryin' to Hannitize her as best as I can
SH:  ((laughs)) that's terrific . I just ask my son
     all the time who's the President . and we li:ke
     Bush . right? right
H:   ((laughs)) that's what I tell her too
SH:  that's all ya gotta do- . it- it's simple at that
     age
H:   ((laughs)) oh yeah . if they'd only stay that way
     . two quick points and then I'll let you comment
     on them?
SH:  okay
H:   first thing with Schwarzeneggar .
```

Broadcast interviewers typically do not use receipts like 'oh', because they suggest that the interviewer (rather than the audience) is the recipient of this information (Greatbatch 1988). Here the host, not the listener, is the recipient. The reference to his sister establishes a shared identity based on place; in other calls the host might remember a visit to the caller's city, or the caller might mention a previous call. The host's question is the sort usually used with someone

one hasn't seen for a long time 'you doin' all right out there?' She
responds in a similarly playful and mock-intimate fashion. Before
she shifts to telling her opinion, she ends the introductory part of the
call with the sort of commonplace used between parents of young
children: 'if they'd only stay that way'. Hannity produces the sound
of local radio, even though (or because) he has the largest audience
of all these phone-ins, and broadcasts across many affiliates in four
time zones.

The one essential part of most of these introductions is that
the caller gives his or her location (it is also a feature of some
focus groups (Myers 2000c)). Place can be defined on several levels
(Lyndhurst, Long Island, in the WABC area, in the suburbs, New
York state, the East) (Schegloff 1972), but callers are never in a
quandary about what is meant when they are asked 'where are you?'.
When Jonathan Dimbleby has trouble connecting to a caller, almost
goes on to the next topic, and returns when the caller is finally con-
nected, the one bit of information he insists on before continuing is
place:

Any Answers 26/10/02
```
JD:  . um Martin Langley is there?
ML:  yes I'm here?
JD:  I'm told you're there
ML:  ((laughs))
JD:  um where are you because
ML:  yes can you hear me Jonathan
JD:  yes I can hear you well where are you
ML:  I'm in Idlewood
JD:  right . fire away
ML:  okay uh . Estelle Morris .
```

The location is apparently an essential part of the para-social interaction. With Sean Hannity, local references assure us of his personal
contact with every affiliate. For *Any Answers*, it is a way of demonstrating this to be a national programme, while on BBC Lancashire
Lunchtime Phone-in, the places show the audience to be identified
with the county. In all cases, the listing of a range of places is part
of breaking out of the studio and generating a sense of shared audi-
enceship (a feature Martin Montgomery noted of a British DJ in the
1970s (1985)). Opinion is scattered and needs to be placed like pins
on a map.

Keeping to topic

We saw in Chapter 5 that focus-group participants and moderator talked with a clear sense of marking the boundaries between one topic and another, but that within these markers the topics tended to shift. In phone-ins, too, it is easier to trace the ways participants mark their keeping, or not keeping, to topic than to name that topic (that issue will be taken up in a later section). In my collection of phone-ins, callers present themselves as responsible for staying on topic. Here a fire-fighter, Paul Totty, shifts from comments on his working conditions to repeat the question as Jonathan Dimbleby posed it to him:

Any Answers 26/10/02
```
PT:   . there is no premium whatsoever for my working
      those time periods and into the weekend . sorry
      but to go back to your question will we feel it's
      worth it . my God no . we don't want anyone to
      lose their life which is why we are actively
      seeking out the public . both in work places and
      in the street .
```

Some callers nominate multiple topics at the outset; we have seen a caller to Sean Hannity saying 'first thing with Schwarzenegger', implying there will be another topic, which she picks up many turns later. As in focus groups, the highly elliptical form for naming topics invites others to recognize a shared frame of reference ('Schwarzenegger', not 'the current campaign for recall of the Governor of California'). Other analysts have noted the kind of control the host has, to comment, interrupt, and formulate to constrain the caller's topic. I am focusing instead on the tact with which the host and callers together display the relevance of each new contribution.

The assumption of host and listeners is that the caller's contribution *is* relevant to the current topic, but the host, even a very patient host, may have to prompt callers to explain this relevance.

BBCRL 26/02/03
```
G:   I never played truant neither did my wife . or my
     children . and I have six
BD:  the point being .
G:   the point I'm making is this
```

Any Answers 26/10/02
```
ML:  so when you get a a a government department which
     . you know can't organize a proverbial in a
     brewery then the contrast is is ever more stark-
JD:  what conclusion do you draw from that
```

In these cases there is the implication that time is limited, and the caller does conclude quickly. More aggressive hosts may point to what they see as lapses from relevance as indicating the caller's evasiveness. In this exchange, Peter Werbe has said there is no connection between Iraq and the events of 9/11, the caller has made a response linking all terrorist groups, and Werbe then makes an assertion marked as a challenge, not information, by his saying 'you know that':

Night Call 24/8/03
```
PW:  the country that most solidly funds Hamas and
     Islamic Jihad and groups like that is United
     States' ally and you know that it's Saudi Arabia
C:   did you uh /
PW:  / well we'll leave that question and go on to
     another one go ahead
C:   well okay fine okay I agree . you oughta take on
     Saudi Arabia
```

When the first words of the caller's response are formed as a question, not a statement, Werbe comments on it (the *we* suggesting the listening audience as addressee) and ironically concedes the caller's right to change the topic (which only highlights the convention that the caller does not have the right to change the topic). It works; the caller comes back to the topic as just defined by Werbe, the identification of Saudi Arabia with terrorism.

The need to stick to a topic would seem to be another instance of the institutional constraints on discussion in phone-ins. But we see here that it is a collaboratively achieved constraint, not a rule. Hosts may bring callers back on topic, or refer indirectly to the need for relevance, or very rarely, challenge the relevance of what they are saying. But callers too work at demonstrating that they know the topic and they are staying on it, and both host and callers refer implicitly to the need to maintain order, not for them, but for an audience out there.

Displaying disagreement

As the hosts' introductions suggest, disagreement between callers
or between host and callers is the point of the phone-in; it is what
distinguishes this genre from other forms of interaction with listeners involving games, news, or advice. But disagreement is always
moderated; opposites never confront each other as on a talk show
(Hutchby 2001; Myers 2001). Hosts and callers have devices both
for emphasizing disagreement and for maintaining face.

   One of the distinguishing features of 'sociable argument' is
that participants diverge instead of seeking grounds for agreement
(Schiffrin 1984). That is certainly the case with phone-ins. Where the
caller and host agree, it is usually by virtue of their demonization of
some other; when they disagree, they seldom work out the grounds
of their disagreement but instead get more and more extreme in
their disagreement. Hutchby has described devices in this institutional forum for emphasizing disagreement, calling the process 'the
pursuit of controversy' (1996). There is, for example, the aggressive
use of formulations:

Night Call 24/8/03
C: yes Peter I'm I'm <u>real</u>ly dismayed at everything
      you say . I mean I disagree with you at virtually
      <u>ev</u>erything when it comes to politics /
PW: /**so you**
      think we should keep giving money to Afghanistan
      and Iraq when we uh we can't even take care of
      our own needs here

Hosts may also shift footing to present themselves as animators of
alternative views, in this case the host repeating to a fire-fighter the
view of the employers.

Any Answers 26/10/02
JD: **the point made a lot by the emplo<u>y</u>ers and the**
      local authorities . is that um your life isn't
      quite as <u>bad</u> as as as it's put about to be you
      have your four days <u>on</u> your four days off
PT: mm
JD: people can work at other jobs in between
PT: .hhh

```
JD:  and . a lot of the time in any case is sitting
     around in a fire station . I put I put it crudely
     but in order to make the point
PT:  well um . thank you for being so um . so um clear
     about it . um the time spent sitting around
     actually isn't spent sitting around .
```

Dimbleby attributes this criticism to other voices, and even apologizes for its bluntness, while the caller rephrases (it is not 'crude' but 'clear') and accepts the bald restatement of views as necessary to the debate.

While hosts and guests use various devices to emphasize disagreement, they also use the same kinds of mitigating devices that we saw used in focus groups in Chapter 6, the same devices we would expect in informal face-to-face conversation. In the first two, callers are responding to the host, the remaining examples to other callers.

- concessions
  ```
  sure . uh uh I take your point but we do feel
  that's scaremongering .
  ```
- hesitation and hedging
  ```
  I just I don't know I saw a little hypocrisy in
  your view
  ```
- stress on personal stance
  ```
  well I'm sorry for me I I couldn't possibly
  trust somebody who uh takes a twelve year old
  dossier from . a student . doctors it a little .
  and presents it
  ```
- agreement followed by disagreement:
  ```
  hello . uh . just a comment . I agree with what
  the education's saying . but . they're at fault
  as well
  ```
- apologies
  ```
  I am ((small laugh)) sorry to disagree with the
  last lady who obviously felt very strongly as
  well . but . ((the previous caller was audibly
  in tears over the resignation of a minister))
  ```

Attention to face seems to be a crucial part of broadcasting decorum, even when talking about a third party. Again this suggests sociable argument that includes the listeners in a para-social relation.

Closing the encounter

I have noted in the radio phone-in a tension between on the one hand the radio interview, with its overhearing audience and its need to fill time, within time, without interruption, in a coherent way (Clayman and Heritage 2002), and on the other hand the personal phone call, with the conventions of greeting and closing designed for open-ended sequential interaction between equal participants passing the time (Schegloff and Sacks 1973; Hopper 1992). This tension is apparent at the closing of calls, which on most of the programmes are so perfunctory that they would seem rude in other situations. Thornborrow, observing truncated closings in a BBC call-in, notes how they are 'designed to exclude the possibility of callers bringing up other "compelling things to say" [(Levinson 1983: 316)] which could cause delays in moving on to the next call' (2002: 84). For my argument, what is notable is not the cutting off, but the need to maintain sociability with, in nearly all cases, a repetition of the caller's name or a salutation. This is not for the benefit of the caller (as Bell and van Leeuwen (1994) suggest is the case with news interviews), since the caller almost never responds, but for the benefit of the audience, who hear the relationship as still civil.

The most frequent transition is just a thank you to one caller, and then a hello to the next, sometimes with the phone-in number repeated in between.

BBCRL 26/2/03
```
N:    now now where's the difference there's double
      standards here
BD:   Neil thanks very much for your call . uh Glyn .
      has called us
```

Where there is a good-bye, we do not usually hear the caller's response. The following example is an exception where the sound was not yet turned down:

Any Answers 26/10/02
```
      . but the government has put us in this position
JD:   Paul Totty thank you
PT:   [faded out] thank you
```

The BBC hosts scrupulously refrain from any evaluative comments at the ends of calls. Peter Werbe, ending the antagonistic call we saw

in the last section, allows himself some evaluative response before
moving on.

<u>Peter Werbe 24/8/03</u>
```
C:   I think you need to fix the infrastructure .
     overseas and the best the dividends we'll reap in
     ten or twenty years will outweigh the costs
PW:  chwhew . oka:y . thank you . 'preciate your call
     . any other thoughts on that?
```

The 'chwhew' sound here can be heard as a receipt indicating astonishment, and thus a kind of evaluation, but the host still closes the call and moves on, without taking his allotted closing turn to get in one more dig.

It is a notable feature of phone-ins that the arguments do not develop or lead to conclusions; nobody changes their mind. The lack of progress and lack of a goal is characteristic of sociable argument; Schiffrin notes, 'very few arguments ended with speakers realigned towards a previously disputed issue' (1984: 321). The one exception in my examples where the host did realign, persuaded of a caller's point, was unusual enough to be commented on. We have seen in earlier examples that Peter Werbe has been arguing in this programme against US aid to rebuild the infrastructure of Iraq or Afghanistan.

<u>Night Call 24/8/03</u>
```
PW:  hi this is Night Call you're on the air good
     evening
C:   hey Pete?
PW:  hi
C:   uh that that last call was really good . uh where
     you said that history doesn't start like six
     months ago like a lot of people think it does .
     and uh that's why I'm kinda surprised at your
     view on . uh sending aid to Afghanistan . because
     I agree that it shouldn't go to the corporations
     . you know . and end up back in Bush's pocket .
     but . if you remember in the 'eighties the United
     States and the Russians . we we destroyed that
     country
PW:  right
C:   and we owe them huge maybe not in aid but . maybe
     a form of reparations or something /
PW:                                      /y'know
```

```
C:   and the . the same argument could be made . uh in
     Iraq . with the sanctions
PW:  y'know that . that is an interesting way to pose
     it . uh . and it it . that does . hey can you
     imagine a talk show host admitting this . it
     leaves me a little confused .
```

The caller makes his point in a very indirect way, praising the host's comments to a previous caller, expressing surprise at the host's view, and mitigating that surprise ('I'm kinda surprised'). Later the caller and host go through a phone call closing routine, which the host cuts off:

```
C:   that's right
PW:  I will think about that
C:   okay tha-
PW:  thank you . I appreciate it for . uh . for
     bringing that up . so . there's the problem . I
     mean a:s our last caller posed it .
```

It is worth noting the rarity of 'I will think about that' as a response on a phone-in. It is rare because it suggests the possibility of a retreat to sort things out, a solution somewhere other than here and now talking to us. So he presents this new view as the basis for further calls: 'there's the problem'. Thinking things out for oneself is not what keeps a talk show moving forward; argument is.

In this section I have been looking at some of the details of the sequential structure of calls. The essential asymmetry in the form of phone-ins, noted by Hutchby and by Thornborrow, holds for my examples. But we can also see in them the collaborative production of this form, in which the hosts offer guests possible roles, guests signal that they are keeping to the topic, disagreements are both aggravated and mitigated, and closures link to an on-going discussion. The result is a kind of argument that confirms instead of threatening the roles and relationships of the participants, and that leaves intact the involvement of the overhearing audience.

Opinions

The definitions of the domain of opinion in the course of phone-in talk are to some extent contradictory, but they share a theme: opinion is already out there, in the everyday routines of listeners.

Thus the references to opinion provide the implicit opening to the engagement with the audience needed for para-social interaction. At the opening of each programme, the host treats opinion as something broken, carried by every listener, scattered across the city, the county, or the nation so that only the broadcast can reassemble it. But opinion can also be reified as an entity or quantity, for instance in polls, opinion not made by discussion but out there to be discussed. There is a third kind of opinion too, in the way participants rely on commonplaces ('education broadens the mind') that assume a shared experience or evaluation. So there is opinion we talk into being, opinion we talk about, and opinion we share without even thinking about it.

Talkable topics

As Hutchby (1996) notes, the topics of phone-ins are constructed as *issues*, things already talked about, refereed to with a definite article because they are given. We have seen this in the programme opening from Peter Werbe, when he refers to '*the* gas prices', '*the* virus', and 'gay marriage'. The givenness of topics is shown by the way guests refer to them in beginning their turns. The topic may be attributed to a previous speaker:

(BBCRL 26/2/03)
```
G:   the reason I I rang up is because . they're
     talking about fine the parents . for taking them
     on holidays
```

(Night Call 24/8/03)
```
C:   uh that that last call was really good . uh where
     you said that history doesn't start like six
     months ago like a lot of people think it does .
```

The caller's turn (after the host names them and gives a place) may begin with just a test that the line is open, a greeting, and the naming of a topic:

Any Answers 26/10/02
```
ML:  okay uh . Estelle Morris . her resignation
*  *
*
FP:  oh hello . this action . by the firemen
```

BBCRW 12/2/03
M: hi: afternoon Nicola . yes I'm going **on the
      fifteenth**

The woman who phoned Sean Hannity with 'two quick points'
names one after the opening small talk we have already considered:

H: first thing with **Schwarzenegger** .

When the host has marked that topic as concluded, she names the
other topic:

H: second point real quick **this whole thing with
      airline security** .

The words 'the fifteenth' or 'Estelle Morris', or 'Schwarzenegger'
can serve as shorthand for topics on which people can have different
opinions, with the assumption the host and listeners share a sense
of the talkable issues.

  The only requirement for a topic is that there has to be something
more to say. Peter Werbe worries about this when he asks for calls
on a recent power blackout in the north-east; he notes that this is
just what every other phone-in will be talking about and hopes his
callers will have something different to offer. Pete Price begins one
of his phone-ins with a response to a caller who apparently found
the topics too trivial for broadcast discussion:

Pete Price 9/9/03
PP: Andrea complained last night about me talking
      about po:nds and now she's complaining about me
      talking about pa:rking. Andrea we deal with many
      many issues and we're on Monday Tuesday Wednesday
      Thursday and also a Sunday and I am making no
      apologies just because you don't want to talk
      about the issues they are issues that need
      dealing with

His next caller is then a bit apologetic:

PP: hello Joe
J: hello
PP: yes Joe
J: I was going to talk about pa:rking but
PP: still talk about parking Joe

Andrea's complaint raises the issue of whether any topic is inappropriate for a phone-in. Pete Price's answer here is that even if the issues seem mundane, 'they are issues that need dealing with' and, more pragmatically, there is a lot of airtime to fill.

Opinion as a topic

Participants in phone-ins refer frequently to opinion as something out there, as news on which they comment. A guest on *Sean Hannity*, Congressman Tom Tancredo, cites a poll saying 70 per cent of Americans support a bill to keep illegal aliens from having driver's licences. Sean Hannity cites polls as determining which candidate Republicans should support in the California recall election. Participants on the BBC Wales discussion consider the size of a demonstration against the invasion of Iraq. In these references to public opinion, it has none of the complexity or ambivalence it might have as enacted on a phone-in; it is a quantity. But these reports of opinion call for more talk:

Night Call 24/8/03
```
PW:  so is there people out there that think we should
     be giving billions of dollars to Afghanistan and
     Iraq when we don't have the billions of dollars
     we need to keep ourselves out of debt? (1) I mean
     I don't get this . I don't get why only seventy
     per cent of Americans think that what do the
     other thirty people- thirty per cent of the
     people thinking . let's go to our phones and find
     out
```

In this case, Werbe agrees with the majority and presents the poll as a provocation to listeners, a reason to look for 'people out there' who could conceivably hold the other view. What would follow (and does) is a broadcastable argument about why one might disagree, and what sort of person would hold this view. But there is no sense that the two versions of public opinion, poll and phone-in, might be part of the same process; they might be talking about football scores.

What's taken for granted: commonplaces

A more subtle invocation of opinion as already out there is in the use of commonplaces, general assertions that can be used across situations and across arguments (see Chapters 2 and 4). We saw that when participants used commonplaces in focus groups (Chapter 5), the moderator often took this as a signal that participants were marking the end of what could be said about a topic. In phone-ins, they are often used to establish solidarity. Here a historian of the 1930s uses a familiar phrase and stance of the time exactly as Shotter (1993) suggests they are used, to crystallize a whole world of shared everyday experience.

BBCRW 12/2/03
```
JD:  and Ramsay Mac had gone over to the enemy
F:   huh huh right . well with the enemy at some times
```

In this case, the phrase 'gone over', the use of the name 'Ramsay Mac' (for Ramsay MacDonald, Prime Minister of the United Kingdom in the 1930s), the stance, and the experience of betrayal are not the historian's own, but are invoked in a gesture of solidarity with the caller, who is being treated on the show as an example of oral history. The caller accepts the historian's commonplace hesitantly and with qualification.

Commonplaces are notable more for what they do than for what they say. Here a familiar charge in all sorts of campaigns for fairness is used by the caller to sum up and give a stance on what he has been saying:

BBCRL 20/2/03
```
N:   now now where's the difference there's double
     standards here
BD:  Neil thanks very much for your call
```

In the following example, the commonplace is used to open a call, responding to a previous caller who was distraught at the resignation of a government minister, and indicating an understanding (shared with listeners but not with the previous caller) of what responsibility must be:

Any Answers 26/10/02
```
BA:  we:ll Estelle Morris was in charge of that
     department . and I think the buck has to stop
     somewhere .
```

The commonplace also conveys a matter-of-factness that contrasts with the sobbing of the previous caller.

A commonplace can be used to respond to a challenge, as in this case in which the host has asked a member of the fire-fighters' union to consider whether other public employees should ask for the same large pay increase.

Any Answers 26/10/02
PT: . each <u>case</u> is worthy of **consideration on its
       own merits**

This is a familiar rejection (usually used by government, not a union) of an across-the-board claim, and it also suggests a kind of care or judgment in distinguishing these claims.

While host or caller might object that this commonplace does not apply in this case – that 'going over to the enemy' is too harsh a phrase for Ramsay Mac, or that 'the buck stops here' does not apply to the particular situation of the Minister for Education – they do not question the commonplaces themselves. (Neither do they do this in focus groups.) The use of commonplaces invokes a shared understanding of how the world works that survives potential disagreement. The sociability of the argument on phone-ins and the intelligibility of the topics as issues depend on the shared sense that we are all sensible people – aren't we?

Broadcasting sociable argument

Why do people listen to phone-ins? I have argued there is pleasure in sociable argument, and that this pleasure is experienced by listeners not as a spectacle but as a kind of para-social interaction. The sense of intimacy-in-conflict is not the same in a broadcast as it is for Schiffrin's (1984) Jewish families and neighbours sitting around the table. But it is there in the way the host and callers interact – in the greetings, naming, shared issues, exaggerated and mitigated disagreement. We in the audience hear phone-ins as a single voice on the phone rather than as a microphone broadcasting to millions, and they incorporate all the conventions and intimacy we associate with the phone. We may watch talk shows as spectacle (Tolson 2001), but we overhear phone-ins. That is why the caller's location and the sense of the present stage of the day and liveness are so important to the shared experience. We need to maintain an imagined link both with the phone call and with other unheard listeners. The definition of opinion used on these shows is one that opens out to such an imagined link.

It may be frustrating for those who look for a media model for deliberative democracy that the host or callers do not change their minds after these calls, that callers do not talk to each other without the intervention of the host, and that neither hosts nor callers present extended rational arguments. And it might be objected that to treat phone-ins as sociable argument is a rather benign and tolerant view of an institution that, in the US at least, may promote extreme political positions with considerable effectiveness. But these criticisms assume that a phone-in with political topics will be experienced as political. People talk about politics, not just to change the world, but to pass the time with other people, just as they talk about work, sports, celebrities (and ponds and parking). And they may listen to such talk, not to participate in the ideal agora, but to experience the pleasure and frustration in sociability, pleasure and frustration made more intimate, not less, by its coming over the phone and the radio.

10

Vox pop television interviews: constructing the public

The phrase *vox populi*, 'the voice of the people', predates broadcasting; the OED gives an instance from 1550. But it is broadcasting that has given the phrase (in its shortened form) a specific meaning, as press or broadcast segments in which a series of usually unidentified people are asked to state an opinion on an issue briefly. The statements are then edited together so that the whole series, rather than any one speaker, is taken to represent the voice of the people.

Just as radio phone-ins would seem to be a drastically attenuated form of public argument, vox pop interviews on television might seem to be a drastically reduced visual representation of public opinion. Who is to say these people on a street in Washington can stand for all the people who make up 'the public'? And who is to say that their offhand thirty-second responses to a question we do not hear can stand for 'opinion'? It is not surprising that vox pops do not seem to be taken very seriously by broadcasters; they may be used at the end of a news report, or as a light introduction to what is seen as an abstract item, or in local news as a kind of filler. I will argue they are important, despite this apparent marginality, because they are key examples of the way broadcasting can categorize people, visually and verbally, and from these categories constitute public opinion.

Constituting public opinion is not, of course, the same thing as summing up the responses of individuals in a representative sample to a specific question in order to project the response of a population. That is what polls do (see the critique of polls in Chapter 4). Vox pops are different: they are analysable documents of how the diverse utterances of individuals can be put together to make something more. To show this process in transcripts, I draw on conversation analysis (CA) again and another approach suggested by Harvey Sacks, Membership Categorization Analysis (MCA) (see Chapter 2 for references). With CA, I will argue that there are different sorts of questions in interviews, that recipients recognize these questions as addressed to different kinds of people, and that they usually answer accordingly. In particular, both interviewers and interviewees distinguish between questions that call for opinions in response and other kinds of question that call for facts, experiences, or emotions.

But what is important about vox pops is not what is said, as news, but the fact of this kind of person saying it here and now. Every vox pop is an exercise in categorization, for the participants and for viewers. This is not as simple as seeing that every package has a representative mix of males and females, young and old, and various races. We will see that there is no general set of schemata that will cover the public, and that what matters in the interactions are the ways categories are offered and taken up (or resisted) by interviewees. The questions in vox pops may have to do with who they are, what actions are associated with this category, where they find themselves, and how they categorize others.

Vox pop questions and answers

Research on broadcast interviews has stressed the way conversational patterns are adapted to the institutional context in which there is a listening audience, a given topic, a set of constraints on questions and answers, a requirement to display neutrality, and a place for such interviews within the structure of a broadcast story (see Chapter 2). All this applies as well to vox pops, but vox pop sequences differ in several ways:

- in broadcast interviews with public figures the interviewee is introduced as having specific entitlement to talk on this issue, while in vox pops we don't know whom we are listening to
- the interviewer and the questions may be omitted entirely in editing without loss of coherence
- the sequence is typically composed, not of a series of questions to one person, but of the same question(s) asked to a series of people
- there is no need for adversarial challenges as part of the display of neutrality

Looked at this way, vox pops are defined by what they may lack: identification, questions, follow-ups and responses, and the possibility of challenge. But the interviewees generally seem to know what is expected of them.

Unidentified members of the public may be asked several sorts of questions, and only some of them call for the kinds of opinions that interest us here. For the beginnings of a classification of such questions, we can turn to Andrew Roth's (2002) analysis of interviews with public figures on the PBS *McNeill-Lehrer Report*. Roth, following Pomerantz's (1980) distinction between two types of 'knowables', distinguishes between 'direct questions' eliciting 'matters of fact' and 'epistemic-framed questions' eliciting 'informed points of opinion' (359). He shows that the questions signal what kind of response this interviewee is expected to give, and that generally interviewees give just that kind of response; even in atypical cases the basic distinction is acknowledged and the deviation accounted for. This defines the kind of relation an interviewee is expected to have to a story, so that, for instance, a member of Congress has direct, first-hand knowledge of his or her vote, but an expert on Congress has only second-hand knowledge, on the basis of which he or she is entitled to an opinion. Even non-experts can have a first-hand knowledge of some issues that concern them; for instance, a set of BBC vox pops in a Manchester coffee bar on people's personal finances assumes they know about their own pension plans. An interview during the 1999 eclipse of the sun asks an old woman about her experience of the previous total eclipse in Britain, decades earlier.

I have argued, in an analysis of vox pops after the death of Princess Diana, that there is another distinction that works in a similar way, between questions calling for an opinion on a public issue and those calling for an emotional response, and that different kinds of entitlement to speak are invoked (Myers 2000b). This is not an epistemological distinction, not a matter of what the interviewee can be expected to have direct knowledge of, but a matter of decorum or appropriateness to the occasion. Displaying one's emotional response is a different kind of speech event from giving information, calling for sincerity rather than fact (see Montgomery 1999). Similarly, I have argued that survivors of the 11 September attack on the World Trade Center, interviewed on the street, were asked questions and gave responses in which experiences, not opinions, were called for (Myers 2003). There was a clear distinction between the interviews with experts expected to *know*, and those with anonymous people expected to *see*.

If we combine Roth's classification of interviews with public figures with mine for interviews with members of the public, we can imagine a grid of entitlements to speak:

	taken as matters of mental states	taken as matters of experience
world	**knowledge** eclipse, pensions	**witness** 11 September
self	**opinion** view of President, reasons for vote, assessment of broadcast	**feelings** response to death of Diana

I argue, following Roth, that these are not just analysts' categories of potential kinds of statement, they are categories to which participants in these interviews respond. Interviewers signal different sorts of relations to interviewees. A question of fact might be posed directly:

```
IR: Reverend Jackson, will you be marching tomorrow?
    (Roth 2002)
```

Roth shows that points of opinion are often epistemologically marked (Here with 'do you think'):

```
IR: Do you think he's gonna endor:se you?  (Roth 2002)
```

Presumably Roth would categorize questions of feeling under direct questions, because the interviewee is assumed to have direct access to the answer:

```
IR: what was it about her that particularly touched
    people like you?
IR: Prime Minister . can we please have your reaction
    to the news? (Myers 2000b)
```

These questions ask, not for a fact that the interviewer wants to know, and not for an evaluative opinion, but for a sincere expression of motives and emotions. The difference in questions is not just a difference in kinds of news events (an election, a march, a funeral);

God's children', the future public in whose name this speech is made, cuts across these and all other possible categorization devices.

In the three examples of vox pop interviews I will now discuss, the interviewees take the categorization as posing some sort of problem. They each respond to the problem, in the first by giving an account of her actions, in the second by redefining the categories and the question, and in the third by recontextualizing the event to which he is supposed to respond. All three interviewees can be seen as exercises in categorization, but also as exercises in construction of a whole, underlying, 'public opinion' that is beyond categories.

Why me?: accounting at the inauguration

In everyday talk, one way to get a more detailed response from someone is to set up an explanation slot, for instance by noticing something about them, or echoing a response they make (Antaki 1994: 76). They are then open to produce an account, an explanation of what you have noticed (the dent in their car, their lateness, a complaint). The same format can be used in vox pop interviews, for instance noting that the interviewee is here on a delayed train, or at Kensington Palace before the funeral of Princess Diana, or in a pub at closing time, or at a demonstration. It is assumed that one has already an opinion (on railways, Diana, licensing laws, the Iraq invasion) by virtue of one's presence, and the task now is to account for it, to explain why you hold it or how it came about. And this involves categorization; the question in a vox pop is not 'what do you say' but 'what does someone like you say' – and it is the interviewee's job to figure out what 'someone like you' means in this case.

Usually this goes smoothly and a string of interviewees give excerptable responses that can be edited together. For instance, at the end of BBC coverage of Bill Clinton's 1992 inauguration, there is a short, live segment of interviews with the well-wishers lining the parade route. The reporter moves the microphone between four different people in the crowd. Though what we see is an undifferentiated crowd, the interviewees were apparently chosen before, because the camera moves smoothly to each new speaker. The first, second, and fourth of the speakers produce responses that refer to the new presidency and offer some issue with which they are personally concerned. The interviews are tightly structured, with each interviewee getting two questions and exactly the same amount of time.

The third of the four inauguration interviews is different because the interviewee must first say what she is doing here if she did not vote for Clinton, and only then can she elaborate on an opinion.

First inauguration of President Clinton - BBC - 20/1/93

	IR	okay perhaps if I can move over here . could I ask you . did you vote for Bill Clinton?	pans to right front - CU
1	IE3	um I- I- I didn't have the	IE gestures
2		chance to vote as a matter	with hand
3		of fact I changed states so	adjusts
4		. kind of out but um . my	glasses looks
5		original choice would have	away
6		been Perot for the economic	
7		policy . at the time I	
8		didn't- hadn't listened to	
9		Clinton that much . but from	
10		what he said he's got the	
11		ball on it you know? he	
12		wants . us to all work as a	
13		group and as long as that's	passerby
14		anyone's purpose I think it	makes two
15		will work out you know. we	finger
16		need definitely to get on	gesture in
17		our feet and. you know we	background
18		have to look at the world as a whole and also concentrate on ourselves	

There is no reason why someone at the inaugural should have voted for the candidate who was elected, and there is no indication of a preferred response in the form of the question, but the interviewee treats it as if it assumes a positive answer. She gives signs of a dispreferred turn, with the hesitation and prefacing in (1). Her explanation trails off unfinished in (4), and she looks briefly away. (She also adjusts her glasses, something she does in each of her turns, another sort of nervous hesitation.) Then she offers an account of herself: if she could have voted, she would have voted for a rival candidate (4–6), as her 'original choice' (this phrasing does not let on if she still supports Perot). She gives a reason for this; it was not an aversion to Clinton, but the 'economic policy'. She refers to her response 'at the time', distinguishing her current state of mind from her previous state. She offers an account for her preference for a rival; she 'hadn't listened to Clinton that much'. In saying this, she revises her statement that she 'didn't' listen (8), which suggests blocking out the message, to one that she 'hadn't' listened, which leaves open the possibility that she just had not had the chance to follow his points.

From there she turns, without further prompting, to her opinion of Clinton's speech. Its first message again is about categorization: 'he wants . us to all work as a group', so her not being a supporter is irrelevant. From there, she talks about 'we' (15,17), not as a party, and not as the whole human race, but as Americans (as shown by the contrast between 'ourselves' and 'the world as a whole'). All this shows both an awareness of the category to which she is assigning herself (Perot supporter) and an insistence that hearers not draw from this category all the possible inferences (for instance, that she is hostile to Clinton).

We can see her careful positioning in her use of discourse markers and commonplaces. The shift from her account to her opinion is marked 'I think' (14); she displays that she is attending to the implication that she should offer an opinion on Clinton, not just a report and account of her vote. This opinion is offered conditionally; 'as long as that's *any*one's purpose'; it is not Clinton she is agreeing with, but his appeal, or anyone making the same appeal. While 'I think' marks what is hers, 'you know' (used three times in quick succession) can mark 'general consensual truths which speakers assume their hearers share through co-membership in the same culture, society, or group' (Schiffrin 1987: 275). The first 'you know' solicits general agreement with in a reference to a speech both she and the interviewer have heard:

but from what he said he's got the ball on it you know?

The second and third 'you know's both follow and precede general commonplaces:

I think it will work out you know
we need definitely to get on our feet
you know we have to look at the world as a whole and also concentrate on
ourselves

Such commonplaces are also a device for giving up one's turn (see Chapter 5 and Chapter 9), but here the interviewer does not step in to take over, and the interviewee is left having to carry on. The end of her turn is signalled, not by her, but by the interviewer moving the microphone back for his next question.

This interviewee's problem is to give a response that is genuinely her own response but is also more than just her own response, a response in keeping with the event she is attending. The inaugural is not just a political celebration, it is a civic ritual. This makes it easy for those who have supported (or strongly opposed) the candidature of the new president to account for their presence and give it a wider significance, whether of acclaim or dissent. It is harder for someone who didn't vote, and who wouldn't have voted for the candidate anyway. So she does some work, honestly disclaiming one category, claiming another, negating that, accounting and appealing with commonplaces to shared feelings. She tries to provide the BBC with an interviewee who can serve (like those before and after her) as the bearer of shared aspirations for Americans.

Why us?: responding to categorization in Harlem

Judging from the broadcasts in 2000, vox pop interviews are not used in US network reports of elections. These expensive, carefully planned, and heavily advertised specials are studio-bound affairs: the voice of the people is out there in the ballot boxes and in here in the form of Voter News Service projections, not in any actual voices. The BBC did use extensive vox pops, perhaps as a substitute for the kind of outside broadcasting from local declarations that is such a feature of UK elections (Marriott 2000). All the sites in which the BBC conducted vox pops were public places, but they were all multiply coded for geography, class, race, and party preference: a café in Harlem, a wine bar in downtown Manhattan, a restaurant on the beach at Santa Monica. So all interviewees were implicitly but not definitively categorized by the fact of where they were. I will consider how two interviewees in one sequence respond to this categorization.

The interviews I will analyse are introduced in three ways, in terms of the relevant electoral unit, the place, and the population. David Dimbleby, the anchor, links to the (pre-recorded) package by referring to the state, because that is the unit in which the election is reported and electoral votes are counted.

```
US Election - BBC - 7/11/00
DD: we join um Michael Crick . who's been out and
    about in New York . and has been talking to
    voters in that state
```

But the opening by the reporter, Michael Crick, codes the place in which the interviews are taking place more specifically:

```
MC: welcome to . Sylvia's Restaurant here in Harlem .
    the heart of Harlem . only three days ago on
    Saturday the restaurant here actually prepared
    food . for Bill Clinton and his team . at a rally
    they gave here across the road
```

The specific location, a café with a long lunch counter, is linked to the campaign and the role of Clinton in it. When Crick shifts from introduction to questioning ('anyway'), he still does not say what category he takes his interviewees to be, apart from their being local:

```
MC: anyway let's see what effect that rally had . on
    the on the local population
```

But in the interviews he implicitly addresses the interviewees as able to speak for 'black voters'. A response involves both accepting the categorization as relevant and answering the question as an issue of fact rather than of one's own opinion. Both interviewees hesitate before responding when addressed in these terms; one responds by taking on the role of local expert, while the other successfully reformulates the question and the categories involved.

The first interviewee displays care in taking on the role of expert on the group.

US Election - BBC - 7/11/00

1.	MC	tell me sir have you have you voted today	MC moves backwards to IE1
2.	IE1	yes I have	CU of IE1
3.	MC	who for (1)	
4.	IE1	Gore and . Clinton? . * Ms. Hilary Clinton?	*IE1 turns to interviewer
5.	MC	and is is Al Gore as popular among . black voters around here as as Bill Clinton was? (3)	
6.	IE1	I would think so . yeah	IE1 closes eyes tight, makes a clicking sound, and then looks at interviewer
7.	MC	you think as many of them will come out	
8.	IE1	yeah they'll come out . they'll show a little later on=	IE1 looks down, nodding
9.	MC	=d'you	
10.	IE1	=before the polls close tonight	
11.	MC	do you think perhaps um . Al Gore should have made a little bit more of Bill Clinton . . .	pan to MC

First there is the kind of yes–no question ('have you voted today') typically used to set up further questioning. The interviewee answers but does not elaborate, and the interviewer asks a further question (3). We might expect (from other vox pops) a follow-up question asking him why he voted this way, that is an opinion that provides an account of the vote. But he is not questioned as a voter. Instead, the next question involves a shift from his knowledge of his own vote to his knowledge of the voting of a category of people, 'black voters' (5). His response to this question (6) is strongly marked, not only by the delay, but also by the interviewee's facial expression, a kind of wry wince, and the post-positioned answer ('yeah'). The conditional form ('I would think so') explicitly categorizes the response as a matter of opinion, rather than knowledge. The interviewer elaborates in formulating this response (7) and the interviewee repeats and elaborates this formulation, now in unhedged form (8). The effect is of a kind of deliberation before responding. As they go on to discuss the decisions in the Gore campaign, the interviewee takes on the offered role as an observer, a strategist, an expert on black voters.

The other interviewee in this sequence revises both the category of actors ('black people') and the action ('not voting') proposed by the interviewer's question. I will quote the whole exchange leading up to the question in turn 11.

1.	MC	thanks very much . *let's let's let's have a word with this lady here . excuse me madam how did how did you vote today	*MC moving toward the camera to a young woman
2.	IE2	um . Ralph Nader	MS - she twists to face the camera
3.	MC	Ralph Nader . was that an an easy choice?	
4.	IE2	uh . no . *because they said a . **vote for Nader was a vote for Bush . but I voted with my conscience	*IE2 glances at camera **IE2 looks at interviewer
5.	MC	would you would you have voted for for Nader in in other places . because of course in New York it may not . make a lot of difference in that=	
6.	IE2	=no	
7.	MC	=Gore will probably win it here	
8.	IE2	if it was a close race? if I was in a state with a close race I would have voted for *Gore . but since . um . I think Gore had New York wrapped up . I voted for Nader	*glances at camera

```
 9. | MC  | do you think a lot of bla-    | pan to MC
    |     | black people will have voted |
    |     | for Nader?=                  |
10. | IE2 |              =no . no        | IE2 smiles,
    |     |                             | looks down
11. | MC  | what about this problem      |
    |     | there is of of a lot of      |
    |     | black people not voting at   |
    |     | all?                         |
12. | IE2 | uh apathy voter apathy and   |
    |     | feeling they don't really    |
    |     | have a choice? . um . I      |
    |     | think we need more than a    |
    |     | two-system party in this     |
    |     | country and they need to     |
    |     | speak more to the needs of   |
    |     | um African Americans . cuz   |
    |     | the Democrats take our vote  |
    |     | for granted that's why I     |
    |     | didn't vote Democrat this    |
    |     | year *                       | nods
```

The interviewer asks five questions (1, 3, 5, 9, 11) and gets different
kinds of responses. In turns 4 and 6–8, the interviewee follows her
'no' unprompted with an elaboration explaining why it was not an
easy decision, or why she would not have voted this way in another
state. The next question is the one I take to be a shift because it is
not about her vote, but about the category of 'black people' and
their 'not voting'. She responds (10) with a latched 'no', but instead
of elaborating repeats the 'no' and looks down, signalling the end
of the turn. (I will not try to interpret the smile.) The interviewer's
question in 11, 'What about this problem' is in a form that presents
it as relevant to the previous question, but she does not take it in
the same way.

There are three stages to her response in 12. First, after a
hesitation, she gives a reason,

```
apathy voter apathy and feeling they don't really
have a choice
```

She can use a nominal and an adverbial rather than a sentence
because these are already recognizable as candidate explanations
for 'not voting'. The rising intonation on 'choice' suggests the turn

is not complete. She marks the second part of her response as an opinion, with 'I think'. In this statement, 'we' apparently refers to all citizens, 'they' to political parties, and 'black people' are recoded as 'African Americans'. The third part of the response begins 'cuz', suggesting a conclusion (as does the nod), and leads back, not to the question in 11, but to the original question about her own vote. She ends with a contrast between what is expected of the category and her individual choice: 'Democrats take <u>our</u> vote for granted' and '<u>I</u> didn't vote Democrat' (stress added).

Both interviewees speak for themselves and then about black or African American voters, but they respond in different ways to the implied categorization, the first interviewee treating the question as calling for an informed prediction, a kind of expertise, the second taking it as an occasion to rephrase a question about black voters into an answer about African Americans and the political system.

What now?: references to people after the Clinton–Lewinsky broadcast

In the inauguration interview and the election interview, the interviewees deal with problems about their past actions (not voting for Clinton) or their categorization (as black). A question can also implicitly challenge a participant's categorizations in the light of some event. The question might not be, 'what do you think', but 'what do you think *now?*'

In the following example, the interviewee has just watched live Bill Clinton's broadcast in 1998 admitting to an affair with Monica Lewinsky. One set of interviews is held at an airport in Dallas, the other, which I am using as an example here, is held at a health club in Los Angeles; they are shot, edited, and introduced so that the two segments in different regions are closely parallel in structure. There are two kinds of categorization here, and they are related: the interviewee is for or against Clinton, and Clinton is either a liar or isn't. The first categorization is not just a matter of political allegiance; the issue was divisive in a way that is very hard for those of us who were not in the US to understand and carries all sorts of potential implications about one's values. The second categorization is also complex; as Michael Lynch and David Bogen argue (1997), the treatment of an account of the past as lying (rather than forgetting, misunderstanding, ambiguity) is constructed in a particular situation, such as cross-examination, not in terms of some generally applicable definition.

We do not know the question here, but the interviewee's response suggests that he was asked what he thought of the speech (not of Clinton or of his actions); he introduces his turn 'I thought', and he starts with two evaluations. This interviewee tries to bring up other issues that were not in the speech but that he sees as related; one of his techniques is to use gestures that literally create a space for these alternative views. Only at the end does he refer directly to the broadcast.

Presidential address (Clinton on Lewinsky) 18 August 1998 - CBS

1	IE2	I thought he was very good	gym
2		and very clear at . uh .	CU
3		throwing the issue on	
4		Kenneth Starr who I believe	
5		is probably more guilty of a	*gestures to
6		crime than uh Bill Clinton .	left
7		he uh if anything *if he	
8		lied under oath he did it on	
9		a question that should have	**gestures to
10		been irrelevant anyway .	right and to
11		**it has nothing to do	left
12		Monica Lewinsky has nothing	
13		to do with Paula Jones .	
14		Monica Lewinsky was	***looks up
15		consensual if it happened	to upper left
16		which . ***uh apparently it	
17		did---	

There is a hesitation (2) before he expands this evaluation so that it applies, not to the speech itself, but to the effect it had, in his view, of shifting the blame to Kenneth Starr (the Special Prosecutor). Then there is an embedded evaluation of Kenneth Starr, marked as an opinion, 'I believe', and hedged, 'probably' (5). So he has shifted from an opinion on the speech to an evaluation of evidence and has acknowledged that this part of what he says is contestable. There is a rhetorical problem, because saying that what Kenneth Starr did is worse than what Bill Clinton did involves saying that Bill Clinton did something (7–8, 15–17). Thus the turn goes on awkwardly, through several possible completion points where the interviewer could break in (6, 10, 13). Like the Clinton–Lewinsky case itself, each new assertion leads to the need for further clarifications and elaborations.

This part of the turn is structured around two conditional clauses, each of them linked to a gesture. The left gesture with 'if he lied under oath' (8) marks this clause as a side point, one that awaits completion with a main clause, that it 'he did it on a question that should have been irrelevant'. Instead of accepting the categorization that Clinton lied, he makes an assertion about the more general grounds of what really counts as lying. The 'anyway' has a similar effect of setting this admission of possible lying aside. The gestures left and right with 'it has nothing to do' (11) mark his repetition of these two cases, which would lead to another possible completion point, after the parallel construction in 'nothing to do with Paula Jones' (12–13). He elaborates the comment in 14–15, 'Monica Lewinsky was consensual', and that has to be elaborated, 'if it happened' and then that has to be elaborated, 'which. apparently it did'. This last phrase is said with a glance to the TV screen that refers the interviewer to their shared knowledge of what they have both just seen. He has granted that Clinton said something that was untrue but has not put this as lying. The editor cuts it here, even though the lack of falling intonation shows the interviewee probably continued or intended to continue. From the producer's point of view, the interviewee has said enough to fill a slot as a defender of Clinton, juxtaposed with others who attack Clinton. The interviewee may have elaborated further, but the elaboration is unnecessary for the contrastive structure of this vox pop sequence.

What links the examples from the inauguration, the election, and the Clinton speech is the way interviewees orient to the categorizations they are implicitly offered. They may finally talk themselves into the appropriate role (in the inauguration interview), or may redefine the category to which they have been assigned (as with the woman in the café in Harlem), or may recategorize the behaviour in which they have been asked to comment (as does the interviewee in the health club). In each case they recognize the kind of question that has been asked and what kind of answer would be appropriate. They show this in the way they frame their answers, with the use of 'you know' and commonplaces in the first example, the echoing of questions and reformulation of terms like 'not voting/voter apathy' in the second, and the performative, gestural use of space to set up alternative views in the third. Though the categories they are offered (having voted for Clinton, speaking for black voters, calling Clinton a liar) seem reductive, their brief responses show the categories to be open to tensions and reinterpretation in specific situations.

Visualizing the public

I have argued that the category of 'public' is constructed, not by enumerating the opinions of individual members of the population, but by packaging a series of interactions that can be seen as suggesting different categorization devices. They construct 'opinion' by showing the expression of a view on an issue as an activity bound to categories of people and actions. Part of this work of construction is done by the production team; except in live segments (like that from the inauguration parade) they can choose and edit interviews to fit into a sequence. (Even in the live segments, there is evidence of careful preparation, for instance in the way the camera follows the movements from one interviewee to the next.) These segments then figure with maps, graphics, outside broadcast interviews with public figures, studio interviews with commentators, and recorded footage as small parts of larger packages that may be broadcast once or may be repeated through the cycle of rolling coverage. The rule seems to be that no one person can speak for 'the public' – but any three can.

Three visual elements contribute to the sense that we are seeing more than just a set of statements: faces, lists, and sites.

Faces might seem to short-circuit any process of collaborative categorization, by making it obvious this person is, say, old, or black, or rich, or a priest. But this is exactly *not* the effect of faces as we watch; they are as individual as a nervous tick, glasses that need pushing up, windblown hair, a mole beside the nose. The face promises a direct encounter of two people with unique identities, face to face. The encounter is not with us but with an unseen interviewer just to the right or left of the camera. This individuality is particularly apparent in the interviews on 11 September, where the experience of the interviewees is written on their faces, figuratively in their jumpy, stunned expressions, literally in the coating of dust (Myers

2003). It is also apparent in the interviews after Diana's death, in the way people present the sincerity of their grief (Myers 2000b). The aural equivalent is the individual distinctiveness of voices in the radio phone-ins, when we conjure up a whole character from a few phonological clues. This sense of some irreducible individuality seems to be essential to constructing a collective visual.

As I have suggested, the underlying visual structure of a vox pop package is that of a *list*. When I said that no one person could represent the public, but any three could, I was echoing Sacks's famous analysis of a dirty joke involving a farmer's three daughters; three, Sacks points out, is the minimum to form a pattern and break it (Sacks 1978; also in Sacks 1992). It is the breaking of the pattern that begins to persuade us we are approaching 'public opinion'. The pattern is visual as well; for instance, interviewees in the inauguration interviews are seen from the same angle and more or less the same distance but are taken from different parts of the crowd, and interviewees at the health club are from the same angle but their gaze is to the right or the left. (I am told that the practice is to film people on one side of the argument with gaze left, those on the other side with gaze right, and to label the clips so that they can be easily edited into a package.)

Vox pops place the abstraction of 'the public' in a *site*, a particular place and moment. They were called 'man in the street' interviews (before codes of non-sexist language) because they were supposed to be encounters with people going about their business, in neutral public space, not trying to express an opinion (as at a demonstration) or tell a story (as at a disaster). Space is public by virtue of what it is not – not someone's house, not a symbolic stage, not the site of an event. The café in Harlem and the health club in Los Angeles correspond to this neutral, unmarked, public space (the route of the inauguration parade is, as we have seen, rather different, because people are assumed to have come there for a reason). Space is also defined as middle distance, not the extreme close-ups sometimes used with the emotional responses of survivors or relatives at a disaster, or the extreme long shots of demonstrations. If the package involves a series of such places (Harlem, Soho, Santa Monica), they follow Sacks's economy rule for categorization devices; if the first is categorized in one way, the others can be categorized by the same device. The café corresponds to a bar and a restaurant in later interviews, places where people are occupied with something else; the health club corresponds to an airport lounge as places where people are passing through (and might see a television). As with faces, places particularize the interviews and make them concrete.

Conclusion

There is a tension in the definitions of opinion underlying vox pops just as there was in the definitions assumed in phone-ins. I have an opinion as an individual, but it is interpreted in terms of the category to which I am assigned. My opinion is mine alone, but I can be called upon to give it publicly. My opinion is inside me, but it follows from this place, this time, or this event. These participants did not call up to volunteer an opinion, but they know what is called for. And they do this effectively even though the final broadcast package is not just their interview (or a bit of their interview) but a collection in which they represent one or more categories.

I have argued throughout this book for attention not just to what members of the public say, but to how they say it. It could be that vox pops, which seem so dubious as social science (no sampling, no testing of the question, no follow-up) and so marginal as broadcasting, survive because of the concreteness and particularity of the faces, places, and even the little hesitations and quirks. The outcome of an interview is never the issue; to count up the numbers taking one side or the other would miss the point. What is fascinating is how people present themselves, represent (or do not) a group, and make their particular contribution relevant. We don't listen for the individual opinions themselves but for the look and sound of the imaginary but necessary category they make together, 'public opinion'.

11

Opinions as talk

In Chapter 1, I argued that when we take a close look at what we mean by 'opinion', we find paradoxes. Opinions are valuable but denigrated, publicly available but protected, personal but shared, unitary but potentially self-contradictory, ephemeral but socially structural, and local but potentially global. These paradoxes arise if we fail to see that opinions are both *situated* and *mediated*. Opinions are situated in that they are actions in on-going talk, interactions with other people, enacted in particular settings of time and place. But if they are to have any effect, they must be mediated, disembedded, and packaged for use, standardized and reproduced in texts, and linked intertextually to other texts. It might seem that this was just a matter of reduction from the complexity of interaction to the simplicity of media summaries. But reports of opinions can be particularly effective in conveying conviction and sincerity when they retain traces of having been said by someone to someone in a particular situation.

In this chapter, I look back over the earlier analyses of focus groups, phone-ins, and vox pops, and explore what it means to say that opinions are talk. I will argue that it means that the expression of opinion is an action in words (not an inner state), an interaction (not just psychological), and that it is enacted at a particular time and place, not as a general statement. This talk can then be packaged (not just collected), mediated (not just spoken), and related intertextually (it doesn't have meaning on its own, but in a chain). One implication of this view, as I have tried to show in Chapters 5–10, is that expressions of opinion need to be analysed as situated acts, not reduced to given categories.

Expressing an opinion is an action in words

A person states an opinion for a reason, for instance to influence, or amuse, or claim membership in a group, or disclaim membership. As I noted in Chapter 1, it is the act of expression at a particular place and time, with a particular hearer, that constitutes the opinion, not the thought in their head. Institutions of opinion, such as polling organizations, study opinions because they are what one can get data about, but usually what they really want to know about is the 'psychological tendency' that is expressed, not only in this particular statement but in future statements and actions. For instance, they want to know not just what someone says just now, but what they will usually say, or how they will vote next month, or what they will buy. This book, along with other recent work on discourse and opinions (Antaki et al. 2000; Houtkoop-Steenstra 2000; Matoesian and Coldren 2002; Puchta and Potter forthcoming), is an attempt to put the focus back on the act of expressing the opinion, here and now.

We know that people do think of opinions as acts, because they can distinguish the expression of opinions from other acts. When they say 'in my opinion' (as they often do in my data), they are saying that this is something challengeable, but that they do not expect a challenge; it is different from 'I know' or 'I've seen' or 'I can promise you.' To call something a matter of opinion is both to claim some space for oneself and to define the kind of conversation we are having now. Of course people need not preface such acts with 'In my opinion', any more than promises must be prefaced with 'I hereby promise' (And the phrase 'in my opinion' can be used before statements that are not taken as opinions, but as statements of fact or even as commands.) This morning on the radio a sports correspondent in the studio asks the cricket commentator in Australia,

Do you think England can win?

The commentator responds with what seems to be a question:

Do you?

The question expresses an opinion, as could an evaluation ('they aren't strong now') or a narrative ('if you had seen them yesterday'), or a facial expression (but this is radio), or even a significant silence. We know that it is an opinion here because the sports correspondent takes it as such, as a satisfactory response to his request. (His answer to the commentator's question, by the way, is 'no'. And they didn't.)

Some social scientists, and not just social psychologists, might want to insist that the important entities are the underlying attitudes, the 'psychological tendency' (Eagly and Chaiken 1993), of which any statement is just one conditional expression. For instance, green campaigners stress the depth of public resistance to genetically modified organisms, and they want this persistent and grounded attitude to influence policy on crop trials. Gun-control campaigners in the US might stress the widespread support for their campaign and argue that congressional votes do not reflect this support. Campaigners in the UK against the invasion of Iraq pointed to public opinion polls and mass demonstrations. If opinions are just talk, and each person could say one thing today and another tomorrow, this would seem to undermine any claims based on public opinion, and to leave all issues to be settled by the mechanisms of elections and representation. These mechanisms are open to manipulation by powerful interests (such as biotechnology firms or the gun lobby), and one might want a strong and unproblematic sense of public opinion as a kind of check, a deeper level of democracy.

There are two lines of response to this focus on the underlying attitudes. One is to remind ourselves that nothing in the sceptical, conversation analytical focus taken here necessarily denies the existence of attitudes (or schema, or stereotypes, or other psychological entities). The argument is that we know about these entities only through some kind of interaction, whether a survey form, an interview, a focus group, or an experiment, and we need to understand first what is going on in those interactions (for arguments for the priority of studying talk, see Edwards 1997; Silverman 1998; ten Have 1999b). The other response is that, even if there are underlying attitudes, and even if we think they are politically important or at least useful, we need to ask whenever they are reported just what sort of interaction was going on, and how it was packaged. In the kinds of debates I mentioned in Chapter 4, shifting legitimacy from legislatures to public attitudes more generally does not necessarily mean opening up democracy; it means giving legitimacy to institutions of opinion such as polling organizations and media reports

(Bourdieu 1993). So we might want to be a bit sceptical about public opinion even when, on a particular issue, it is on our side.

Since opinions are actions, one can perform them in ways that do not require words: raising one's hand, marching, wearing an armband, clapping, even just remaining silent when a response is expected. But these actions all depend on the more typical case in which one expresses the opinion in speech or writing, in response to another opinion with which one agrees or disagrees. Even a silent protest has its meaning verbalized elsewhere, in posters, pamphlets, or speeches. Common expressions for opinion suggest action – 'stand up and be counted', but also verbal action – 'have your say', 'speak up', 'get on your soap box'.

One implication of the essentially verbal nature of opinions is that one cannot rephrase them without some loss of meaning. If one codes a number of different statements in interviews as saying, more or less, 'genetically modified organisms are unnatural', one loses the particular meaning of each expression and imposes a similarity on different forms. Since opinions are also actions, one cannot even count every instance in which someone says the words, 'genetically modified organisms are unnatural'. As we have seen in Chapters 5–8, the same words could be offered as setting out a shared consensus, offering a devil's advocate position, making a concession before disagreement, opening up a new topic or closing an old one. One can of course search a body of textual data using corpus linguistic tools to see if one phrase is used consistently with positive or negative associations (Stubbs 2001). Such searches are likely to turn up interesting and sometimes counter-intuitive insights about how people use these phrases. But they do not tell us about opinions as situated actions.

Opinions are expressed in interaction

A person states an opinion for a reason and states it in relation to other people; they design each expression for this audience and this moment in the on-going interaction. Treating statements of opinion in isolation would be like practising the perfect tennis serve without considering how the opponent might hit it back, or learning to overtake on a highway on which there are no other cars. So it matters whether they are talking to an interviewer on the doorstep, another parent outside the school gate, a teacher in a class, a group of strangers in a hotel meeting room, or a microphone and camera in a studio. Professional market research and public-opinion research and many academic projects try to get around this variability by making the interviewer as neutral as possible, an unaffiliated stranger, training them to restrict their prompts to what can be planned and standardized across interviewers, and presenting the research organization as a neutral bystander to the issues discussed. This should make responses more reliable, that is, more reproducible, but it won't make them valid as indicators of opinion. As we have seen, people will assign an identity to the person they are talking to, and interests to the organization behind them, reasons for wanting to know, whether as messenger, representative, agent, or critic.

As people attribute identities to their interlocutors (Chapters 4 and 9), they present identities for themselves (Chapters 8 and 10). People present themselves as entitled to speak on this issue at this moment, because their experience or places they have lived are relevant, or because they speak for others, or just because they have been asked. The need to display entitlement is often missed by institutions of opinion, because they set up situations in which entitlement should not be an issue: we say we want your opinion, we want anyone's opinion, we want public opinion that includes everyone and no one. But a respondent may hold back because they feel that someone else in the room is more entitled, or they may design their response to say what is appropriate for the only farmer in the room, or the only person who has worked in a nuclear plant, or the only single mum, or retired person, or resident alien. These categories do not have to correspond to those for which the respondent was chosen to participate in the research; they are offered and sometimes revised, moment to moment (Antaki and Widdicombe 1998).

In the same way as research organizations try to present a neutral interlocutor and an open role for the interviewee, they often try to create a neutral space, whether in a dedicated research lab with a one-way mirror, a rented meeting room in a hotel, or a living room (Macnaghten and Myers 2004). Similarly, the studio sets of talk shows may be designed to look informal and domestic, public inquiries may be held in places that do not seem to affiliate them with the bureaucracy, polls and vox pops may meet people on the street, which is taken to be just anywhere. But no space is neutral; people transform the space by the way they sit, look at each other or at the walls, respond to noises and interruptions. The same space can be a meeting room, a classroom, a private corner for an inside joke, all within minutes.

Interaction means talking to someone in particular, somewhere in particular; it also means saying something at the right moment. One of the puzzles for me throughout this study has been why people talk about their opinions. It is easy enough to see why people write angry letters to the editor or go on marches – they want to change something. But why sit in a room with eight strangers and talk about issues one has not thought about much, for just a beer and ten quid? One answer that has run through this book is that there is pleasure in the interaction for its own sake. Following Simmel (1949), I have argued that this sociability is not just a by-product of real social organization but is an essential quality of society. Following Schiffrin, Blum-Kulka, Eggins and Slade, and others, I have shown empirically the traces of sociability in what one might think were highly unsociable encounters, for instance radio phone-ins.

Because focus groups are sociable, they develop over the course of the session, and contributions that would fit at one stage would seem odd or awkward at another. More subtly, each contribution is assumed to follow the one before it – or perhaps glaringly fails to follow – and each contribution sets up possibilities for who can talk next and what they can say (Chapters 5 and 6). This is true of all conversation of course, but it is particularly relevant to expression of opinions, because such expressions are appropriate only in certain slots in the conversation. Or, more accurately, statements in some slots in the conversation are likely to be taken as expressions of opinions. And the opinion expressed is interpreted in terms of what came before. After a powerful or extreme statement, anything that follows that is not chiming in at the same level of enthusiasm is taken as disagreement, even when its literal content would seem to be agreement.

Considerations of action and interaction keep taking us back to the particular situation in which an opinion was expressed: who and where, and at what stage, and for what purpose, and in exactly what words. It might seem that this approach would severely restrict what one could find. But the analysis does not lead to a list of endlessly varying particulars. As we have seen in Chapters 5–8, there are regularities in the ways people express opinions, in relation to other opinions, and define the topic and their own identities in relation to these opinions. Examples of these regularities include the forms of greetings and introductions, agreement and disagreement, the ways of defining and redefining topics, and the ways of invoking the voices of others, expert and non-expert. We do not find an answer to one question – 'What do they really think, deep down? – but we find the beginnings of an answer to another question – 'What do they think they are doing when they say what they think?'

Opinions are packaged

Opinions are packaged in two ways, as they are reproduced by institutions of opinion, and as they are designed by speakers for that reproduction. Polling agencies, market-research firms, and academic researchers know they need certain kinds of relevant opinions that can be counted or quoted. Their instruments are designed to channel interactions into usable forms, whether in a questionnaire that allows only certain responses (Belson 1981; Low 1999), or in a focus group in which the moderator probes until he or she has a stand-alone quotable response (Puchta and Potter 1999). Then a qualitative researcher chooses only some passages or responses; we do not usually hear how the interaction began or ended. These selected passages are then further truncated, so that typically the report does not include what happened just before and just after this statement, or how the speaker might have prefaced it or followed it up. And they are categorized or grouped in some way, so that various utterances are taken to say the same thing. All this brings some order to the crowd of statements jostling for our attention, but it also has the effect of abstracting opinions from any context of utterance, and from any action being performed in uttering them.

It is not just the institutions of opinion that do the packaging. Subjects of research design their utterances to be collected in this way, just as subjects of photographs lift their heads, look at the camera, and smile so that the image produced will simulate a direct gaze at any viewer (on such posing, see Scollon 1998). Interviewees think they know what is needed; indeed, it requires careful design to elicit in these genres of interaction anything other than an opinion. We can see this packaging when a focus group moderator asks an open question and the participants hesitate before one participant hazards a candidate answer; when an answer is accepted as appropriate, the participants may rapidly pour out a list of the items that they now see are wanted, words or phrases that might fit in this slot.

We have seen other kinds of packaging as well, when a speaker prefaces an utterance with his or her entitlement to speak, or tells a rambling story and then gives it relevance to the topic, or initiates his or her phone call to a radio station with a list of topics. The devil's advocate statements in Chapter 6 have participants speaking for another to provide the researchers with a full range of possible opinions. Participants show care in reformulating their responses, sometimes repeating various forms of a statement until it is acknowledged by the researcher or by other participants as an appropriate and usable response. They are like screen actors repeating a line again and again, knowing that just one version will be in the final cut. At the end of a session, as we saw in Chapter 3, they are concerned to know just what will be done with their opinions, what channels they will take. Participants can do all this packaging and imagine the possible channels, because they have seen how opinions are carried in media interviews, phone-ins, vox pops, and poll results.

Opinions are mediated

Opinions are talk, but they cannot remain just talk if they are to have an effect. They have to be mediated, whether through polls, or focus-group reports, or news interviews, or legislative representatives who have received letters. Even utopian schemes of a public sphere broadened by unlimited community cable television, or speeded up by direct Internet access to legislators, assume the loss of face-to-face interaction and the packaging of opinions. To imagine earlier forms of democracy in which mediation was not central, one has to go back to the eighteenth century, to New England town meetings with all male citizens required to attend (as discussed in Schudson 1998), or hustings with local grandees marshalling the voters (as seen in William Hogarth's series of satirical paintings), or the coffee houses where merchants and literary men exchanged news (Habermas 1989). It is difficult now to tell how much nostalgia distorts our view of this period. What is clear is that by the middle of the nineteenth century, the time of Lincoln and Gladstone, the press reports of the speech mattered more than the speech, and opinion was a matter of estimates of crowd size, straw polls, and published letters (Herbst 1993; Schudson 1998), not face-to-face conversation.

Mediation poses problems for my view of opinions as talk. Broadcast talk may not be two-way, it may be performed for an overhearing audience, it involves institutional conventions of turn-taking and control, and it must be edited to fit the genre of broadcast and the slot assigned. Letters to the editor, protest marches, and symbolic actions also have to fit into the kinds of slots media make possible. Broadcasters may attempt to change the terms of expression of public opinion, by inviting audience feedback, or incorporating a studio audience into the interview, or allowing access to cable channels, or providing Internet chatrooms and bulletin boards to discuss programmes, but none of these make up for what is lost in mediation, the moment-to-moment engagement with another person present. Opinion becomes a slot, usually towards the end of the news or in the corner of the front page, in which 'you' have 'your say'.

Some would see this packaging, distancing, and emphasis on entertainment as the commodification of public opinion, rendering it no longer public and no longer effective. I have argued that this view underestimates the affective power of experiencing a broadcast as part of one's daily life. Viewers engage in para-social interaction with the personae they hear and see, and they can do this only because the broadcast interactions are in some ways left open for them. Only by assuming something like para-social interaction can one account for the extraordinary effects of broadcasts on audiences, the experience of talk radio for a late-night trucker, the identification with Princess Diana in her *Panorama* interview, or the empathy aroused by faces of interviewees on 11 September. These effects are not just a matter of changing people's minds on given issues – the broadcasts do less and more than that.

I have been concerned with the ways interaction is stripped away from opinions, but even in some reduced forms opinions can carry traces of their origins in talk. Opinions are taken to be more authentic when they bear the marks of interaction: hesitation and repetition, stiff control and flooding out of emotions. That is why phone-ins continue to be popular when we have Internet chat available, and vox pops remain a powerful device even when they would seem to have been replaced by professional polls: we still want to hear voices and see faces. It is also why brief phrases from such interviews can become symbols in a media event of the 'voice of the people'. Newspaper and magazine interviews with members of the public may be printed in a way that reminds us of their origins in an encounter, with ellipses, colloquialisms, and a picture of the person speaking. Talk that still sounds like talk remains the touchstone of authenticity.

Opinions are intertextual

When people state opinions, they are usually asked to do so using their own words. But these words come to them already used. This is of course true for all discourse, from poetry to management talk to advertising (Bakhtin 1986; Fairclough 2003); it has become a constant theme of recent text analysis. But it is particularly true for discourses of public opinion, because familiar words are the prompts that elicit expressions of opinion, tools for steering the discussion, and categories for the packaging of the opinions for reproduction.

How do people know when an opinion is called for and when it is not? As we have seen (Chapter 5 and Chapter 9), one set of cues is in the language already used to define the issue. In the example I gave at the beginning of Chapter 4, Americans were offered the following responses to the 11 September attacks: 'Shock', 'Sorrow', 'Anger'. Every issue is defined in the media, not just in a given vocabulary, but in set phrases. Even if one tries to elicit opinions without putting words in the mouths of participants, for instance by using pictures rather than verbal questions (Miller et al. 1998; Meinhof and Galasinski 2000; Szerszynski et al. 2000), participants supply the words as soon as they identify the referents of the pictures. We could make a negative evaluation by calling these set collocations clichés or slogans. In Chapter 2, I take up the terminology of 'commonplaces', as a way of recognizing their function in encapsulating a sense of shared experience, 'shared moments in the flow

of social activity which afford common reference' (Shotter 1993:
53). Expressions of opinions typically make some reference to these
shared moments as a way of evoking responses from others, even
if the familiar words are re-used obliquely or ironically. It could be
argued that the function of media discussion of opinions is not to tell
us what to think (as in conspiracy-theory approaches to the media)
but to tell us how we might say it.

The reliance on familiar phrases make expressions of opinion an
easy target for irony and parody. In the television opera *When She
Died* . . . (Dove and Harsent 2002), broadcast on the fifth anniver-
sary of the death of Princess Diana, phrases from the speeches, interviews, and headlines of the time are chanted over and over by a chorus behind the soloists: 'Diana the People's Princess, Diana Queen
of Hearts, Diana We Love You.' The effect is both ironic and oddly
moving, as if these banal phrases had finally found an appropriate
musical setting. On *The Day To-Day*, a parody news series from
the 1990s, a reporter conducts a vox pop with vague but plausible
questions like 'Should the law be tightened up?' He then repeats and
develops the question until it becomes absurd, offering the interviewee a rubber band and asking him to determine just how much it
should be tightened up. The humour comes from the recognition
that the passer-by has been drawn into playing along with a discussion that has the conventional form of a vox pop, and words of an
issue, but no content.

Intertextual references are not just prompts and resources for
talk; as we saw in Chapters 5 to 9, they can be useful to participants
in shaping the interaction. A commonplace can serve to close off
a topic, because it is assumed that the commonplace is what other
people share however much they differ. Intertextual references can
serve as openings to make a bid for the floor: 'I saw a documentary
last night . . .', 'I read in the paper . . .', 'a friend of mine works
there and says . . .'. People can quote named or unnamed others,
real or hypothetical talk, experts and those to whom expertise is
attributed. This does not mean they take positions that are already
fixed by what they have heard. The positions given in these references provide material against which their own statements can be
compared, coordinates for placing opinions as sensible or extreme.
To express an opinion, one must, apparently, both show it is one's
own, and show it is not just one's own.

The common sense of opinions

I outlined in Chapter 1 some of the academic sources for a view of opinions as things rather than as talk, in cognitive psychology proposing schema, in social psychology separating attitudes from expressions of attitudes, in the public-opinion research focusing on the reliability rather than the validity of results, and in techniques of content analysis. But these academic disciplines are drawing on a much broader commonsense way of talking about opinions as things. Part of this common sense arises from our reflexive sense of how opinions have been and will be packaged. We treat opinions as psychological entities when we think of them as utterances that could be either spoken or unspoken (so a teenager might withhold her opinions around her boyfriend's father). We treat them as things when we compare one to another or juxtapose something we've just heard with something read in the newspaper, as being on the same issue. We treat opinions as a store of things we have, like jokes for an after-dinner speaker, stories of a war veteran, or the cultural references of a critic. There may even be a sense of spending opinions, using them like capital in the conversation. These are all ways of making opinions into things.

Yet there is also a commonsense view of opinions that accords more with the perspective offered in this book. We draw on this view when we remember that the purpose of most conversations is not to express opinions or change the opinions of others (except in a few genres set up by institutions for these purposes). Many conversations, ones that are not focus groups, public inquiries, classes, or interviews, take place so that the participants can be with people, enjoy the play of similarity and difference, pass the time. The expression of opinions, the discovery of how one's opinions dovetail with others (or don't) in a complex on-going interaction, is part of the excitement of being with other people, and the pleasure of talk.

References

Abercrombie, N. and B. Longhurst (1998). *Audiences: A Sociological Theory of Performance and Imagination*. London, Sage.

Adams, K. L. (1999). 'Deliberate dispute and the construction of oppositional stance'. *Pragmatics* 9: 231–48.

Agar, M. and J. MacDonald (1995). 'Focus groups and ethnography'. *Human Organization* 54: 78–86.

Antaki, C. (1994). *Explaining and Arguing: The Social Organization of Accounts*. London, Sage.

(1998). 'A conversation-analytic approach to arguments'. In M. Bondi, ed., *Forms of Argumentative Discourse*. Bologna, CLUEB (Cooperativa Libraria Universitaria Editrice Bologna): 57–70.

Antaki, C., S. Condor, and M. Levine (1996). 'Social identities in talk: speakers' own orientations'. *British Journal of Social Psychology* 35: 473–92.

Antaki, C., F. Diaz, and A. F. Collins (1996). 'Keeping your footing: conversational completion in three-part sequences'. *Journal of Pragmatics* 25(2): 151–71.

Antaki, C., H. Houtkoop-Steenstra and M. Rapley (2000). '"Brilliant. Next question . . .": high-grade assessment sequences in the completion of interactional units'. *Research on Language and Social Interaction* 33(3): 235–62.

Antaki, C. and M. Rapley (1996a). '"Quality of life" talk: the liberal paradox of psychological testing'. *Discourse and Society* 7: 293–316.

(1996b). 'Questions and answers to psychological assessment schedules: hidden troubles in "quality of life" interviews'. *Journal of Intellectual Disability Research* 40: 421–37.

Antaki, C. and S. Widdicombe (1998). *Identities in Talk*. London, Sage.

Arendt, H. (1963). *On Revolution*. London, Faber and Faber.

Atkinson, J. M. and P. Drew (1979). *Order in Court: The Organisation of Verbal Interaction in Judicial Settings*. London, Macmillan.

Atkinson, J. M. and J. Heritage, eds. (1984). *Structures of Social Action: Studies in Conversation Analysis*. Cambridge, Cambridge University Press.

Auer, P., ed. (1998). *Code-Switching in Conversation: Language, Interaction and Identity*. London, Routledge.

Auer, P. and A. di Luzio, eds. (1992). *The Contextualisation of Language*. Amsterdam, Benjamins.

Aukrust, V. G. and C. E. Snow (1998). 'Narratives and explanations during mealtime conversations in Norway and the U.S.' *Language in Society* 27: 221–46.

Baker, R. and R. Hinton (1999). 'Do focus groups facilitate meaningful participation in social research?' In R. S. Barbour and J. Kitzinger, eds., *Developing Focus Group Research*. London, Sage: 79–98.

Bakhtin, M. (1986). *Speech Genres and Other Late Essays*. Austin, University of Texas Press.

Banfield, A. (1982). *Unspeakable Sentences: Narration and Representation in the Language of Fiction*. Boston, MA, Routledge and Kegan Paul.

Barber, B. (1996). 'Foundationalism and democracy'. In S. Benhabib, ed., *Democracy and Difference: Contesting the Boundaries of the Political*. Princeton, Princeton University Press: 348–59.

Bateson, G. (1972). *Steps to an Ecology of Mind*. New York, Ballantine.

Bauer, M. W. (2000). 'Classical content analysis: a review'. In M. W. Bauer and G. Gaskell, eds., *Qualitative Researching with Text, Image, and Sound*. London, Sage: 131–51.

Baynham, M. (1996). 'Direct speech: what's it doing in non-narrative discourse?' *Journal of Pragmatics* 25(1): 61–81.

(1999). 'Double-voicing and the scholarly 'I': on incorporating the words of others in academic discourse'. *Text* 19: 485–504.

Baynham, M. and S. Slembrouck (1999). 'Speech representation and institutional discourse'. *Text* 19: 439–57.

Beach, W. A. (1990). 'Language as and in technology: Facilitating topic organization in a videotext focus group meeting'. In M. J. Medhurst, A. Gonzalez, and T. R. Peterson, eds., *Communication and the Culture of Technology*. Pullman, WA, Washington State University Press: 199–219.

Beck, U. (1992). *Risk Society: Towards a New Modernity*. London, Sage.

(1995). *Ecological Politics in an Age of Risk*. Cambridge, Polity Press.

Becker, H. S. (1998). *Tricks of the Trade: How to Think About Your Research While You're Doing It*. Chicago, University of Chicago Press.

Bell, A. (1991). *The Language of News Media*. Oxford, Blackwell.

Bell, A. and P. Garrett, eds. (1998). *Approaches to Media Discourse*. Oxford, Blackwell.

Bell, P. and T. van Leeuwen (1994). *The Media Interview: Confession, Context, Conversation*. Kensington, University of New South Wales Press.

Belson, W. A. (1981). *The Design and Understanding of Survey Questions*. Aldershot, Hampshire, Gower.

Berlant, L. (1997). *The Queen of America Goes to Washington City: Essays on Sex and Citizenship*. Durham, NC, Duke University Press.

Bertrand, J. T., J. E. Brown, and V. M. Ward (1992). 'Techniques for Analyzing Focus Group Data'. *Evaluation Review* 16(2): 198–209.

Billig, M. (1978). *Fascists: A Social Psychological View of the National Front*. London/New York, Academic Press.

(1987). *Arguing and Thinking: A Rhetorical Approach to Social Psychology*. Cambridge, Cambridge University Press.

(1991a). *Ideology and Opinions: Studies in Rhetorical Psychology*. London, Sage.

(1991b). *Talking of the Royal Family*. London, Routledge.

(1995). *Banal Nationalism*. London, Sage.

(1999). 'Whose terms? Whose ordinariness?' *Discourse & Society* 10: 543–58.

Billig, M., S. Condor, D. Edwards, M. Gane, D. Middleton, and A. Radley (1988). *Ideological Dilemmas: A Social Psychology of Everyday Thinking*. London, Sage.

Bilmes, J. (1988). 'The concept of preference in conversation analysis'. *Language in Society* 17: 161–81.

Bloor, M., J. Frankland, M. Thomas, and K. Robson (2001). *Focus Groups in Social Research*. London, Sage.

Blumer, H. (1948). 'Public opinion and public opinion polling'. *American Sociological Review* 13: 242–9.

Blum-Kulka, S. (1997a). *Dinner Talk: Cultural Patterns of Sociability and Socialization in Family Discourse*. Mahwah, NJ, Lawrence Erlbaum Associates.

(1997b). 'Discourse pragmatics'. In T. A. van Dijk, ed., *Discourse as Social Interaction*. London, Sage: 38–63.

Blumler, J. G. and M. Gurevitch (1996). 'Media change and social change: linkages and junctures'. In J. Curran and M. Gurevitch, eds., *Mass Media and Society*. London, Arnold: 120–40.

Boden, D. (1994). *The Business of Talk*. Cambridge, Polity Press.

Boden, D. and D. Zimmerman, eds. (1991). *Talk and Social Structure: Studies in Ethnomethodology and Conversation Analysis*. Cambridge, Polity Press.

Boltanski, L. (1999). *Distant Suffering*. Cambridge, Cambridge University Press.

Bourdieu, P. (1971/1993). 'Public opinion does not exist'. In *Sociology in Question*. London, Sage: 149–57.

Boyle, R. (2000). 'Whatever happened to preference organisation?' *Journal of Pragmatics* 32(5): 583–604.

Brannigan, A. (1981). *The Social Basis of Scientific Discoveries*. Cambridge, Cambridge University Press.

Briggs, C. L. (1986). *Learning How to Ask*. Cambridge, Cambridge University Press.

Brown, G. and G. Yule (1983). *Discourse Analysis*. Cambridge, Cambridge University Press.

Brown, P. and S. Levinson (1987). *Politeness: Some Universals in Language Use*. Cambridge, Cambridge University Press.

Brown, R. and A. Gilman (1960). 'The pronouns of politeness and solidarity'. In T. A. Sebeok, ed., *Style in Language*. Cambridge, MA, MIT Press: 253–76.

Bryce, J. (1888). *The American Commonwealth*, 2 vols. London, Macmillan.

Bucholtz, M. (2000). 'The politics of transcription'. *Journal of Pragmatics* **32**: 1439–65.

Burgess, J., M. Limb, and C. M. Harrison (1988a). 'Exploring environmental values through the medium of small groups: 2. Illustrations of a group at work'. *Environment and Planning A* **20**(4): 457–76.

  (1988b). 'Exploring environmental values through the medium of small groups: 1. Theory and practice.' *Environment and Planning A* **20**: 309–26.

Buttny, R. (1997). 'Reported speech in talking race on campus'. *Human Communication Research* **23**(4): 477–506.

  (1998). 'Putting prior talk into context: reported speech and the reporting context'. *Research on Language and Social Interaction* **31**(1): 45–58.

  (1999). 'Discursive constructions of racial boundaries and self-segregation on campus'. *Journal of Language and Social Psychology* **18**(3): 247–68.

Buttny, R. and P. L. Williams (2000). 'Demanding respect: the uses of reported speech in discursive constructions of interracial contact'. *Discourse & Society* **11**(1): 109–33.

Button, G. (1991). 'Conversation-in-a-series'. In D. Bowen and D. Zimmerman, eds., *Talk and Social Structure: Studies in Ethnomethodology and Conversation Analysis*. Cambridge, Polity Press: 251–77.

Button, G. and N. Casey (1984). 'Generating topic: the use of topic initial elicitors'. In J. M. Atkinson and J. Heritage, eds., *Structures of Social Action: Studies in Conversation Analysis*. Cambridge, Cambridge University Press: 167–90.

Button, G. and J. R. E. Lee (1987). *Talk and Social Organisation*. Clevedon, Avon, Multilingual Matters.

Caldas-Coulthard, C. R. (1994). 'On reporting reporting: the representation of speech in factual and factional narratives'. In M. Coulthard, ed., *Advances in Written Text Analysis*. London, Routledge: 295–308.

Calhoun, C., ed. (1992). *Habermas and the Public Sphere*. Studies in contemporary German social thought. Cambridge, MA, MIT Press.

Carter, R. and M. McCarthy (1995). 'Grammar and the spoken language'. *Applied Linguistics* **16**(2): 141–58.

Catterall, C. and P. MacLaren (1997). 'Focus group data and qualitative analysis programmes: coding the moving picture as well as the snapshots'. *Sociological Research Online* **2**(1).

Clark, H. H. and R. J. Gerrig (1990). 'Quotations as demonstrations'. *Language* **66**(4): 764–805.

Clayman, S. E. (1988). 'Displaying neutrality in television news interviews'. *Social Problems* **35**(4): 474–92.

(1991). 'News interview openings: aspects of sequential organization'. In P. Scannell, ed., *Broadcast Talk*. London, Sage: 48–75.

Clayman, S. E. and J. Heritage (2002). *The News Interview: Journalists and Public Figures on the Air*. Cambridge, Cambridge University Press.

Coates, J. (1996). *Women Talk: Conversation Between Women Friends*. Oxford, Blackwell.

Coates, J. (2000). 'Small talk and subversion: female speakers backstage'. In J. Coupland, ed., *Small Talk*. Harlow, Longman: 241–64.

Coates, J. and J. Thornborrow (1999). 'Myths, lies and audiotapes: some thoughts on data transcripts'. *Discourse & Society* **10**(4): 594–7.

Collins, H. M. (1985). *Changing Order: Replication and Induction in Scientific Practice*. London, Sage.

Cook, G. (1995). 'Theoretical issues: transcribing the untranscribable'. In G. Leech, G. Myers, and J. Thomas, eds., *Spoken English on Computer*. Harlow, Longman: 35–53.

Coupland, J., ed. (2000). *Small Talk*. Harlow, Pearson Education.

Coupland, N. and V. Ylänne-McEwen (2000). 'Talk about the weather: small talk, leisure talk, and the travel industry'. In J. Coupland, ed., *Small Talk*. Harlow, Pearson: 163–82.

Dahlgren, P. and C. Sparks, eds. (1991). *Communication and Citizenship: Journalism and the Public Sphere in the New Media Age*. London, Routledge.

Dayan, D. and E. Katz (1992). *Media Events: The Live Broadcasting of History*. Cambridge, MA, Harvard University Press.

Delin, J. (2000). *The Language of Everyday Life*. London, Sage.

Douglas, M. and A. Wildavsky (1982). *Risk and Culture: An Essay on the Selection of Technological and Environmental Dangers*. Berkeley, CA, University of California Press.

Dove, J. and D. Harsent (2002). 'When she died . . .' Channel 4 (UK), August 2002.

Drew, P. and K. Chilton (2000). 'Calling just to keep in touch: regular and habitualised telephone calls as an environment for small talk'. In J. Coupland, ed., *Small Talk*. Harlow, Longman: 137–62.

Drew, P. and J. Heritage, eds. (1992). *Talk at Work: Studies in Interactional Sociolinguistics*. Cambridge, Cambridge University Press.

Drew, P. and E. Holt (1998). 'Figures of speech: figurative expressions and the management of topic transition in conversation'. *Language in Society* **27**: 495–522.

Drew, P. and M.-L. Sorjonen (1997). 'Institutional dialogue'. In T. A. van Dijk, ed., *Discourse as Social Interaction*. London, Sage: 92–118.

Drew, P. and A. Wootton (1988). *Erving Goffman: Exploring the Interaction Order*. Cambridge, Polity Press.

Dunbar, R. (1995). *The Trouble with Science*. London, Faber and Faber.

Dunwoody, S. and R. J. Griffin (1993). 'Journalistic strategies for report-ing long-term environmental issues: a case study of three superfund sites'. In A. Hansen, ed., *The Mass Media and Environmental Issues*. Leicester, Leicester University Press: 22–50.

Durant, J. and M. Bauer (1997). *Public Understanding of Science in Britain: 1996 National Survey*. London, The Science Museum.

Duranti, A. and C. Goodwin (1992). *Rethinking Context: Language as an Interactive Phenomenon*. Cambridge, England/New York, Cambridge University Press.

Eagly, A. H. and S. Chaiken (1993). *The Psychology of Attitudes*. Fort Worth, TX, Harcourt Brace Jovanovich.

Edelsky, C. (1981). 'Who's got the floor?' *Language in Society* 10: 383–421.

Edwards, D. (1997). *Discourse and Cognition*. London, Sage.

Eggins, S. and D. Slade (1997). *Analysing Casual Conversation*. London, Cassell.

Fairclough, N. (1988). *Language and Power*. London, Longman.

(1992). *Discourse and Social Change*. Cambridge, Polity Press.

(1995). *Media Discourse*. London, Edward Arnold.

(2003). *Analysing Discourse: Text Analysis for Social Research*. London, Routledge.

Fairclough, N. and R. Wodak (1997). 'Critical discourse analysis'. In T. A. van Dijk, ed., *Discourse as Social Interaction*. London, Sage: 258–84.

Fowles, J. (1996). *Advertising and Popular Culture*. Thousand Oaks, CA, Sage.

Frankland, J. and M. Bloor (1999). 'Some issues in the systematic analysis of focus group materials'. In R. S. Barbour and J. Kitzinger, eds., *Developing Focus Group Research*. London, Sage: 144–55.

Fraser, N. (1992). 'Rethinking the public sphere: a contribution to the cri-tique of actually existing democracy'. In C. Calhoun, ed., *Habermas and the Public Sphere*. Cambridge, MA, MIT Press: 109–42.

Gallup, G. H. and S. F. Rae (1940). *The Pulse of Democracy: The Public Opinion Poll and How It Works*. New York, Simon and Schuster.

Garfinkel, H. (1967). *Studies in Ethnomethodology*. Englewood Cliffs, NJ, Prentice-Hall.

Georgakopoulou, A. and D. Goutsos (1997). *Discourse Analysis: An Introduction*. Edinburgh, Edinburgh University Press.

Gilbert, G. N. and M. Mulkay (1984). *Opening Pandora's Box: A Socio-logical Analysis of Scientists' Discourse*. Cambridge, Cambridge University Press.

Ginzberg, C. (1994). 'Killing a Chinese Mandarin: the moral implications of distance'. *New Left Review* (298): 107–19.

Goffman, E. (1959). *The Presentation of Self in Everyday Life*. Garden City, NY, Doubleday.

(1963). *Behavior in Public Places: Notes on the Social Organization of Gatherings*. New York, Free Press.

(1971). *Relations in Public: Microstudies of the Public Order*. London, Penguin.

(1974). *Frame Analysis: An Essay on the Organization of Experience*. New York, Harper and Row.

(1981). *Forms of Talk*. Oxford, Blackwell.

Goodwin, C. (2000). 'Action and embodiment within situated human interaction'. *Journal of Pragmatics* **32**: 1489–522.

Goodwin, C. and M. H. Goodwin (1990). 'Interstitial argument'. In A. D. Grimshaw, ed., *Conflict Talk: Sociolinguistic Investigations of Arguments in Conversations*. Cambridge, Cambridge University Press: 85–117.

(1992). 'Assessments and the construction of context'. In A. Duranti and C. Goodwin, eds., *Rethinking Context: Language as an Interactive Phenomenon*. Cambridge, Cambridge University Press: 147–90.

Goodwin, M. H. (1990). *He-Said-She-Said: Talk as Social Organization Among Black Children*. Bloomington, IN, Indiana University Press.

Greatbatch, D. (1988). 'A turn-taking system for British news interviews'. *Language in Society* **17**(3): 401–30.

Grice, P. (1989). *Studies in the Way of Words*. Cambridge, MA, Harvard University Press.

Gumperz, J. J. (1982). *Discourse Strategies*. Cambridge, Cambridge University Press.

Gunthner, S. (1999). 'Polyphony and the "layering of voices" in reported dialogues: an analysis of the use of prosodic devices in everyday reported speech'. *Journal of Pragmatics* **31**(5): 685–708.

Haarman, L., ed. (1999). *Talk About Shows*. Bologna, CLUEB (Cooperativa Libraria Universitaria Editrice Bologna).

Habermas, J. (1962/1989). *The Structural Transformation of the Public Sphere: An Inquiry into a Category of Bourgeois Society*. Cambridge, Polity Press.

Hall, C., S. Sarangi, and S. Slembrouck (1999). 'Speech representation and the categorisation of the client in social work discourse'. *Text* **19**: 539–70.

Hamilton, H. (1998). 'Reported speech and survivor identity in on-line bone marrow transplanation narratives'. *Journal of Sociolinguistics* **2**(1): 53–67.

Handelsman, D. (2002). 'Towards virtual encounter: Horton's and Wohl's "Mass communication and para-social interaction"'. In E. Katz, J. D. Peters, T. Liebes, and A. Orloff, eds., *Canonic Texts in Media Research*. Cambridge, Polity Press: 137–51.

Harris, S. (1991). 'Evasive action: how politicians respond to questions in political interviews'. In P. Scannell, ed., *Broadcast Talk*. London, Sage: 76–99.

Hartford, B. S. and K. Bardovi-Harlig (1992). 'Closing the conversation – evidence from the academic advising session'. *Discourse Processes* **15**(1): 93–116.

Heath, C. (1986). *Body Movement and Speech in Medical Interaction.* Cambridge, Cambridge University Press.

Herbst, S. (1993). *Numbered Voices: How Opinion Polling Has Shaped American Politics.* Chicago, IL, University of Chicago Press.

Heritage, J. (1984a). 'A change of state token and aspects of its sequential placement'. In J. M. Atkinson and J. Heritage, eds., *Structures of Social Action: Studies in Conversation Analysis.* Cambridge, Cambridge University Press: 299–345.

(1984b). *Garfinkel and Ethnomethodology.* Cambridge, Polity Press.

(1985). 'Analysing news interviews: aspects of the production of talk for an overhearing audience'. In T. A. van Dijk, ed., *Handbook of Discourse Analysis*, vol. III. New York, Academic Press: 95–117.

(1997). 'Conversation analysis and institutional talk: analysing data'. In D. Silverman, ed., *Qualitative Research: Theory, Method, and Practice.* London, Sage: 161–82.

Hester, S. and P. Eglin, eds. (1997). *Culture in Action: Studies in Membership Categorization Analysis.* Lanham, MD, University Press of America.

Hoijer, B. (1990). 'Studying viewers' reception of television programmes: theoretical and methodological considerations'. *European Journal of Communications* 5: 29–56.

Holbrook, B. and P. Jackson (1996). 'Shopping around: focus group research in North London'. *Area* 28(2): 136–42.

Holmes, J. (2000). 'Doing collegiality and keeping control at work: small talk in government departments'. In J. Coupland, ed., *Small Talk.* Harlow, Longman: 32–61.

Holmes, J., M. Stubbe, and B. Vine (1999). 'Constructing professional identity: "Doing power" in policy units'. In S. Sarangi and C. Roberts, eds., *Talk, Work, and Institutional Order: Discourse in Medical, Mediation, and Management Settings.* Berlin, Mouton de Gruyter: 351–85.

Holt, E. (1996). 'Reporting on talk: the use of direct reported speech in conversation'. *Research on Language and Social Interaction* 29(3): 219–45.

(1999). 'Just gassing: an analysis of direct reported speech in a conversation between employees of a gas company'. *Text* 19(4): 505–38.

Hopkins, C. (1995). *My Life in Advertising and Scientific Advertising.* Lincolnwood, IL, NTC Business Books.

Hopper, R. (1992). *Telephone Conversation.* Bloomington, IN, Indiana University Press.

Horton, D. and R. Wohl (1956). 'Mass communication and para-social interaction: observations on intimacy at a distance'. *Psychiatry* 19: 215–29.

Houtkoop-Steenstra, H. (2000). *Interaction and the Standardized Survey Interview: The Living Questionnaire.* Cambridge, Cambridge University Press.

Houtkoop-Steenstra, H. and C. Antaki (1997). 'Creating happy people by asking yes–no questions'. *Research on Language and Social Interaction* **30**(4): 285–313.

Hutchby, I. (1996). *Confrontation Talk: Arguments, Asymmetries, and Power on Talk Radio.* Mahwah, NJ, Lawrence Erlbaum Associates.

(2001). 'Conversation as spectacle: the argumentative frame of the *Ricky Lake* Show'. In A. Tolson, ed., *Television Talk Shows: Discourse, Performance, Spectacle.* Mahwah, NJ, Lawrence Erlbaum Associates: 155–72.

Hutchby, I. and R. Wooffitt (1998). *Conversation Analysis: Principles, Practices and Applications.* Cambridge, Polity Press.

Hyland, K. (1998). *Hedging in Scientific Research Articles.* Amsterdam, John Benjamins.

Hymes, D. (1972). 'Models of the interaction of language and social life'. In J. J. Gumperz and D. Hymes, eds., *Directions in Sociolinguistics: The Ethnography of Communication.* New York, Holt, Rinehart, and Winston: 35–71.

Jacquemet, M. (1996). *Credibility in Court: Communicative Practices of the Comorra Trials.* Cambridge, Cambridge University Press.

Jefferson, G. (1984a). 'On step-wise transition from talk about a trouble to inappropriately next-positioned matters'. In J. M. Atkinson and J. Heritage, eds., *Structures of Social Action: Studies in Conversation Analysis.* Cambridge, Cambridge University Press: 191–222.

(1984b). 'On the organization of laughter in talk about troubles'. In J. M. Atkinson and J. Heritage, eds., *Structures of Social Action: Studies in Conversation Analysis.* Cambridge, Cambridge University Press: 346–69.

Jefferson, G., H. Sacks, and E. A. Schegloff (1987). 'Notes on laughter in the pursuit of intimacy'. In G. Button and J. R. E. Lee, eds., *Talk and Social Organisation.* Clevedon, Avon, Multilingual Matters: 152–205.

Johnstone, B. (1993). 'Community and contest: Midwestern men and women creating their worlds in conversational storytelling'. In D. Tannen, ed., *Gender and Conversational Interaction.* Cambridge, Cambridge University Press: 62–80.

Jucker, A. (1993). 'The discourse marker "well": a Relevance-Theoretical account'. *Journal of Pragmatics* **19**: 435–52.

Kasper, G. (1990). 'Linguistic politeness: current research issues'. *Journal of Pragmatics* **14**: 193–218.

Katz, E. and P. F. Lazarsfeld (1955). *Personal Influence: The Part Played by People in the Flow of Mass Communications.* Glencoe, IL, Free Press.

Katz, E., J. D. Peters, T. Liebes, and A. Orloff, eds. (2003). *Canonic Texts in Media Research.* Cambridge, Polity Press.

King, Martin Luther (1963). 'I have a dream', speech given at the March on Washington, Washington DC, 28 August 1963.

Kitzinger, J. (1994). 'The methodology of focus groups – the importance of interaction between research participants'. *Sociology of Health and Illness* 16(1): 103–21.

(1995). 'Qualitative research – introducing focus groups'. *British Medical Journal* 311(7000): 299–302.

(1998). 'Resisting the message: the extent and limits of media influence'. In D. Miller, J. Kitzinger, K. Williams, and P. Beharrell, eds., *The Circuit of Mass Communication*. London, Sage: 192–212.

Kitzinger, J. and C. Farquhar (1999). 'The analytical potential of "sensitive moments" in focus group discussions'. In R. S. Barbour and J. Kitzinger, eds., *Developing Focus Group Research*. London, Sage: 156–72.

Klewitz, G. and E. Couper-Kuhlen (1999). 'Quote-unquote? The role of prosody in the contextualization of reported speech sequences'. *Pragmatics* 9(4): 459–85.

Kotthoff, H. (1993). 'Disagreement and concession in disputes – on the context-sensitivity of preference structures'. *Language in Society* 22(2): 193–216.

Kress, G., C. Jewitt, J. Ogburn, and C. Tsatsarelis (2001). *Multimodal Teaching and Learning: The Rhetorics of the Science Classroom*. London, Continuum.

Kress, G. and T. van Leeuwen (2001). *Multi-modal Discourse: The Modes and Media of Contemporary Communication*. London, Arnold.

Krueger, R. A. (1994). *Focus Groups: A Practical Guide for Applied Research*. Thousand Oaks, CA, Sage.

(1998). *Moderating Focus Groups*. Thousand Oaks, CA, Sage.

Lakoff, G. (1973). 'Hedges: a study in meaning criteria and the logic of fuzzy concepts'. *Journal of Philosophical Logic* 2: 458–508.

Lakoff, R. (1973). 'The logic of politeness, or, minding your p's and q's'. In C. Corum, T. C. Smith-Stark and A. Weiser, eds., *Papers from the Ninth Regional Meeting*. Chicago, Chicago Linguistics Society: 292–305.

Lane, R. E. and D. O. Sears (1964). *Public Opinion*. Englewood Cliffs, NJ, Prentice-Hall.

Latour, B. (1987). *Science in Action: How to Follow Scientists and Engineers Through Society*. Milton Keynes, Open University Press.

Latour, B. and S. Woolgar (1979). *Laboratory Life: The Social Construction of Scientific Facts*. London, Sage.

Lazarsfeld, P. (1944). 'The controversy over detailed interviews – an offer for negotiation'. *Public Opinion Quarterly* 8: 38–60.

Leech, G. (2000). 'Grammars of spoken English: new outcomes of corpus-oriented research'. *Language Learning* 50(4): 675–724.

Leech, G. N. and M. Short (1981). *Style in Fiction: A Linguistic Introduction to English Fictional Prose*. London, Longman.

Leudar, I. and C. Antaki (1996). 'Backing footing.' *Theory & Psychology* 6(1): 41–6.

Levinson, S. (1983). *Pragmatics*. Cambridge, Cambridge University Press.

(1988). 'Putting linguistics on a proper footing: explorations in Goffman's concepts of participation'. In P. Drew and A. Wootton, eds., *Erving Goffman: Exploring the Interaction Order*. Cambridge, Polity Press: 161–227.

(1992). 'Activity types and language'. In P. Drew and J. Heritage, eds., *Talk at Work: Interaction in Institutional Settings*. Cambridge, Cambridge University Press: 66–100.

Liebes, T. and J. Curran (1998). *Media, Ritual and Identity*. London, Routledge.

Lippmann, W. (1922). *Public Opinion*. New York; London, Free Press.

Livingstone, S. and P. Lunt (1994). *Talk on Television: Audience Participation and Public Debate*. London, Routledge.

Low, G. (1999). 'What respondents do with questionnaires: accounting for incongruity and fluidity'. *Applied Linguistics* 20(4): 503–33.

Lucy, J. A. (1993). *Reflexive Language: Reported Speech and Metapragmatics*. Cambridge, Cambridge University Press.

Luhmann, N. (2000). *The Reality of the Mass Media*. Cambridge, Polity Press.

Lury, A. (1994). 'Advertising: moving beyond the stereotypes'. In R. Keat, N. Whiteley and N. Abercrombie, eds., *The Authority of the Consumer*. London, Routledge: 91–101.

Lynch, M. and D. Bogen (1997). 'Lies, recollections, and categorical judgements in testimony'. In S. Hester and P. Eglin, eds., *Culture in Action: Studies in Membership Categorization Analysis*. Lanham, MD, University Press of America: 99–121.

Lyons, J. (1977). *Semantics*. Cambridge, Cambridge University Press.

Macgregor, B. and D. E. Morrison (1995). 'From focus groups to editing groups – a new method of reception analysis'. *Media Culture & Society* 17(1): 141–50.

Macnaghten, P., R. Grove-White, M. Jacobs, and B. Wynne (1995). *Public Perceptions and Sustainability in Lancashire: Indicators, Institutions, Perceptions*. Lancaster, Centre for the Study of Environmental Change, Lancaster University.

Macnaghten, P. and G. Myers (2004). 'Focus groups: the moderator's view and the analyst's view'. In J. G. Giampietro Gobo, Clive Seale, David Silverman, eds., *Qualitative Research Practice*. London, Sage: 65–79.

Malone, M., J. (1997). *Worlds of Talk: The Presentation of Self in Everyday Conversation*. Cambridge, Polity Press.

Marriott, S. (2000). 'Election night'. *Media Culture & Society* 22: 131–48.

Matoesian, G. M. (2000). 'Intertextual authority in reported speech'. *Journal of Pragmatics* 32: 879–914.

Matoesian, G. M. and J. R. J. Coldren (2002). 'Language and bodily conduct in focus groups evaluations of legal policy'. *Discourse & Society* 13(4): 469–93.

May, R. M. and R. Pitts (2000). 'Communicating science behind the global change issues'. In J. Smith, ed., *The Daily Globe: Environmental Change, the Public, and the Media*. London, Earthscan: 15–25.

Maybin, J. (1997). 'Story voices: the use of reported speech in 10–12 year olds' spontaneous narratives'. *Current Issues in Language and Society* 3: 36–48.

(1999). 'Framing and evaluation in ten- to twelve-year-old school children's use of repeated, appropriated, and reported speech in relation to their induction into educational procedures and practices'. *Text* 19(4): 459–84.

Maynard, D. W. (1980). 'Placement of topic changes in conversation'. *Semiotica* 30: 263–90.

(1984). *Inside Plea Bargaining: The Language of Negotiation*. New York, Plenum.

(1997). 'The news delivery sequence: bad news and good news in conversational interaction'. *Research on Language and Social Interaction* 30(2): 93–130.

Maynard, D. W. and D. H. Zimmerman (1984). 'Topical talk, ritual, and the social organization of relationships'. *Social Psychology Quarterly* 47: 301–16.

McCarthy, M. (1998). *Spoken Language and Applied Linguistics*. Cambridge, Cambridge University Press.

McGuigan, J. (1998). 'What price the public sphere?' In D. K. Thussu, ed., *Electronic Empires: Global Media and Local Resistance*. London, Arnold: 81–107.

McHoul, A. (1978). 'The organisation of turns at formal talk in the classroom'. *Language in Society* 19: 183–213.

Mehan, H. (1979). *Learning Lessons: Social Organization in the Classroom*. Cambridge, MA, Harvard University Press.

Meinhof, U. and D. Galasinski (2000). 'Memory and the construction of identities on the former East-West German Border'. *Discourse Studies* 2: 323–53.

Mercer, N. (2000). *Words and Minds: How We Use Language to Think Together*. London, Routledge.

Merton, R. K. (1987). 'The focused interview and focus groups – continuities and discontinuities'. *Public Opinion Quarterly* 51(4): 550–66.

Merton, R. K., M. Fiske, and P. L. Kendall (1956). *The Focused Interview: A Manual of Problems and Procedures*. New York, Free Press: London, Collier Macmillan.

Merton, R. K. and P. L. Kendall (1946). 'The focused interview'. *American Journal of Sociology* 51: 541–57.

Meyrowitz, J. (1985). *No Sense of Place: The Impact of Electronic Media on Social Behavior*. New York, Oxford University Press.

Michael, M. (1996). 'Ignoring science: discourses of ignorance in the public understanding of science'. In A. Irwin and B. Wynne, eds.,

Misunderstanding Science: The Public Reconstruction of Science and Technology. Cambridge, Cambridge University Press: 107–25.

Middleton, D. and D. Edwards, eds. (1990). *Collective Remembering.* London, Sage.

Miller, D., J. Kitzinger, K. Williams, and P. Beharrell (1998). *The Circuit of Mass Communication.* London, Sage.

Mitchell, P. (1998). 'Authorial voice in radio news: a framework for the linguistic and pragmatic analysis of "Objective" discourse representation'. PhD dissertation, Centre for Language and Communication, Cardiff University.

Mitchell-Kiernan, C. (1972). 'Signifying and marking: two Afro-American speech acts'. In J. J. Gumperz and D. Hymes, eds., *Directions in Sociolinguistics: The Ethnography of Communication.* Oxford, Blackwell: 161–79.

Moerman, M. (1988). *Talking Culture: Ethnography and Conversation Analysis.* Philadelphia, University of Pennsylvania Press.

Mondada, L. (1995). 'L'entretien comme lieu de negotiation d'objets de discours'. *Cahiers de Linguistique Sociale* (28–9): 219–24.

Montgomery, M. (1985). 'DJ Talk'. *Media Culture & Society* 8: 421–40.
  (1999). 'Speaking sincerely: public reactions to the death of Diana'. *Language and Literature* 8: 5–34.

Morgan, D. L. (1988). *Focus Groups as Qualitative Research.* Thousand Oaks, CA, Sage.

Morgan, D. L. and R. A. Krueger (1993). 'When to use focus groups and why'. In D. L. Morgan, ed., *Successful Focus Groups.* Newbury Park, CA, Sage: 3–19.

Morgan, D. L. and R. A. Krueger (1998). *The Focus Group Kit.* Thousand Oaks, CA, Sage.

Morrison, D. (1998). *The Search for a Method: Focus Groups and the Development of Mass Communication Research.* Luton, University of Luton Press.

Muhlhausler, R. and R. Harre (1990). *Pronouns and People.* Oxford, Blackwell.

Mulkay, M. (1979). *Science and the Sociology of Knowledge.* London, George Allen and Unwin.

Myers, G. (1998). 'Displaying opinions: topics and disagreement in focus groups'. *Language in Society* 27(1): 85–111.
  (1999). *Ad Worlds: Brands, Media, Audiences.* London, Arnold.
  (2000a). 'Becoming a group: face and sociability in moderated discussions'. In S. Sarangi and M. Coulthard, eds., *Discourse and Social Life.* Harlow, Pearson Education: 121–37.
  (2000b). 'Entitlement and sincerity in broadcast interviews about Princess Diana'. *Media Culture & Society* 22(2): 167–85.
  (2000c). *Talking to Strangers: Constructing Local Place in Focus Group Discussions.* Sociolinguistics Symposium 2000, Bristol.

(2000d). 'Unspoken speech: hypothetical reported discourse and the rhetoric of everyday talk'. *Text* **19**: 571–90.

(2001). '"I'm out of it; you guys argue": making an issue of it in the Jerry Springer Show'. In A. Tolson, ed., *Television Talk Shows: Discourse, Performance, Spectacle.* Mahwah, NJ, Lawrence Erlbaum Associates: 173–92.

(2002). '"In My Opinion": the place of personal views in undergraduate essays'. In M. Hewings, ed., *Academic Writing in Context: Implications and Applications. Papers in Honour of Tony Dudley-Evans.* Birmingham, University of Birmingham Press: 63–78.

(2003). '*Vox Pop Interviews in Media Events*'. Paper presented at conference. Staging Reality, Stirling Media Centre.

Myers, G. and P. Macnaghten (1998). 'Rhetorics of environmental sustainability: commonplaces and places'. *Environment and Planning A* **30**(2): 333–53.

(1999). 'Can focus groups be analysed as talk?' In R. S. Barbour and J. Kitzinger, eds., *Developing Focus Group Research: Politics, Theory and Practice.* London, Sage: 173–85.

Ochs, E. (1979). 'Transcription as theory'. In E. Ochs and B. Schieffelin, eds., *Developmental Pragmatics.* New York, Academic Press: 43–72.

O'Connell, D. C. and S. Kowal (2000). 'Are transcripts reproducible?' *Pragmatics* **10**: 247–69.

Ogburn, J., G. Kress, I. Martins, and K. McGillicuddy (1996). *Explaining Science in the Classroom.* Buckingham, Open University Press.

Ogilvy, D. (1983). *Ogilvy on Advertising.* London, Pan Books.

Petts, J., T. Horlick-Jones and G. Murdock (2001). 'The social amplification of risk'. London, Health and Safety Executive. http://www.hse.gov.uk/research/crr.pdf/2001/crr01329.pdf.

Philips, S. (1993). 'Evidentiary standards for American trials: just the facts'. In J. Hill and J. Irvine, eds., *Responsibility and Evidence in Oral Discourse.* Cambridge, Cambridge University Press: 248–59.

Pidgeon, N., J. Walls, A. Weyman, and T. Horlick-Jones (2003). Perceptions of and Trust in the Health and Safety Executive as a Risk regulator. London, Health and Safety Executive. http://www.hse.gov.uk/research/rrpdf/rr100.pdf.

Pomerantz, A. (1980). 'Telling my side: "limited access" as a fishing device'. *Sociological Inquiry* **50**: 186–98.

(1984). 'Agreeing and disagreeing with assessments: some features of preferred/dispreferred turn shapes'. In J. M. Atkinson and J. Heritage, eds., *Structures of Social Action.* Cambridge, Cambridge University Press: 57–101.

(1986). 'Extreme case formulations: a way of legitimising claims'. *Human Studies* **9**: 219–30.

Potter, J. (1996). *Representing Reality: Discourse, Rhetoric and Social Construction.* London, Sage.

Potter, J. and M. Wetherell (1987). *Discourse and Social Psychology: Beyond Attitudes and Behaviour*. London, Sage.

Psathas, G. (1995). *Conversation Analysis: The Study of Talk-in-Interaction*. Thousand Oaks, CA, Sage.

Puchta, C. and J. Potter (1999). 'Asking elaborate questions: focus groups and the management of spontaneity.' *Journal of Sociolinguistics* 3: 314–35.

(2003). *Focus Group Moderation: Discourse, Opinion, and Market Research*. London, Sage.

Ravatsos, D. and C. Berkenkotter (1999). 'Voices in the text: the uses of reported speech in psychotherapists' initial assessments'. *Text* 18(2): 211–39.

Richards, J., S. Wilson, and L. Woodhead (1999). *Diana, the Making of a Media Saint*. London/New York, I. B. Tauris.

Richardson, K. (2001). 'Risk news in the world of Internet news groups'. *Journal of Sociolinguistics* 2: 50–72.

(2003). 'Health risks on the Internet: establishing credibility on-line'. *Health Risk and Society* 5(2): 171–84.

Roberts, C. (2000). 'Professional gatekeeping in intercultural encounters'. In S. Sarangi and M. Coulthard, eds., *Discourse and Social Life*. Harlow, Longman: 102–20.

Roberts, C. and S. Sarangi (1999). 'Hybridity in gatekeeping discourse: issues of practical relevance for the researcher'. In S. Sarangi and C. Roberts, eds., *Talk, Work and Institutional Order: Discourse in Medical, Mediation and Management Settings*. Berlin, Mouton de Gruyter: 473–503.

Roth, A. (2002). 'Social epistemology in broadcast news interviews'. *Language in Society* 31: 355–81.

Rothenberg, R. (1994). *Where the Suckers Moon: An Advertising Story*. New York, Knopf.

Royal Society of London (1985). 'The public understanding of science'. London, The Royal Society.

Royal Society of London (1992). 'Risk: analysis, perception, management'. London, The Royal Society.

Sacks, H. (1972). 'An initial investigation of the usability of conversational data for doing sociology'. In D. Sudnow, ed., *Studies in Social Interaction*. New York, Free Press: 31–74.

(1978). 'Some technical considerations of a dirty joke'. In J. N. Schenkein, ed., *Studies in the Organization of Conversational Interaction*. New York, Academic Press: 249–70.

(1987). 'On the preferences for agreement and contiguity in sequences in conversation'. In G. Button and J. R. E. Lee, eds., *Talk and Social Organisation*. Clevedon, Avon, Multilingual Matters: 54–69.

(1992). *Lectures on Conversation*. Oxford, Blackwell.

250 References

Saville-Troike, M. (1989). *The Ethnography of Communication*. Oxford, Blackwell.

Scannell, P. (1991). *Broadcast Talk*. London, Sage.

(1996). *Radio, Television and Modern Life: A Phenomenological Approach*. Oxford, Blackwell.

(2000). 'For-anyone-as-someone structures'. *Media Culture & Society* 22: 5–24.

Schegloff, E. A. (1968). 'Sequencing in conversational openings'. *American Anthropologist* 70: 1075–95.

(1972). 'Notes on a conversational practice: formulating place'. In D. Sudnow, ed., *Studies in Social Interaction*. New York, Free Press: 75–119.

(1982). 'Discourse as an interactional achievement: some uses of 'uh huh' and other things that come between sentences'. In D. Tannen, ed., *Analyzing Discourse: Text and Talk*. Washington, DC, Georgetown University Press: 71–93.

(1984). 'On some questions and ambiguities in conversation'. In J. M. Atkinson and J. Heritage, eds., *Structures of Social Action*. Cambridge, Cambridge University Press: 28–52.

(1997). 'Whose text? Whose context?' *Discourse & Society* 8(2): 165–87.

(2000). 'Overlapping talk and the organization of turn-taking for conversation'. *Language in Society* 29(1): 1–63.

Schegloff, E. A. and H. Sacks (1973). 'Opening up closings'. *Semiotica* 8: 289–327.

Schiffrin, D. (1984). 'Jewish argument as sociability'. *Language in Society* 13(3): 311–35.

(1987). *Discourse Markers*. Cambridge, Cambridge University Press.

(1990). 'The management of a co-operative self during argument: the role of opinions and stories'. In A. D. Grimshaw, ed., *Conflict Talk: Sociolinguistic Investigations of Arguments in Conversations*. Cambridge, Cambridge University Press: 241–59.

(1993). '"Speaking for another" in sociolinguistic interviews: alignments, identities, and frames'. In D. Tannen, ed., *Framing in Discourse*. Oxford, Oxford University Press: 231–63.

(1994). *Approaches to Discourse*. Oxford, Blackwell.

(1996). 'Narrative as self-portrait: sociolinguistic constructions of identity'. *Language in Society* 25(2): 167–203.

Schudson, M. (1984). *Advertising: The Uneasy Persuasion*. New York, Basic Books.

(1998). *The Good Citizen: A History of American Civic Life*. Cambridge, MA, Harvard University Press.

Scollon, R. (1998). *Mediated Discourse as Social Interaction: A Study of News Discourse*. Harlow, Longman.

Scollon, R. and S. W. Scollon (2003). *Discourses in Place: Language in the Material World*. London, Routledge.

References 251

Semino, E., M. Short, and J. Culpeper (1997). 'Using a corpus to test a model of speech and thought presentation'. *Poetics* **25**: 17–43.

Semino, E., M. Short, and M. Wynne (1999). 'Hypothetical words and thoughts in contemporary British narratives'. *Narrative* 7(3): 307–34.

Short, M. (1988). 'Speech presentation, the novel, and the press'. In W. van Peer, ed., *The Taming of the Text*. London, Routledge.

Short, M., M. Wynne, and E. Semino (1999). 'Reading reports: discourse presentation in a corpus of narratives, with special reference to news reports'. In Hans Jurgen Diller and Erwin Otto Gert Stratmann, eds., *English via Various Media (Anglistik & Englischunterricht)*. Heidelberg, Universitatsverlag C. Winter: 39–66.

Shotter, J. (1993). *Conversational Realities: Constructing Life Through Language*. Thousand Oaks, CA, Sage.

Shuman, A. (1993). '"Get outta my face": entitlement and authoritative discourse'. In J. Hill and J. Irvine, eds., *Responsibility and Evidence in Oral Discourse*. Cambridge, Cambridge University Press.

Silverman, D. (1998). *Harvey Sacks: Social Science and Conversation Analysis*. Cambridge, Polity Press.

Simmel, G. (1949). 'The sociology of sociability'. *American Journal of Sociology* **55**(3).

Sinclair, J. and M. Coulthard (1975). *Towards an Analysis of Discourse: The English Used by Teachers and Pupils*. Oxford, Oxford University Press.

Slembrouck, S. (1992). 'The parliamentary Hansard "verbatim" report: the written construction of spoken language'. *Language and Literature* 1(2): 101–19.

  (1999). 'Translation, direct quotation and decontextualisation (reported speech, process of translation, cultural criteria)'. *Perspectives-Studies in Translatology* 7(1): 81–108.

Sparks, C. (1998). 'Is there a global public sphere?' In D. K. Thussu, ed., *Electronic Empires: Global Media and Local Resistance*. London, Arnold: 108–24.

Sperber, D. and D. Wilson (1981). 'Irony and the use-mention distinction'. In P. Cole, ed., *Radical Pragmatics*. London, Academic Press: 295–318.

Stubbs, M. (1996). *Text and Corpus Analysis: Computer Assisted Studies of Language and Institutions*. Oxford, Blackwell.

  (2001). *Words and Phrases: Corpus Studies of Lexical Semantics*. Oxford, Blackwell.

Suchman, L. and B. Jordan (1990). 'Interactional troubles in face-to-face survey interviews'. *Journal of the American Statistical Association* **85**(409): 232–41.

Summerfield, P. (1998). *Reconstructing Women's Wartime Lives: Discourse and Subjectivity in Oral Histories of the Second World War*. Manchester, Manchester University Press.

Szerszynski, B. (1999). 'Risk and trust: the performative dimension'. *Environmental Values* 8(2): 239–52.

Szerszynski, B., J. Urry, and G. Myers (2000). 'Mediating global citizenship'. In J. Smith, eds., *The Daily Globe: Environmental Change, the Public, and the Media*. London, Earthscan: 97–114.

Tannen, D. (1984). *Conversational Style: Analyzing Talk Among Friends*. Norwood, NJ, Ablex.

(1989). *Talking Voices: Repetition, Dialogue, and Imagery in Conversational Discourse*. Cambridge, Cambridge University Press.

ed. (1993). *Gender and Conversational Interaction*. Oxford, Oxford University Press.

Tannen, D. and C. Wallat (1987). 'Interactive frames and knowledge schema in interaction: examples from a medical examination/interview'. *Social Psychology Quarterly* 50: 205–16.

ten Have, P. (1991). 'Talk and institution: a reconsideration of the "asymmetry" of doctor–patient interaction'. In D. Boden and P. Zimmerman, eds., *Talk and Social Structure; Studies in Ethnomethodology and Conversation Analysis*. Cambridge, Polity Press: 138–63.

(1999a). *Doing Conversation Analysis: A Practical Guide*. London, Sage.

(1999b). 'In the presence of the data'. Paper presented at conference. Ethnomethodology: An Improbable Science, Cerisy la Salles, France. http://www2.fmg.uva.n1/emca/presence.htm.

Thomas, J. (1995). *Meaning in Interaction: An Introduction to Pragmatics*. Harlow, Longman.

Thompson, G. (1996). 'Voices in the text: discourse perspectives on language reports'. *Applied Linguistics* 17(4): 501–30.

Thompson, J. (1995). *The Media and Modernity*. Cambridge, Polity Press.

Thornborrow, J. (1997). 'Having their say: the function of stories in talk show discourse'. *Text* 17: 241–62.

(2000). 'The construction of conflicting accounts in public participation TV'. *Language in Society* 29(3): 357–77.

(2002). *Power Talk: Language and Interaction in Institutional Discourse*. Harlow, Longman.

Times, The (1999). 'Internet offers a new world of democracy' (by Philip Gould), 15 November: 17.

Titscher, S., M. Meyer, R. Wodak, and E. Vetter (2000). *Methods of Text and Discourse Analysis*. London, Sage.

Tolson, A. (2001). *Television Talk Shows: Discourse, Performance, Spectacle*. Mahwah, NJ, Lawrence Erlbaum Associates.

Tomlin, R. S., L. Forrest, M. M. Pu, and M. H. Kim (1997). 'Discourse semantics'. In T. A. van Dijk, ed., *Discourse as Structure and Process*. London, Sage: 63–111.

Tracy, K. and J. M. Naughton (2000). 'Institutional identity-work: a better lens'. In J. Coupland, ed., *Small Talk*. Harlow, Longman: 62–83.

Turnock, R. (2000). *Interpreting Diana: Television Audiences and the Death of a Princess*. London, British Film Institute.

van Dijk, T. A. (1997a). *Discourse as Social Interaction*. London, Sage.
 (1997b). *Discourse as Stucture and Process*. London, Sage.
van Dijk, T. A., S. Ting-Toomey, G. Smitherman, and D. Troutman (1997). 'Discourse, ethnicity, culture, and racism'. In T. A. van Dijk, ed., *Discourse as Social Interaction*. London, Sage: 144–80.
Volosinov, V. N. (1986). *Marxism and the Philosophy of Language*. Cambridge, MA, Harvard University Press.
Walter, T. (1999). *The Mourning for Diana*. Oxford, UK/New York, Berg.
Waterton, C. and B. Wynne (1999). 'Can focus groups access community views?' In R. S. Barbour and J. Kitzinger, eds., *Developing Focus Group Research*. London, Sage: 127–43.
Wetherell, M. and J. Potter (1992). *Mapping the Language of Racism: Discourse and the Legitimation of Exploitation*. London, Harvester/Wheatsheaf.
Wetherell, M., S. Taylor, and S. Yates, eds. (2002). *Discourse as Data*. London, Sage.
Wilkinson, S. (1998). 'Focus groups in feminist research: power, interaction, and the co-construction of meaning'. *Women's Studies International Forum* **21**: 111–25.
 (1999). 'How useful are focus groups in feminist research?' In R. Barbour and J. Kitzinger, eds., *Developing Focus Group Research: Politics, Theory, and Practice*. London, Sage: 64–78.
Williamson, J. (1978). *Decoding Advertisements: Ideology and Meaning in Advertising*. London, Marion Boyars.
Wodak, R. (1996). *Disorders of Discourse*. Harlow, Longman.
Wodak, R., R. de Cillia, M. Reisigl, and K. Liebhart (1999). *The Discursive Construction of National Identity*. Edinburgh, Edinburgh University Press.
Wodak, R. and M. Meyer, eds. (2001). *Methods of Critical Discourse Analysis*. London, Sage.
Wooffitt, R. (1992). *Telling Tales of the Unexpected: Accounts of Paranormal Experiences*. Hemel Hempstead, Harvester/Wheatsheaf.
Wooffitt, R. (2001). 'Researching psychic practitioners: Conversation Analysis'. In M. Wetherell, S. Taylor, and S. Yates, eds., *Discourse as Data: A Guide for Analysis*. London, Sage: 49–92.
Woolgar, S. (1988). *Science: The Very Idea*. Chichester, Ellis Horwood: Tavistock Publications.
Worcester, R. (2000). 'Public and "expert" opinion on environmental issues'. In J. Smith, ed., *The Daily Globe: Environmental Change, the Public, and the Media*. London, Earthscan: 33–45.
Wynne, B. (1995). 'Public understanding of science'. In S. Jasanoff, G. E. Markle, J. C. Peterson and T. Pinch, eds., *Handbook of Science and Technology Studies*. Thousand Oaks, CA, Sage: 361–88.
 (1996a). 'May sheep safely graze? A reflexive view of the expert-lay knowledge divide'. In S. Lash, B. Szerszynski and B. Wynne, eds., *Risk, Environment, and Modernity*. London, Sage: 44–83.

(1996b). 'Misunderstood misunderstandings: social identities and the public uptake of science'. In A. Irwin and B. Wynne, eds., *Misunderstanding Science? The Public Reconstruction of Science and Technology*. Cambridge, Cambridge University Press: 19–46.

(2001). 'Creating public alienation: expert cultures of risk and ethics on GMOs'. *Science as Culture* 10: 445–81.

Yngve, V. H. (1970). 'On getting a word in edgewise'. In *Papers from the 6th Regional Meeting of the Chicago Linguistics Society*. Chicago, Chicago Linguistics Society: 567–78.

Young, I. M. (1996). 'Communication and the other: beyond deliberative democracy'. *Democracy and Difference: Contesting the Boundaries of the Political*. S. Benhabib, ed. Princeton, Princeton University Press: 120–36.

Yule, G., T. Mathis, and M. F. Hopkins (1992). 'On reporting what was said'. *ELT Journal* 46(3): 245–51.

Index